Caligula and the Fight for Artistic Freedom

Caligula and the Fight for Artistic Freedom

The Making, Marketing and Impact of the Bob Guccione Film

WILLIAM HAWES

McFarland & Company, Inc., Publishers
Jefferson, North Carolina, and London

ALSO BY WILLIAM HAWES
AND FROM MCFARLAND

Live Television Drama, 1946-1951 (2001)
Filmed Television Drama, 1952-1958 (2002)

Frontispiece: Malcolm McDowell as Gaius Caesar Augustus Germanicus/Caligula. Courtesy Photofest.

LIBRARY OF CONGRESS CATALOGUING-IN-PUBLICATION DATA

Hawes, William, 1931–
    Caligula and the fight for artistic freedom : the making, marketing and impact of the Bob Guccione film / William Hawes.
       p.   cm.
    Includes bibliographical references and index.

    ISBN 978-0-7864-3986-7
    softcover : 50# alkaline paper ∞

    1. Caligula (Motion picture : 1979)   I. Title.
PN1997.C2423H39   2009
791.43'72 — dc22   2008038807

British Library cataloguing data are available

Copyright ©2009 William Hawes. All rights reserved

No part of this book may be reproduced or transmitted in any form or by any means, electronic or mechanical, including photocopying or recording, or by any information storage and retrieval system, without permission in writing from the publisher.

Cover photograph: Malcolm McDowell as the title character from the 1979 film *Caligula* (Independent Artists/Photofest).

Manufactured in the United States of America

McFarland & Company, Inc., Publishers
   Box 611, Jefferson, North Carolina 28640
      www.mcfarlandpub.com

Acknowledgments

I have seen hundreds of traditional and pornographic movies of all kinds and I have met an untold number of participants—from fan dancer Sally Rand to Seka to Jeff Stryker, from Rosaland Russell to Charlton Heston to Clint Eastwood. Much of this has been made possible through my friends: the late Alvin Guggenheim, of Alvin Guggenheim and Associates; Walter Coblenz, producer of *All the President's Men*, which emphasizes the importance of journalism in a democracy; the late Delbert Mann, director of live television dramas and the Academy Award–winning *Marty*, which was the prelude to merging the television and motion picture industries; Joe Spiegel,

Pliny the Younger had a villa on the thirty acres of land behind the structure pictured here.

president, Universal Entertainments, Inc.; and the late Jack Valenti, president of the Motion Picture Association of America, who began bringing major directors and pictures to the University of Houston in 1967.

In 2003 the Rockefeller Foundation invited me to its Study and Conference Center in Bellagio, Italy, to meditate, outline, and write an early draft of this, my seventh media-related book. I am indebted to the Rockefeller Foundation's Susan Garfield, Gianna Celli, and distinguished colleagues at Bellagio, and to the University of Houston Small Grants Program for encouraging this work. Italian translations are by Michael Cloud and French translations are by Stephanie Proutheau. Most photographs are courtesy of General Media Communications, Inc. and Robert C. Guccione and used by permission of assistant general counsel Marilyn Peck Francescon; and Ron and Howard Mandelbaum at Photofest, New York. Photo processing was provided by The Production Company, Austin, Texas.

TABLE OF CONTENTS

Acknowledgments v
Preface 1

1. Divine Metamorphosis 5
2. Tablets and Parchment 42
3. A Movie Marriage 77
4. Editions of *Caligula* 120
5. Release, History and Impact 190

Chapter Notes 229
Bibliography 237
Index 245

PREFACE

No film of the 1970s symbolizes the fervent effort to expand artistic freedom in the movies more than *Caligula*.

Caligula is the most expensive attempt ever made to produce a film that combines sexually explicit and traditional scenes. Initially, it was written to contrast the sexual and violent practices of pagan times with those of today. The film was born in controversy, litigated for four years, released worldwide after arguable editing and censorship, and today enjoys profitable sales to adults and continues to receive recognition due to new editions, the cast that was assembled for the film, and various awards.

Despite receiving unfavorable reviews and weak distribution at the outset, *Caligula* today draws attention from the popular press, as does its producer, Bob Guccione. It is available in bookstores and via many Web sites. More recent reviews, placing it in a contemporary context, refer to it as a cult classic, which has led the way for the adult-traditional movie merger and foreshadowed the cultural changes that have taken place since it first appeared. It was released in 1980 at the time the lights were being turned off at adult cinemas and switches were being turned on for home videotape players. Adult and traditional motion pictures were on the verge of raising profits from millions to billions of dollars by entertaining international audiences. *Caligula* is the seminal Z-to-A film that signifies this cultural change — the end of most viewing and having sex in small adult theaters and book stores, and the beginning of watching videos while engaging in live sex, not only in adult theaters and book stores but also at home. Traditional movies often substitute violence for sex, and pornographic films may use violence with sex, but more often adult films show sex exclusively for pleasure, without violence. *Caligula* displays separately and together both sex and violence.

Caligula is one of those films that has not received proper recognition in cinema history. Like other subjects I have written about — the first public television station and that almost forgotten era of live television dramas — *Caligula* has yet to receive its rightful place as a benchmark in popular culture.

My first film viewing was *Three Little Pigs* (1933), Walt Disney's Depression-era entertainment that was appealing to children and adults. "All we have to fear is fear itself," President Franklin D. Roosevelt told the nation, and Frank Churchill's lively tune "Who's Afraid of the Big Bad Wolf?" reflected that sentiment. In those days going to a movie was a family event. Who would have noted the gleam in the wolf's eyes or the pigs' rumps as sexual temptation? This was a simple story of good and evil. It was lighthearted, funny, and carried the message that building a house, or anything else that is meant to endure, required strong materials and sound construction, if it is to survive adversity.

Six years later I saw Disney's *Snow White and the Seven Dwarfs* (1937). During a time when little kids never feared being snatched off the streets, I walked a mile on Saturdays to the local cinema to see famous players in shows of the 1930s and 1940s, family pictures that inspire filmmakers to this day. World War II came along and the movies introduced the public to a great deal of violence, human sorrow, and death. Movie stars did what they could to alleviate the pain at home and abroad. The first big movie star I saw was Bob Hope, who landed near Michigan's Willow Run bomber plant in the mid–1940s when he did one of his road shows. Thereafter, I saw many important stars of stage and screen in person, including Sonja Henie, Vivien Leigh, Mae West, Judy Garland, Lucille Ball, Elvis Presley, Henry Fonda, and Gary Cooper; and ones I did not see, I wrote to for autographed photographs—10 cents for a 5 × 7 and 25 cents for an 8 × 10-inch photo. Of course, many pictures were free—including those of Humphrey Bogart and the GI's favorite, Betty Grable. As a naive teenager, sex was an incomprehensible mystery. By contrast, love had many forms—love of country, of home, of family, maybe of a girl. My home town was sacrificed to the war effort. Its quaint, friendly, easy-going way of life and innocence ended. During the Korean War, the Air Force enabled me to see well-endowed topless ladies sway their endowments in early examples of absurdly plotted nude films that coincided with the Supreme Court's decision to protect motion pictures under the First Amendment.

By the mid–1960s I was teaching cinema history at a time when there was a resurgence of interest in movies on college campuses. Gerald Mast identified the focus of this interest as the New American Cinema. I projected real film in class until 1988, when reduced university budgets forced me to show videotapes, which, of course, are not the same thing. As a frequent visitor to New York City since my Air Force days, I watched the country's culture change. Broadway, the pinnacle of theatrical success shown in *42nd Street* (1933), had become a hustlers' paradise pictured in Warhol/Morrissey's *Trash*, (1970). Broadway to Eighth Avenue was a microcosm of the scene, and offered drugs, live or filmed intercourse on stage, or prostitution. In the center of the south side of the block was the New Amsterdam Theatre, a 1903 vaudeville house built for Klaw and Erlanger, and where Florenz Ziegfeld glorified the American girl during the Gilded Age. I would take a peak inside the lobby hoping someday to see the theater restored. Decades later, the Walt Disney Company restored most of it for the stage presentation of *The Lion King*. During the 1970s, however, the Times Square area became seedier. Touring sex shows were common. Al Parker, John Holmes, Kip Knoll, Georgina Spelvin, and Gloria Leonard appeared in person to promote their hardcore movies.

In 1970 the Commission on Obscenity and Pornography, appointed by President Lyndon B. Johnson, concluded that pornography is a nuisance rather than evil, with no measurable ill effects. Its recommendations, rejected by President Richard M. Nixon, included repealing prohibitions against the sale and exhibition of such materials to consenting adults. In 1973 the U.S. Supreme Court decided that unlawful *obscene* material must be patently offensive to community standards, appeal to prurient interest, and have no serious literary, artistic, political or scientific value. Discussions about the place of hardcore movies, adult cinemas, and book stores in society were popular. In 1975, I offered what may be the first university seminar on pornographic films and community standards. Fifteen senior adult students conducted a twelve-hundred-person telephone survey in Houston, and they went gratis, courtesy of Joe Spiegel and friends, to eighteen cinemas to review pornography. By summer, the study was published and the exercise was repeated in 1982, 1993, and 2006. The studies showed public attitudes changing toward sexually explicit movies; the public wanted to make its own viewing choices, and believed adult movies would increase. While the study drew national attention in 1975, it was ignored by 2006. Though principal photography ended in 1976, *Caligula* did not have its New York premiere until 1980, when I saw it at the Penthouse East Theatre.

Unlike sex, an increase in intense violence, especially after the 1960s assassinations and the Vietnam War, was acceptable in traditional films for adults and for many youngsters who attended these pictures. Being interested in cultural change through entertainment, I have taught the history of cinema as a reflection of our lives and times.

Caligula emerged as a favorite villain from the contrasting works of Robert Graves and Albert Camus during the mid–20th century. The first chapter places the minor emperor in an unlikely context — Caligula, who combined his wicked ways with charm and capricious temperament, would become a media darling thanks to the interpretations of various film actors. Chapter 2 is a brief historical account of Caligula's life to provide a basis for the narratives in the screen and stage versions. Although the scholarly research has been diligent, much more is unknown than is known about his life. In Chapter 3 we see that however complicated Caligula's life may have been, making a movie about him was no less complex, as a multitude of artists contributed their best efforts to transform diverse visions into one film reality. In Chapter 4, *Caligula* is finally completed after intense artistic struggles, only to be challenged by numerous lawsuits and censorship decisions. These resulted in releasing the film in various editions so that the collision between the objectives of art and business could market the film worldwide. Chapter 5 tells of *Caligula's* impact on film culture, its references to changing social behavior, and its continuing place as a harbinger of product distribution in a new media world.

Once during the famed and fading 1970s I invited a traveling porno film director to visit my university class. He defined "pornography" for us: "Penetration and wet. That's a porno film." This is recognized as *hardcore* pornography; it is distinguished from *softcore,* which is neither penetration nor wet, and a multitude of vague sexual and violent references covered by a nicer sounding word *erotica.*

Later, when I learned he had his family with him, my wife and I invited him to our home. They had two children younger than our two boys. We enjoyed a Texas cookout in the backyard, while he kept the motor of his old white Cadillac running at the curb. The kids looked fine but life seemed tough, so I asked him as they left, "What keeps you making porno films?" "Hope," he said and his wife beside him added, "Who knows? He could hit it big tomorrow." Whether the movies are pornography or multi-million dollar features, the stalwarts of the motion picture business risk whatever they have by placing their work before the gods and a public that craves entertainment. As far as I can tell, they would not live any other way.

This study combines three stories—those of Emperor Caligula, Bob Guccione, and the artists who created *Caligula.* They asked the question, "What would happen if sexually explicit frames, along with many violent ones, were included in a traditionally produced motion picture?" This study is an effort to provide the clearest, most accurate narrative to date about the film's production, distribution, exhibition, and impact.

1

DIVINE METAMORPHOSIS

According to historians, after a month-long illness, Roman Emperor Gaius Caesar Augustus Germanicus, aka Caligula (A.D. 12–41), thought he had become a god and forced the senate to confirm his status. Augustus Caesar had been voted a god after his death, and Emperor Claudius, who would succeed Caligula, would be voted deity status also. The idea that a mortal could have such a transformation was the central theme in popular culture treatments of Caligula during the mid–twentieth century. Though Caligula was believed to be possibly insane, this idea of divinity cannot be set aside quickly. Caligula was no doubt aware that the Egyptians thought Alexander the Great was a god, and he may have heard about the promised Messiah from his Jewish confidant Herod Agrippa. The lives of Jesus and Caligula overlapped for about fifteen years. Perhaps Caligula simply wanted assurance that he would live as a god with his ancestors. In any case, the concept of divine metamorphosis is fascinating and pervasive in these works. Of course, Caligula's alleged vile activities, especially while in office, have prompted much of the inquiry as to whether he *really* thought of himself as a god, and so the parameters of his belief and the violent background in which he lived his short life are the variable tenets of imagination and some history.

Thanks to the books of the English-born American classical scholar Robert Graves (1895–1985) — who wrote *I, Claudius*, a 1934 novel based on the lives of the Julio-Claudian emperors, and was responsible for several translations, including *The Twelve Caesars* (1957) by Gaius Suetonius Tranquillus, a second-century historian — Caligula and the other emperors emerge immortal from ancient scrolls and parchment. This study, however, not only concerns Caligula's personal and political struggles, but how Caligula's story was used during the 1970s to expand artistic freedom in filmmaking by marrying adult and traditional components in the motion picture *Caligula* (1979) and its subsequent editions.

Pagan Pictures

During three decades of silent screen stories, depicting pagan times was very popular. The silver screen genius David Wark Griffith (1875–1948) directed his first feature, *Judith of Bethulia*, in 1914. The story takes place in ancient times and tells about a young woman who risks her life to prevent the imminent siege of her home town by murdering the invading general with whom she has fallen in love. Once drink has overtaken him, she commits the violent act and rallies the people to save the town. Griffith's repertoire company, unaffected by the star system, consisted of loyal actors who could convey their intentions with a look, a leer, or a smile. Murder to improve the common good is universally understood and explodes in action, an ingredient most movies must have; peaceful negotiations are neither dynamic nor dramatic. While filming *Intolerance* (1916), Griffith became so enthralled with the construction of his imaginary Babylon that he devoted most of his four-part story of inhumanity with massive battles outside and inside the city. Newlyweds King Belshazzar and Princess Beloved send love notes to each other in a tiny cart drawn by doves, while King Cyrus (600?–529 B.C.), founder of the Persian empire, is bringing their world to an end. The human slaughter is impressive as heads are lopped off during close combat. These early feature pictures were experiments in what the public was willing to buy a ticket to see, and violence — killing people in graphic ways — was an obvious favorite.

Producers soon learned that the public does not know in advance what it wants to see; consequently, they present their pictures and hope that their great financial risk will be rewarding. After Theda Bara (aka Theodosia Goodman, 1890–1955), a rather shy starlet, was transformed by Hollywood publicity to match her sexual encounters on screen, she became the personification of "Arab Death," a dangerous but available woman. Bara vamped her way through *A Fool There Was* (1914) by tapping a gunman's arm with a long-stemmed rose, hinting that it meant more than a flower, and in the lost *Cleopatra* (1918), viewers knew they liked the sexual inferences she was bold enough to offer them. It was implicit, not explicit, sex. Besides a sway of the torso, it was a look of promise in her darkly lined eyes and expressions in her face. The film-going public carefully read actors' faces for their true beliefs and intentions. The actors, who could convey in close-up shots subtle inner thoughts to audiences, heightened their emotions. Neither Griffith nor his contemporary, Cecil B. De Mille (1881–1959), were very good at directing sex in silent films. Griffith went in for close-ups that allowed his principal actors to convey their desires without speaking, and De Mille praised this technique and used it in his films.

Then De Mille added another dimension by intensifying the environment with sexual objects that were less blatant than the Romans' display of phalluses but were stimulating just the same. His main star, Gloria Swanson (1899–1983), dressed beautifully and undressed even more enticingly as she got in and out of bathtubs, as Roman women would do in later films. And De Mille inserted dream sequences. In *Male and Female* (1919) Swanson's wealthy character, Mary, could switch economic status with her butler (Thomas Meighan). Mary imagines him as the King of Babylon saving her from an encounter with a lion.

Incessant European influences changed American movie content. When German director Ernst Lubitsch (1892–1947) went to Paramount to perfect the sophisticated sex romps with European finesse, De Mille turned to greater opulence in *The Ten Commandments* (1923) and *The King of Kings* (1927). In *The Ten Commandments* De Mille tells the familiar story of Moses guiding the Israelites from Egypt, pursued by Rameses' army into the parted Red Sea, as a moral basis for sin in modern times. Then he contrasts a wandering, wastrel son abandoning his kindly religious mother (Edythe Chapman) and eventually his loving wife (Leatrice Joy) in search of an irresponsible materialistic life that includes a wanton Eurasian seductress (Nita Naldi) who has contracted leprosy and infects him. De Mille realized that stories set in pagan times had many sinners who surrounded themselves with sexual enticements. After they enjoyed participating in huge orgies (whether or not historically accurate), they sought forgiveness. This cycle enabled De Mille to bring even more hedonistic values into the film. De Mille's films were criticized as "vulgar"; his directing as straightforward and mundane; but his insight for what bourgeois audiences wanted to see was uncanny.

The movies of Griffith and De Mille established the main characteristics of successful traditional films—stars, story, director, and high production values, including beautiful costumes and lavish settings. All of these film experiments were verified at the box office before the movies said a word aloud.

Italian Competition

During this same period, Italian film influences were especially strong. Although men wore tunics and sandals in a silent, short, American version of Sidney Olcott's *Ben-Hur* (1907) when Ben-Hur and Messala first ran their famous chariot race, European films shot on location showed authentic panoramas, massive crowds, and meticulous settings introduced by Giovanni Pastrone in *The Fall of Troy* (*La caduta di Troia*) in 1910. His impressive adaptation of Gabriele D'Annunzio's novel *Cabiria* (1914) is "the acknowledged masterpiece of the Italian silent costume film."[1] The backdrop for this epic story is the Second Punic War, the battle for supremacy between Rome and Carthage. The narrative concerns a Roman child, Cabiria, who is separated from her family during an eruption of Mt. Etna in Sicily. Cabiria and her nurse are captured by pirates and taken to Carthage. Cabiria is about to be sacrificed to Moloch, the god of bronze, but she escapes with the help of Maciste (Bartolomeo Pagano), the muscleman servant of Roman spy Fulvius Axilla (Umberto Mozzato), who wears a ring of commitment to Cabiria. After years of momentous events, including scenes of Hannibal crossing snow-covered mountains, destruction of the Roman fleet by reflected sunlight, and trend-setting decors with elephant statues, leopard pets, and white love birds, Cabiria and Fulvius are reunited.[2]

Pastrone's *Cabiria,* Mario Caserini's *The Last Days of Pompeii* (1913) and Enrico Guazzoni's *Quo Vadis?* (1913), also adapted from novels, established the ancestry for pagan historical costume dramas and muscle-bound heroes. The horse race in *Quo Vadis?* shows an arena much like the one in Caligula's day, with its very wide dirt track and garlanded center-post columns separating the oval in halves. *Quo Vadis?* opened at the Astor Theatre on Times Square in 1913. It ran for twenty-two weeks for a record admission of one dollar and fifty cents.

In *Messalina* (1923), another monumental and accurate spectacle, Guazzoni established the standard for a Roman chariot race by recreating a breathtaking event, cutting from the master shot to the drivers, to close-ups, and to the potentially treacherous points at which the chariots might collide and throw their riders to defeat. The Circus Maximus is in fact a short walk from the emperors' palaces on Palatine Hill. A similar race in Antioch was replicated for an American silent classic, Fred Niblo's *Ben-Hur: A Tale of the Christ* (1926). The narrative takes place over several years when Augustus is rebuilding Rome and Jesus is growing up as a teenager. Enhanced by some scenes in two-strip Technicolor, Judah Ben-Hur (Ramon Novarro) meets a childhood friend, Messala (Francis X. Bushman), a prominent Roman soldier. Messala boasts that Rome rules the world while a Jew crawls in the dust. The pair soon become enemies, and Ben-Hur is enslaved as an oarsman on a Roman galley. Filmed before the Motion Picture Production Code was established, *Ben-Hur* pictures a vessel filled with scores of half-naked men, including the back view of a totally naked man being whipped. Ironically, Ramon Novarro, a handsome, muscular homosexual, whose sexual preference was not reported at the time, was purposely kept as naked as the censors would allow to the applause of his female fans, who were assured by one reviewer that he was "without doubt a man's man and 100 percent of that." Matinee idol Francis X. Bushman is less convincing in his role as the adversary because of excessive make-up applied to enhance his comeback. Later in a scene of triumph, bare-breasted women accompany a parade of Roman soldiers. Both men and women appeared partially nude in some 1920s pictures.[3]

The main attraction was spectacle: fierce naval battles, and, of course, the anticipated chariot race held in an enormous arena, where a dozen or more charioteers drive four-horse teams. The film has comprehensive shots of the arena, the stands, the race track, and the crowds. The contest is fast and challenging as the participants are eliminated. In the final moments Messala is overturned and Ben-Hur wins the race. By now Augustus has died and Tiberius reigns; Caligula is in his mid-teens. Ben-Hur attributes his good fortune to Jesus, and he is further rewarded by having his mother and sister cured of leprosy. After Ben-Hur is reunited with his family, the crucifixion is enacted, with storms and an earthquake, followed by the resurrection—"He will live forever in the hearts of men." Remembrance throughout history is a characteristic of a god. Though the competition depicts Roman versus Jew, *Ben-Hur* broadens the scope, excitement, environments, degree of nudity, potential for color, and identification of god-like attributes—an ability to cause miracles, to be worshipped, and to be remembered for a long time. Most of these attributes are identified or sought by Caligula.

Early Censorship

Fearing federal censorship, industry leaders attempted to self-regulate the movies in 1909 by forming the National Board of Censorship of Motion Pictures. Some cities' censors had already cut passionate embraces, kissing, seduction of men, and even scenes of people lying on the floor, as being vulgar, immoral, and dangerous. Some of these films were projected in incoherent tatters. The challenge was clear. When the first state censorship board was established in Pennsylvania in 1911, additional causes gained prominence, such as eliminating content that might create racial tension, using age to restrict viewing, and omitting scenes of cigarette smoking and drunkenness. Ohio, Kansas, and Maryland formed censorship boards. There was no uniformity in matters that were censored; local opinion was the controlling factor.

By 1914 the movies graphically presented social problems regarding the abuse of alcohol and narcotics, child labor practices, and mistreatment of women to an audience of ten million people. Censorship groups then blamed the movie industry for revealing, and supposedly even causing, these social ills. Federal legislation for censoring movies was introduced in the U.S. Congress, but it failed to pass. A debate over the parameters of artistic freedom and censorship in the public marketplace continues to this day. In 1915, the

Supreme Court ruled in *Mutual Film Corporation v. Ohio Industrial Commission* that moving pictures were not important enough to be protected by the First Amendment: "The exhibition of motion pictures is a business pure and simple, originated and conducted for profit ... not to be regarded, nor intended to be regarded by the Ohio Constitution, we think, as part of the press of the country or as organs of public opinion."[4] So state and municipal censoring groups could do as they pleased about editing or banning films for the next thirty-seven years. The film industry, therefore, tested the limits of artistic freedom with varying degrees of caution, trying to tantalize, but not outrage, the public. As each decade went by, liberalization of public views on a wide range of film subjects expanded. This was essential for *Caligula* to exist.

Doughboys returning from World War I were not satisfied with the homespun, dominantly rural life America offered when they grew up. It seemed old fashioned; the boys who had seen Paris knew their lives back home could be improved. Movie attendance showed that audiences wanted to view more complex narratives in comfortable, sumptuous theaters. Anticipating the postwar trends with remarkable insight, Cecil B. De Mille noted that the rising middle class liked contemporary stories that challenged the values of common experience. De Mille presented characters involved in naughty activities, usually within a wealthy environment, and they always abided by what had become traditional silent film standards. Then in 1919 the film industry's more adventuresome producers outside mainstream Hollywood accelerated the distribution of exploitation movies that showed nakedness, drug abuse, vice lords, teenage promiscuity, and pregnant high-school girls. All of these subjects had been dealt with before, but exploitation films capitalized on the sensational aspects of human behavior and strongly preyed upon its degrading tendencies.[5] After the war and the influenza epidemic ended, pleasure-seeking was all the rage.

The Jazz Age danced to frantic tunes, intensified by publicity-seeking producers and actors who sought attention at any price. Prohibition, which was federally banned from 1920 to 1933, became the currency of mobsters as the public sought a popular illegal pastime in alcohol. Just as Theda Bara's biography was fiction, stories featuring the women who imitated her, called femmes fatales, received outlandish attention. Many were Europeans, who made it to the United States as producers' mistresses, respectably referred to as protégées. Their publicity said that they were lonely, worldly women seeking something, but they did not know what. They were mysterious and beautiful too, after Hollywood make-over departments changed their appearances and educated them. Many of them played mistresses lost in a cruel world of endless pleasure. The movie industry was mainly interested in romantic escape, and an alliance developed between the movies and the press. The studios gave the press inside information, and the press exaggerated it. During the 1920s the femme fatale became a glamorous, almost ethereal, untouchable woman who was groomed to be a heavenly vision on the screen. This vision was a sex goddess, a blend of the evil powers of the vamp and a woman with good intentions. Her affairs on- and off-screen were followed in detail. This basic tenet of the movies would one day be one of the underlying elements of *Penthouse* magazine; therefore, the magazine had to have an obvious connection with *Caligula*. How the sources were exploited mattered less and less so long as the public bought magazines and attended the feature pictures.

Marlene Dietrich (1901–1992) had just arrived from Germany after starring in her European triumph, Josef von Sternberg's *The Blue Angel* (1930). Dietrich's blond hair, lustrous in overhead lighting, her cheekbones framing her large eyes and face, her beautiful legs, and throaty songs left no doubt that von Sternberg's discovery was just what he had been looking for. As Lola Lola, the naughty Lola, she enchants a distinguished, old professor (Emil Jannings). On a tiny stage in Weimar Berlin she puts a net-stockinged, gartered leg on a chair and sings in her husky contralto voice "Falling in Love Again." "Marlene Dietrich, by that one image, became femme fatale for the ages."[6] After the professor gives her everything he has, she leaves him humiliated and miserable. Under von Sternberg's guidance and directorial skills demonstrated in six pictures, Marlene Dietrich became a mythic screen untouchable. In her later years when I saw her, still on stage, she shimmered in jewels and furs while singing her nostalgic songs.

None of these women — Mae West, Jean Harlow — could quite live up to the their ancient rivals Messalina and Poppaea. Once again Cecil B. De Mille, aware of changing times, gave the public another Christian drama set in pagan Rome. Reigning one emperor later (A.D. 54–86) and more treacherous than Caligula was Emperor Nero. The black-and-white, two-hour sound film *The Sign of the Cross* (1932) takes place in Rome in A.D. 64. A fire has been raging in the old district of wooden buildings for three nights. Nero (Charles Laughton), strumming a lyre, likes the fire and plans to blame it on the Christians. Nero's trusted Prefect Marcus (Frederic March) meets a pretty Christian girl Mercia (Elissa Landi) on the street and is smitten with her immediately. The dashing officer is also the favorite lover of the notorious power behind Nero, the enchantress Poppaea (Claudette Colbert). She is seen taking a milk bath.

Nero issues an edict declaring that the Christians are to be killed. Knowing Mercia is in danger, Marcus hides her in his villa, and during a banquet he tries to seduce her to a salacious song, "Naked Moon," but the Christians

Marlene Dietrich, Sternberg's femme fatale, appeared on stage in concerts after her movie career ended. This picture was autographed in her Paris apartment.

singing outside and the appearance of his military rival ruin Marcus's plans, and Mercia is taken away. A crowd gathers in the arena where the Christians are to be sacrificed to lions. De Mille carefully shoots just what the public wants to see. Gladiators exhibit their skills, elephants crush men, sword fights draw blood, crocodiles enter to eat a nearly naked girl, and tall women battle dwarfs. These scenes, filmed before the Code took effect, add sexuality and violence before redemption. In prison, the Christians are resigned to their fate. Marcus pleads to Nero for the life of Mercia. Poppaea does not want any competition, and Nero denies his request. Marcus joins Mercia as she is about to go into the arena, and the scene dissolves to a cross.

As movie studios tried to survive the depths of the Great Depression in 1933, after spending fortunes in converting to sound, the principal survivor seemed to be Mae West (1892–1980). West specialized in comedies with one-line gags. She wrote and flaunted her promiscuity without retribution. She flirted with criminals and *Night After Night,* her 1932 film debut, had a ring of truth. At the depth of the Depression she became the highest-paid woman in the country. The message was not lost on producers—sex, like violence, pays and pays well.[7] Meanwhile moralists closed ranks. The next year the Episcopal Committee on Motion Pictures condemned the movies as immoral, and the Catholic Legion of Decency established a classification guide for its parishioners. Jewish movie-industry owners and the protestant Will Hays (1879–1954), who headed the Motion Picture Producers and Distributors Association (MPPDA), seemed to welcome the establishment of a special office within the MPPDA headed by Catholic newspaper reporter Joseph I. Breen. Breen felt it was his mandate to scrub every picture of suggestive inferences and he issued guidelines that the studios agreed to enforce under threat of being fined. Rip-

Mae West toured as Diamond Lil during the 1950s.

pling effects influenced radio and later live television to the mid–1960s, as similar regulations were written. The influence of the Motion Picture Production Code cycled from reasonable to petty over the years. Some directors took it on as a personal challenge, devising ways to circumvent it.

By the early thirties, Julius Caesar, Augustus, Tiberius, and Nero had feature pictures made about their exploits. The most popular female depicted was probably the nymphomaniac Messalina, Claudius's third wife. Then in 1934 the Julio-Claudian line received a substantial boost when Robert Graves published his remarkable epic novel *I, Claudius*. While reading Suetonius and Tacitus years earlier, Graves said he knew something was wrong with the story, and that when he had need of the money he would write his own version. The complex and exciting story became a popular success, and British producer-director Alexander Korda (1893–1956) bought the rights. Ordinarily, he would have directed the film himself, but he was overwhelmed with keeping his new Denham Studios occupied with film projects. Significantly, the forty-four-year-old Korda was seeking a major property for his romantic interest Merle Oberon (1911–1979). Born in Bombay, the beautiful twenty-three-year-old was to play Messalina, as a fifteen-year-old virgin. Korda had also cast the difficult British genius Charles Laughton (1899–1962) as the stammering, limping, sly, contemporary historian Claudius. Korda wanted someone famous to replace himself as director of his protégée, and so he hired American Josef von Sternberg, who had become an internationally famous "woman's director." Von Sternberg's career was an attempt to bring high art and European culture into the Hollywood system that recognized stars and a strong story over director contributions. He purposefully tried to control everything in a picture from the actors' movements to the details of the *mise en scène*.

Von Sternberg's films are largely based on character studies

Merle Oberon, whose role as Messalina was aborted in 1937, costarred with Laurence Olivier in *Wuthering Heights* in 1939.

and feature unique, impressionistic lighting. He also enjoyed working in large studio settings where he had complete control. He thought the material for *I, Claudius* was "magnificent." British actor Emlyn Williams was chosen to play the psychopath Caligula and Flora Robson, a fine character actress in her thirties, was to play the eighty-six-year-old Livia, his grandmother.

I, Claudius begins during the mid-reign of Augustus, covers the periods of Tiberius and Caligula, and ends with the ascendancy of Claudius. To emphasize the roles of Claudius and Messalina, the screenplay varies somewhat from the novel, which spends considerable time on the lives of Augustus, Livia, and Tiberius. Von Sternberg's films often show the growing impotence of the male and the ruthlessness of the female, which is handily illustrated by Livia's influence over Tiberius and Augustus. Caligula is a central character, however, because he takes pleasure in forcing the marriage of the disabled Claudius to his young and beautiful cousin, Messalina.[8]

Huge sets were built and principal photography began on 15 February 1937, when Josef von Sternberg walked onto the set in riding boots, britches, and with a silk bandana in the form of a turban wrapped around his head. (Similar outfits, sans turban, were worn by Griffith and De Mille.) The initial scenes record the arrival of Livia, Claudius, and Caligula after the death of Tiberius. In another scene, the simple, decent Claudius is shown on his farm taking care of a runt pig and tending to his flowers. Caligula summons him to the palace where Messalina briefly flirts with him from a distance. When he has his visit, Caligula tells Claudius he has been transformed into a god, and Claudius plays right along with this absurdity. Caligula says he is going to kill Claudius by sexual exhaustion; presumably because Messalina was so young. Later Messalina acquired the reputation of having an obsession for sex.

Laughton complained that he could not find the right voice for his role. For an actor to be completely credible, he must develop, at least in theory, a character with the appearance, voice, and movement different from his own persona. At last he hit upon the notion that the voice of Edward the Eighth (1894–1972), who had abdicated the throne of England for the woman he loved the previous year, would be suitable for Claudius. Laughton was said to hate his appearance, being overweight and unattractive in a celluloid universe that idolized beautiful people. His incredible insecurity was compounded in part by his secret life as a homosexual. In rather childlike ways he craved constant attention and encouragement from his director. Korda could be a father figure, but von Sternberg was not. Von Sternberg and Laughton had a peculiar personal connection. Some time earlier, Laughton had decided to commit suicide when he thought he had contracted syphilis.

Von Sternberg talked him out of it by insisting that he be retested. The laboratory had made an error.[9]

Von Sternberg gave Laughton the direction he thought the part required; namely, for Claudius to be ignored "with distain," like his relatives had treated him. The technique was debatable. Laughton was continuously frustrated and often distraught, literally crying to Merle Oberon for assurance and sympathy. Despite his anxieties, Laughton's scenes in the senate show him gaining strength as he gradually assumes leadership on his terms. He insists, appropriate stammers and pauses included, that the senate rid itself of corruption and that the murderers of Caligula's wife and child be punished. The movement of his body from standing to sitting, the effective minimal use of his stuttering, and the compassionate look in his eyes illustrate his metamorphosis from perceived idiot to emperor.

Emlyn Williams (1905–1987), who toured as a murderer in his own play, *Night Must Fall* (1935), was excellent as the smug, spiteful, lecherous, and cruel Caligula. *I, Claudius* by all accounts was all set to be a triumph for von Sternberg, the cast, and Alexander Korda, since Laughton found his voice, which sounded, when recorded, like his own. Then the unexpected happened. Rushing to the studio one morning, Merle Oberon and her driver were in an accident. Oberon was thrown through the windshield and out on the pavement. She was hospitalized for a concussion and cuts to her face. With the impossibility of shooting around her, *I, Claudius* was canceled and Lloyd's had to pay out a great deal in insurance. Amused, Robert Graves insisted that Claudius did not want his story told, which, of course, seemed inconsistent with his having written it in the first place.

As frequently happens in the movies, when *I, Claudius* was attempted again, it would be bigger and better than ever.

Caligula on Stage

During the Second World War few pictures drew upon ancient characters and settings. Public attention was focused on the human devastation occurring daily across Europe, Africa, and Asia. With heavy emphasis on wartime heroes and romantic musicals attempting to assure the public that the lights would go on again all over the world, 1946 became the highest grossing year in the history of motion pictures. Then, rather quickly the box office went into decline.

In Europe, the British assembled a brilliant cast and stunning sets, which they are so capable of constructing, to offer *Caesar and Cleopatra* (1945). This was an adaptation of George Bernard Shaw's play, starring thirty-two-year-old Vivien Leigh (1913–1967) and fifty-six-year-old Claude Rains (1889–

1967); but, despite Shaw writing dialogue changes himself, the movie rendition, first staged in Berlin in 1906, turned out to be slow and dull, a common complaint about the conversion of a stage play into a movie, since a stage play requires lots of dialogue and a movie demands a great deal of movement. Since 1930, Shaw, who had hesitated to sell control of his plays to television or film, entrusted his work to producer-director George Pascal (1894–1954), who had successfully filmed three of Shaw's plays previously. The failure of *Caesar and Cleopatra* virtually ruined Pascal's career and was an ill omen for the return of the ancient genre to the screen.

Meanwhile, Caligula, who was not the principal figure in earlier films about the period, drew unexpected attention from Albert Camus (1913–1960), a left-wing French director, writer, and actor, who was working with the Théâtre du Travail in Algiers from 1936 to 1939. While there he read Suetonius and wrote a version of *Caligula* for the stage and planned to play the lead. During the war his intentions were put on hold while he edited an underground newspaper, delaying the premiere until 1945, when it opened at the Théâtre-Hebertot, Paris. With Gerard Philipe as Caligula, the play was very successful. Some French critics wrote that the play was philosophical, a notion that Camus seemed to have difficulty understanding. The play concerns Caligula's belief that he has attained the unattainable; he has become a god. The prospect of attaining the impossible lends itself more to discussion than to an emotional expression, more suitable to rhetorical treatise than dramatic art.

The four-act play begins after the death of Drusilla. Caligula is missing but soon returns to declare that "men die and they are not happy," the only philosophy Camus admitted to in the play. Yet, Camus' characters take positions about the purpose and importance of life that viewers must weigh. The ideas, once spoken, may or may not be supported by other characters. These views, though not necessarily new, are generally cynical and reinforce the theme that humans beings do not change. They repeat mistakes made throughout history, as Griffith reminded viewers in *Intolerance*. Such updated reasoning leads to the view that human life has no value and is inconsequential. Caligula's ideas are sometimes non sequitur, devoid of continuity. Caligula says every man should leave his money to the state and disinherit his children. If money is important, he claims, human life is of no importance. Caligula says he is the only free man in Rome and he intends to make the impossible possible. Often Caligula, does not explain his conclusions.

Three years have gone by when Act II opens. Caligula has seriously hurt most of his supporters. A conspiracy is being planned, but Prefect Cherea says Caligula is not mad because he knows what he wants. Caligula sets no limits on his power, says humankind is of no value, and that the world is no reason for living. Caligula knows about a conspiracy, perhaps more than one, being planned, but he deliberately carries out executions and acts to provoke those around him. They cower in his presence. Scipio, Caligula's young friend, says, "The only mistake one makes in life is to cause others suffering." Caligula acknowledges that Scipio is single-mindedly for good, but says he is for evil.

As Act III begins, Helicon, a condescending supporter of Caligula, calls everyone to adore Caligula, who is dressed as Venus, and to hear the truth about the gods of Olympus. Caligula's wife, Caesonia, repeats a poem to Venus and collects alms for her, after which Caligula says he is going to have his audience killed. He tells Scipio that the smallest war he could wage would exceed in causalities whatever personal executions he sanctions. Scipio responds that at least war made some sense. Caligula insists he plays the part of a god, and Scipio tells him a multitude of human gods are rising against him. Caligula abruptly dismisses Scipio so that he can paint his toenails. He ignores the warnings of conspiracy. He summons Cherea to speak honestly. Cherea agrees, saying there is nothing likable about Gaius, but he is no coward. Cherea prefers being happy, not extraordinary like Caligula. Caligula has collected enough proof to execute Cherea, but melts the tablet of evidence over a candle.

In the final act, Scipio says he cannot join the assassins. After Caligula enters, poets are called upon to speak about death, but they are disappointing to him. He claims he is comfortable only with those he has killed, and he expects that those he has ridiculed will kill him. His only tenderness is for Caesonia, whom he strangles, so that he can have the happiness of loneliness. Caligula is afraid. He faces a mirror and declares that his life has been all wrong: "I have chosen a wrong path, a path that leads to nothing." This idea sets up a search for validation; Caligula has sought value in life and not found it. This declaration seems to expand the theme that life is futile, and consequently, justifies suicide and even murder. Led by Cherea, the conspirators descend on Caligula. His last words after being stabbed: "I'm still alive." Camus contended that for the dramatist the passion for the impossible is just as valid a subject for drama as avarice or adultery, two traits the Romans knew well. Truth is the one thing an artist cannot renounce without giving up his art, he said.[10]

There is no effort here to preserve Caligula's personality or history consistent with ancient records. Instead, Camus extracts traits attributed to him to discuss truth by juxtaposing opposites: "This world has no importance; once a man realizes that, he wins his freedom." He seeks to be above the gods. "I am taking over a kingdom where the impossible is king." Some of these ideas seem to have consciously or unconsciously seeped into *Caligula*, although they may not be obviously presented. Instead, such references are offered subtly in dialogue that suggests a growing acceptance of pessimism, cynicism, and futility. These views are among the tenets of disparagement promoting the contemporary outlook: live for today. Camus wrote about the theory of absurdity in novels and papers that indicate he was striving for a wider theatrical technique, eventually called Theatre of the Absurd. Three years before he died in an automobile accident, Camus received the Nobel Prize for Literature.

Faith in the Fifties

The World War II years did not produce many films of the ancient genre. Public attention was focused on the current dramas staged in the Atlantic and Pacific theaters. The year 1946 became the highest-grossing year for the silver screen. Then, rather quickly, the box office went into decline. The U.S. government declared a new menace in the land—communism. This was a replay of the Red Scare after World War I. Various federal investigations sought communists in the movie industry, government, and military. Innovative cinematic trends from overseas; depressing, unresolved social issues in America; the public's unexpected enthusiasm for high-priced, small screen television; the federal government's insistence on breaking up the major studios; and the rise of the independent motion picture and television producer—all had an effect on a twenty-year period for the industry.

To compete, industry leaders immediately turned to improved wartime technology in color and sound, and to taking over most aspects of television distribution, for the television had long been considered as a probable means for distributing motion pictures. With decision-making power and money remaining on the East Coast, the only division seemed to be in programming. The East Coast would keep the news, in part because New York, Washington, and London were relatively close, and most other programs would gradually move to Los Angeles. By the 1950s, television had begun to make a profit, it was linked from coast to coast, color standards were adopted by the Federal Communications Commission, and the public found primetime television dramas, comedies, and variety programs were acceptable if prerecorded on film or videotape.

In addition to violence, one other ingredient was about to be added so that the public could truly enjoy the lives of the ancients—sex, protected, so to speak, at long last by the First Amendment.

Film Under the First Amendment

The atomic bomb, the Cold War, and an overload of social anxieties stirred a renewed public interest in faith.

In 1952 the Supreme Court recognized the social relevance of motion-picture content and effectively put it under the protection of the First Amendment in *Burstyn v. Wilson*. This benchmark case considered whether Roberto Rossellini's *The Miracle*, which is about a peasant woman (Anna Magnani) who believes she has been impregnated by St. Joseph, was sacrilegious and should be prohibited from public exhibition. The court reasoned that though this opinion may be held by one religion (Catholic) it could not be imposed on the general public, and *The Miracle* could not be prohibited from public viewing. A multitude of new cases resulted from this decision, and they established the basis for the abiding theme of this study—the fight for greater artistic freedom of expression in motion pictures, as exemplified by *Caligula*. In one case, *Roth v. United States*, in 1957, the Supreme Court worked toward defining obscenity, and in *Freedman v. Maryland*, 1965, it described legal procedures for movie censors to follow.

Biblical Temptations

Adult themes of violence, sex, and forgiveness made a big comeback in a cycle of ancient-genre pictures after an absence of nearly a decade. None other than Cecil B. De Mille, "the greatest showman on earth," a reference to circus impresario P. T. Barnum, was recognized, for telling solid stories and spending money on production values rather than expensive stars. After a successful career of over a decade, Hedy Lamarr (1913–2000) was known as one of Hollywood's great beauties, certainly a femme fatale, but she had no big box-office success until she was partnered with Victor Mature (1915–1994) in De Mille's *Samson and Delilah* (1949). Regardless of what viewers thought of his acting, Mature looked like Samson, and Lamarr was undeniably a seductress a man might give up his locks

Hedy Lamarr, playing opposite Victor Mature, initiated the biblical cycle in *Samson and Delilah* in 1949.

for. It was typecasting at its best: Lamarr was wonderful at posing and uttering a few lines in her mysterious Viennese accent, and Mature would be enabled by God to deliver the Israelites from the Philistines by killing a thousand of them with the jawbone of an ass. Like Judith of Bethulia, a great man is enticed and then betrayed by the enchanting Philistine Delilah. He resists her as she asks what makes him so strong, but he loves and trusts her when he finally reveals it is his hair, which had never been cut. Samson is delivered to the Philistines who torture him, but he gets some measure of revenge when years later he destroys the temple of Dagon. According to historian Jon Solomon, the colorful biblical spectacle did not exist previously. "*Samson and Delilah*, in fact, created the genre and served as the prototype that was to culminate in De Mille's hands seven years later."[11]

With a narrative and scenes similar to those used by Cecil B. De Mille for *Sign of the Cross*, Mervin LeRoy rebuilt Rome of A.D. 64 in twentieth-century Italy, hiring bigger stars for a lavish production of *Quo Vadis?* (1951), prior to widescreen. In the opening scenes, Nero (Peter Ustinov) is practicing his songs and being pampered, when Roman general Marcus Vinicus (Robert Taylor) arrives in his chariot expecting to enter the city in triumph. Delayed, he stays at an officer's villa where he takes a bath (Claudette Colbert took a bath in the *Sign of the Cross*) and is shaved by a slave, a common practice for many Roman men. He meets Lygia (Deborah Kerr), who awaits the arrival of Paul, a Jew from the Middle East. Though some settings are different, the romantic situation is identical. Poppaea, guarded by a leopard, wants Marcus as her lover. Marcus and his legion enter Rome in triumph, but Lygia is assigned to Nero's women's quarters, where he cannot find her. The presence of Christians becomes more noticeable, as Peter and Paul tell crowds about Jesus, in a montage of scenes. Marcus finds Lygia, who is protected by strongman Ursus, reminiscent of *Cabiria*. Marcus and Lygia are in love and Paul wants Marcus to put down his arms and conquer only through love.

Marcus learns too late that Nero has torched the old wooden part of Rome and intends to blame the Christians. Marcus tries to save Lygia by leading her and others through the sewer system to the river. Petronius, who has lost his favored advisor position to Nero, commits suicide. Peter and Lygia are imprisoned, and so he marries Lygia and Marcus there. The Christians enter the arena singing, as in the previous film; however, in contrast to *Sign of the Cross*, the violence in *Quo Vadis?* is visualized and prolonged. Several animals attack scantily clad women dressed up as sacrifices. Marcus is forced to watch Lygia as she is about to be killed by a bull, but she is saved by Ursus. Marcus escapes his captors, dashes into the arena, and denounces Nero. He and Poppaea flee; Nero strangles her and commits suicide. With the arrival of a new emperor, Marcus and Lygia return to the location where earlier Peter had his vision answering, "Quo vadis?"

The debut in major features of 3-D screen images having depth rather than just height and width, and the application of this technology to the location films for Cinerama provided breathtaking effects, but the public was still mainly interested in plot, character, and fresh ideas. In an attempt to restore the family movie-going habit, industry leaders pondered the benefits of spectacle. Widescreen attempts had been made since the late 1920s. The most commercially promising endeavor reached the screen as CinemaScope, developed by 20th Century–Fox (TCF), which had a wartime reputation for lush Technicolor musicals and escapist films with endless vistas. Producer Frank Ross (1904–1990) decided to adapt *The Robe*, a popular 1941 novel written by Lutheran clergyman Lloyd C. Douglas (1877–1951) and based on the New Testament, using TCF's CinemaScope at a cost of five million dollars. With a cast of famous names, direction by Henry Koster, a screenplay by Philip Dunne, and an impressive score by Alfred Newman, *The Robe* (1953) brought in seventeen million.

To adjust the time frame, narration describes Tiberius as secluded and elderly. It is Caligula as his heir and regent in Rome who makes the decisions that drive the story. (In fact, Caligula would have been about fifteen.) The movie opens on a slave market. Demetrius (Victor Mature) is purchased by Marcellus Galleo (Richard Burton), a tribune and son of a senator. Marcellus outbids Caligula (Jay Robinson), who is displeased and sends them to Jerusalem, where Pontius Pilate (Richard Boone) asks Marcellus to execute three criminals. Jesus is one of them. During the stormy event, Demetrius acquires Jesus's robe. Marcellus is deeply disturbed by what has happened — he cannot even touch the robe, presumably being steeped in guilt. Believed to be mentally unstable, he is sent to Capri (of all places) to recover. Marcellus tells Emperor Tiberius (Ernest Thesiger) about his strange and bewildering experience. The emperor, who studies occult signs, sends him on a secret mission back to Jerusalem to learn more about the mysterious man and to find the robe. Tiberius speculates that the force behind Jesus is the greatest sickness of all, "Man's desire to be free." This major theme, built into the movie, was on the rise in the 1950s for artists and social movements forming throughout the nation. Marcellus hears about more miracles and meets Christian leaders, including Peter (Michael Rennie), while seeking the robe that he finds Demetrius has kept hidden.

Tiberius dies and Caligula becomes emperor. Marcellus tells Peter that he crucified Christ, and Peter assures him that he was forgiven from the cross. Marcellus pledges to serve Jesus. Knowing that he has returned to Rome, Caligula thinks Marcellus may be a Christian conspirator. Meanwhile,

Demetrius has been captured and is being tortured; but Marcellus and other Christians free him. Demetrius is taken to the villa of Marcellus's father, Senator Galleo, where Peter, who evidently has miraculous powers, heals him. Roman soldiers arrive and Marcellus is taken into custody, but Demetrius escapes. (He was a principal character in the sequel already underway.) Caligula interrogates Marcellus and Diana (Jean Simmons), the woman who loves him. They are defiant Christians. Caligula sentences them to death. When the couple leave the throne room, Diana hands the robe to a slave, indicating that it too will be part of the sequel. The lovers look happy as an unseen chorus sings "Hallelujah," and the palace dissolves into clouds.

The careful use of painted backgrounds and large crowd scenes created an impression of scope, even though most of the settings were shot in rather small locations. Jay Robinson,

Susan Hayward plays Messalina in *Demetrius and the Gladiators*, 1954.

as Caligula, using a harsh voice and a fast-paced walk, yells his commands to those whom he had taken prisoner. He gained a good deal of favorable press for his biting style and dominant character. His memorable performance, acted with more frenzy than fear, defined a niche for Caligula among the pantheon of emperors. *The Robe* received Academy Awards for art direction and costumes, and honorary recognition for the development of Cinemascope.

The next year's *Demetrius and the Gladiators* (1954) begins with a replaying of the final scenes from *The Robe*, showing Caligula sentencing Marcellus and Diana to death. They embrace their future, and Diana passes the robe on to a slave to give to the Big Fisherman. This scene, however, is observed by newcomers Messalina (Susan Hayward) and Claudius (Barry Jones), as the opening titles roll. The picture takes advantage of the elements most favorably mentioned in regard to *The Robe*. With Demetrius as the leading character (Victor Mature), screenwriter Philip Dunne wrote a mainly original screenplay and some of the principal contributors to *The Robe* assisted in continuing their work, notably producer Frank Ross, and the award-winning production designers for settings and costumes.

Once again the story itself opens with a storm. Caligula (Jay Robinson) is escorted to the chambers of Claudius and Messalina. Robinson remains consistent in his characterization of Caligula, and bald British actor Barry Jones, sixty-one, plays Claudius without a stammer or limp. Caligula is troubled because Marcellus and Diana were not afraid to die. Perhaps they did not die, Claudius suggests. Caligula wonders why he should die, which contradicts the notion that he considers himself a god. This story adjustment is essential because it rests on the premise that Jesus and the robe may have the secret to eternal life. Messalina, young, beautiful, and apparently faithful to Claudius, complains about how unpredictable Caligula is, and Claudius makes reference to Attia's important statement mentioned in *Caligula*. He may be mad, but "men do not kill what they despise, only what they fear." At a Christian gathering in front of Marcellus's tomb, Peter (Michael Rennie) reviews the importance of Jesus and reassures Demetrius of his faith. Peter is going on a trip and gives the robe to Demetrius. In a busy marketplace, Demetrius talks to Lucia (Debra Paget), a young Christian woman who loves Demetrius. Soldiers enter looking for the robe and say that concealment means death. Lucia runs off as a decoy so that Demetrius can hide the robe, but when he hears her scream at a soldier, he defends her. The fight results in Demetrius being sentenced to gladiator school. In the Italian tradition established by Bartolomeo Pagano, Victor Mature had an outstanding physique that was exhibited whenever possible in his roles.

There is a private arena in the palace, where Claudius and Messalina plan to entertain Caligula on his birthday. While they are announcing their plans to the gladiators, Demetrius tries to escape and, when captured, reveals that he is a Christian who will not kill his opponent. Messalina wants to test whether the law of the jungle will prevail—kill or be killed. She tells Strabo (Ernest Borgnine), head of the gladiator school, that she wants a special event staged for Caligula's birthday. Caligula attends reluctantly and complains about the poor quality of previous contests, but he is mainly preoccupied with finding the robe. The gladiators salute the emperor and several pairs fight to the death. Glycon (William Marshall), a Nubian who is friendly with Demetrius, is paired with him. He says if they fight convincingly without killing each other, the crowd may save them. Glycon falls and Demetrius

1. Divine Metamorphosis 25

awaits for a thumbs-up or thumbs-down signal from Caligula; the crowd saves the Nubian. These battles illustrate how emotionally effective and superior they are to the decapitation scene presented in *Caligula*. Messalina insists that Demetrius also fight the tigers. Four tigers attack him, and he kills them. He is badly hurt so Messalina tends to his wounds in the gladiator cell, while Glycon stands guard. Claudius calls Demetrius to the palace and talks about the robe. Demetrius becomes Messalina's guard.

Caligula summons Messalina to the palace; she is accused of conspiracy. She denies the charge. Caligula says he "aspires" to be a god. Messalina, a priestess of Isis, says he is a god. This response is similar to Caligula's confrontation with Claudius in the 1937 *I, Claudius*. Later, Messalina confides her conspiracy plans to Demetrius and wants him to protect her at her seaside villa. There she tries to seduce Demetrius, but he rejects her and returns to the gladiator school. This was an important decision, inasmuch as Mature was better flexing his muscles in the arena than in bed. Demetrius expects to fight, but Messalina tells Strabo he is not to fight, thus denying him contact with a woman. When the women arrive that night, Lucia, concealed among them, tells Demetrius she loves him, but they are separated. Demetrius is locked up, and Lucia is abused by another gladiator (Richard Egan). Demetrius prays to God to protect her, but she faints and Strabo carries her away. Demetrius believes she is dead and that God has failed him.

Caligula recognizes Demetrius in the arena, where a group of men surround him and he then kills them. Cassius Chaerea asks freedom for life for Demetrius. Demetrius has rejected God and is promoted to tribune. Demetrius and Messalina make love at the villa. Glycon, expressing Christian leanings, guards them. Peter comes to see Demetrius, but he is bitter; therefore, Peter leaves.

Caligula complains that his statues are being torn down; the guards are not protecting them. Caligula threatens the guards and he slaps Chaerea. This sets up the rapid ending so as not to prolong the story. Messalina convinces him that the robe has the power of eternal life, so he tells Demetrius to find it. Demetrius discovers that Lucia, who is in a coma, clutches the robe. Peter appears and says to pray for her. A flashback retells how Demetrius got the robe at the crucifixion. By praying, Demetrius redeems himself and Lucia is restored. Peter says to take the robe to Caligula. Caligula kills a man and tries to bring him back to life with the robe, only to realize it has no magic restorative powers. Macro, the greatest fighter to appear in the arena, is to fight Demetrius. The robe is given to Glycon. Demetrius will not fight; he is knocked down and ready to die. Mercifully, a spear thrown from somewhere, rather like a *deus ex machina* ending, kills Macro and a second one kills Caligula. Claudius is immediately proclaimed emperor by the guards, and

Messalina reassumes her role as his wife. Demetrius, Peter, and Glycon leave the palace.

With two major pictures back to back, Jay Robinson and Caligula received a great deal of attention. Caligula was defined as wicked, even though he was less so than some other emperors. Claudius is reintroduced without paying any attention to his disabilities, Messalina is untainted by her extraordinary desire to seduce men, and even Pontius Pilate vacillates sufficiently to generate some sympathy for the difficulty of his decision. The villain is the Jewish high priest and several cruel Roman soldiers, as later in Mel Gibson's *The Passion of the Christ*. The gladiators appear as righteous and muscled protectors, a sexy combination. Some nudity is seen in ancient and biblical stories that followed. What was eventually extracted from these pictures for *Caligula* was enlarging the parameters for violence, sex, and nudity. Touching as the Christian cause may be, the licentious sex, the arena slayings of human and beast, and demonstrations of inhumanity tend to override any religious messages that these films convey.

In 1956, Cecil B. De Mille, the grand master of the biblical film, was able to revive another of his storied hits, *The Ten Commandments*, into a $13.5 million, VistaVision spectacular for Paramount. In this revival, Charlton Heston as Moses parts the Red Sea and allows the children of Israel to enjoy another explicit, exuberant orgy, worshipping the Golden Calf; therefore, they could be redeemed by verbal presentations of Christian ethics. With a much-rehearsed story, famous stars, all of the production values that De Mille could muster in the tradition of Barnum and Bailey, and the theatrical perfection of David Belasco, he presented to the public his last hurrah, his crowning biblical screen achievement. *The Ten Commandments* lives on as one of the most endurable and popular masterworks of the cinema. It was introduced with his own voice assuring viewers that the film was morally acceptable to watch. De Mille died two years later. Guccione wanted to emulate this cinematic standard.

A rival in the same category is yet another remake, *Ben-Hur* (1959), for which director William Wyler received his third Academy Award. *Ben-Hur* was on the verge of disaster for the lack of a convincing script when producer Sam Zimbalist enticed Gore Vidal to rewrite several scenes. According to Fred Kaplan, Gore Vidal's biographer, Zimbalist thought Karl Tunberg's script was "unshootable."[12] With a budget of $15 million from MGM, it took ten months to complete the sets depicting ancient Rome and Jerusalem, already under construction at Cinecittà Studios in Rome. Vidal and British playwright Christopher Fry were to be the fourth and fifth writers to work on the script. One of Vidal's principal contributions was to provide motivation for Messala and Judah's intense rivalry and hatred. He convinced Zimbalist and

Wyler that Messala was Judah's spurned lover, and, in a key confrontation, British actor Steven Boyd as Messala conveys this idea using only his eyes. Vidal was on the set and at work until his day of departure about five weeks later. When the Screen Writers' Guild met to acknowledge the credits for the film, Norman Tunberg was given exclusive credit, although Vidal insists that he wrote one-third of it, and Fry wrote almost as much. Vidal really wanted this recognition; but his disappointment foreshadowed a bitter controversy in reverse over his script for *Caligula*.

From the end of the war to 1959, six biblical films were ranked among the top ten box-office successes. During the following forty years, several ancient features with the same production values failed to attract big audiences. The biggest failure in the category supposedly was *Cleopatra* (1963). The story suffered from the same over-length and complications experienced in Pascal's *Caesar and Cleopatra*. It had stars Richard Burton and Elizabeth Taylor. Joseph L. Mankiewicz (1909–1993) replaced the previous director, the production was moved from wet England to sunny Italy, and there were many delays because of illness and lawsuits. Taylor had a million-dollar contract, the highest amount ever paid to a Hollywood star. With sumptuous sets and twenty-six thousand costumes, the cost ran to forty million dollars by the time it opened at the Rivoli Theater in New York. Similar problems plagued *Caligula*. The important lesson learned was that off-screen controversy may pay the bills, as the Taylor-Burton romance became international news

The Convergence of Violence and Sex

Other contributors to cultural progress during the 1950s were the little-publicized but highly individualized "art" film creators, who had gone virtually unnoticed, but were beginning to seek recognition and respect. Similar to the development of traditional movies, art films were often produced in Europe and pornographic films were shot in the United States. Frequently, the French were given credit for the naughty books, playing cards, and stage shows, just as they led the way in early traditional movies. In America, amateurs were the early subjects of inexpensive 8mm and 16mm sex films; then, as burlesque faded from the stage, those performers appeared in movies that featured strippers for male-only viewers. Producer Florenz Ziegfeld revealed nude sixteen-year-olds on the *Follies*' stage in the first quarter of the century; Sally Rand, who did her famous nude fan dance at the Chicago World's Fair in 1933, was still doing it at state fairs in the fifties; and Candy Barr was already a legend as a burlesque queen during the decade she filmed *Smart Aleck*. A proportionally rounded body, rather large breasts, a welcoming look from innocent eyes, long legs, and mid-teen youth when she began performing were among Barr's assets.

Pornographic films fell into various categories. "Loops," ten-minute soft- or hardcore films, featured sexual activity shown repeatedly and were referred to as "stag," "beaver," or "experimental" movies. Occasionally, they were shown on military bases during the Korean War. Pioneer sex-film producers and adult-magazine publishers increased during the fifties. Ruben Sturman became the most significant distributor of pornography in the country, according to Luke Ford in *A History of X*. He exerted more influence than later magazine publishers Hugh Hefner, Bob Guccione and Larry Flynt, Ford claims.[13] The first cover for Hefner's *Playboy* featured Marilyn Monroe. Both the magazine and the actress would become cultural icons, gaining general approval for women who appeared in states of undress without offending moral standards. They offered a rite of passage at a time when even underground sexually explicit films were almost nonexistent. In the late 1950s the principal distributors in the United States were Bill Mishkin and Joe Brenner in New York, David Friedman in Chicago, and Dan Sonney in Los Angeles. The picture output was a mere eight or ten a year; and so they were played continuously. Huge profits were made on little production. No one realized that 8mm and 16mm sex films would become so popular that they would continue to be widely advertised and distributed into the eighties.

Within the same period, the first traditional filmmaker to ignore the establishment's Motion Picture Code was Otto Preminger (1905–1986), a versatile Jewish producer, director, and actor who played Prussian officers. He startled the industry when he directed *The Moon Is Blue* (1953), using prohibited words "virgin" and "pregnant" in the dialogue. In *The Man with the Golden Arm* (1955), he introduced the hazards of drug addiction by showing Frankie Machine (Frank Sinatra) injecting himself and later going berserk trying to kick the habit. In *Advise and Consent* (1962), he has a homosexual congressman (Don Murray), under threat of exposure, commit suicide, just as a compromised Roman might have done.[14]

Further European competition encouraged nudity when French director Roger Vadim attracted world attention by featuring his twenty-two-year-old wife Brigitte Bardot in his first film, *And God Created Woman* (1956). The widescreen, Eastmancolor film displayed Bardot as an exotic "sex kitten" and was an international sensation.

In *Samuel Roth v. United States*, 1957, the Supreme Court defined obscene material as "utterly without redeeming social importance."[15] Under the ruling another French import, *The Game of Love*, also showing nudity, was not considered obscene, nor were heterosexual- and homosexual-oriented nude magazines. Over the next two decades French cinema would keep the pressure on American producers to expand artistic freedom. French filmmakers risked the loss of government subsidies in 1976 for such erotic films as Just Jaeckin's *The Story of O* and Walerian Borowczyk's *The Beast*. In 1957, the first nudist-colony film was licensed for distribution, but it failed to appeal to the general public, illustrating that nudity in itself would not sell these pictures.

In 1959, adult directors Russ Meyer, David Friedman, Ted Paramour, and Radley Metzger sought audiences beyond those who watched short loops. Russ Meyer (1922–2004) made the raunchy pop-culture feature *The Immoral Mr. Teas* (1959), often regarded as America's first "skin flick." Meyer, a former *Playboy* photographer, cast a friend as the comical Mr. Teas. Teas, under the influence of dental anesthesia, sees all women in the nude, but without genitalia, for Meyer had no interest in displaying genitalia; and of course, Teas does not touch the women. Produced for $24,000, *The Immoral Mr. Teas* grossed a million dollars. This low cost-to-high profit ratio was (and is) fundamental to the adult-movie business. This was the period of the "nudie-cutie," films with nudity and a modest story. Tinto Brass thinks of himself as working similarly to Russ Meyer. Meyer had a successful 23-picture traditional film career with such films as *Vixen* (1968) and *Beyond the Valley of the Dolls* (1970). Lewis Segal wrote in *Show*: "*Beyond the Valley of the Dolls* preserves virtually every film cliché of the 1960s in the most intricate narrative since *War and Peace*—and assembles these elements with an astounding combination of directorial zeal and unerring bad taste."[16] In *Lorna* (1964), Meyer opened the way for lurid exploitation films to return to the business. Ted Paramore's *Not Tonight, Henry* combines continuity with breasts, which for some are virtually a genre in themselves and David Friedman's *Adventures of Lucky Pierre* does something similar, but in addition he introduced violence in *Blood Feast* (1963). Violence was relatively uncommon in sexually oriented nude movies, although vigorous sexual acrobatics were prevalent and may have seemed violent.

By the mid–1960s various cultural changes allowed feature pictures to have more flexibility in their content. The macho male who protected home and country during the wars could sense the growing demands for equal rights among women, especially after birth-control pills were made available to the public in 1960. Pop culture artist Andy Warhol (1927–1987) produced a film collection of funny, ad-libbed, rough-cut, and sometimes naked acquaintances out of his New York studio. These examples of cinéma vérité illustrate the lifestyle of many rich, famous and unknown drug users and addicts. Warhol figured that if he just kept working he would produce some distinguished art pieces from happenstance. While at a loss for new ideas, he came upon the notion of filming his guests with a 16mm Bolex camera, which he set up and turned on as an experiment. He was the ultimate minimalist director of art films. With long-time friend Paul Morrissey he shaped the sixties' experiences into a commercial collection, consisting of *Flesh* (1968), *Trash* (1970), and *Heat* (1972), that revealed the human devastation caused by narcotics. Warhol, himself a teetotaler, used drugs only to keep awake.

Another outlet for sexual exploitation was publishing, where Bob Guccione saw a place in the United States for *Penthouse* magazine, already established in England. He believed there was a market for something more daring than *Playboy*. In cinema circles, film buffs had taken a serious liking to discussions about the artistic, social, and scientific merits of the new American cinema, as historians Gerald Mast and Bruce F. Kawin refer to it in *A Short History of the Movies*.[17] The label "auteur" was being applied to a body of work by unusually talented directors; and universities, which had little more than essential production classes and equipment, began film-studies classes that were listed in a range of intellectual disciplines, suggesting that the Supreme Court got it right: motion pictures *do* impact the lives of millions of citizens.

In 1968, the Motion Picture Production Code was replaced by an age-based rating system introduced by the Motion Picture Association of America. This system allowed everyone of any age to see a movie so long as children were accompanied by a parent. For example, a screaming child could see a violent version of *Macbeth*. Adults were eighteen or older; those who were younger were considered children in the United States. Unobjectionable pictures, like those produced under the obsolete Code would provide a splendid library of motion pictures that, regardless of what rating they received originally, would be reintroduced to the public. Society is fortunate to have inherited from those filmmakers the stories and cultural events that contributed to the twentieth century.

1969

The liberal tenets of Supreme Court decisions, the competition from Europe, restlessness of artists in the United States, and the groundswell of social movements provided the environment for producing *Caligula*. One film that influenced *Caligula* directly was *Fellini Satyricon* (1969), which contributed to *Caligula*'s visual depth as the second golden age of the Italian cinema was coming to a close. Another factor leading to *Caligula* was the American film industry's one-up advantage on world cinema by recognizing the increased importance of hardcore adult films, which reached their pinnacle with the box-office attendance of *Deep Throat*.

The neorealistic Italian directors showed substance and a wide-range of intimate and sweeping narratives in numerous films during what some critics refer to as the second golden age of the Italian cinema. Likewise, in the United

States, some called the overlapping period of the late 1960s and early 1970s the "golden age" of adult cinema, which had a life just long enough to encourage a risk-taker like Bob Guccione to invest in a major crossover production.

The Italian Connection

Among the prominent directors of the neorealistic period were Roberto Rossellini with *Rome, Open City* (1945), *Paisan* (1946), and *Germany Year Zero* (1947); Vittorio De Sica's *Shoeshine* (1946), *The Bicycle Thief* (1948), and *Umberto D.* (1951); and Luchino Visconti's *The Earth Trembles* (1948). "These seven works," wrote Peter Bondanella in *Italian Cinema from Neorealism to the Present*, "do not by any means exhaust the wealth of neorealism, but neorealism's contribution to the evolution of cinema must in large measure be ultimately judged by their achievements."[18] These directors' works and the brilliant works of those following them slowly shifted Italian attendance at American movies since the war to Italian movies dominated by Italian filmmakers. By the 1960s and 1970s, Italy, like the United States, had an abundance of fine directors of superb films. It was the golden age of Italian filmmaking. Multi-talented as writers, designers, actors, and directors, most of them were equally at home in the theater, and most of them had worked on each others' films and films for major artists in France. These directors were involved in politics, often as communists or Marxists, and expressed their beliefs in their films, upsetting wary censors either in the state or the church. Similar political views and filmmaking relationships have contributed to Tinto Brass's background as a movie director. Several American artists who went to Hollywood from live television were also talented in various artistic fields, and they stimulated the American film renaissance of the sixties.

Caligula is particularly indebted to Federico Fellini. Fellini was known for his early work *La dolce vita* (1960), banned in some American cities for sexual content, and *8½* (1962), an "exciting, stimulating, monumental creation," according to *Variety*, about a film director who has gone to a spa looking for inspiration and experiences intense introspection. Fellini's *Juliet of the Spirits* (1965) concerns a wife's frantic attempts to keep her adulterous husband. It is *Fellini Satyricon*, however, his 1969 Technicolor feast, that had the most influence on *Caligula*. Although his early films were neorealistic, "Beginning with *La dolce vita*, Fellini creates a high idiosyncratic and surrealistic world of images and dream fantasies which leave behind forever any connection to traditional cinematic 'realism.'"[19]

Accepting the premise that decadence is indispensable to rebirth, Fellini drew upon his subconscious to create new forms and images in his pictures. Just as *La dolce vita* suggests that much of the past is lost, and that life is facade and masquerade, he bases a surreal fantasy on an incomplete manuscript of *The Satyrica* (aka *Satyricon*) by Gaius Petronius Arbiter (died A.D. 66), an adviser to Emperor Nero, mentioned earlier. Patronius's comic text is about two young men who are in love with a sixteen-year-old boy. The narrative consists of a collection of unusual sequences and images that were created largely from Fellini's imagination. "The visionary is the only true realist," Fellini said. Though directing terrified him, he liked working extemporaneously, seeing shapes and unanticipated actions on the set while shooting was in progress. He loved to capture unusual, bizarre, time-ravaged faces and extraordinary images of all kinds. So the fragments of *Satyrica* were well suited to him.[20] Fellini constructed his dream world at Cinecittà. Very little was shot outside the studio. Similarly, *Caligula* was shot at nearby Dear Studio. In *Fellini Satyricon,* according to Bondanella, "The controlling vision that links the film's many disparate episodes together is a vision of a dehumanized, chaotic, disintegrating, pagan world with important analogies to our own times. This symphony of corruption concentrates upon two major concerns—the status of the arts in ancient Rome, and the ancient myths or religions of pagan times."[21]

In Petronius's *The Satyrica*, two bisexual young men, Encolpius and Ascyltus, are in love with the same beguiling slave, Gitone, a pretty little boy whom everyone wants. The trio are fascinating thieves who live by their wits and sexual favors. After a visit with some friends, they steal enough gold to set out on a journey to seek sexual adventures and plunder. The first-century narrative of social criticism is believed to protest the orgies and debaucheries during Nero's reign. The fragments lend themselves to interpretation and a narrative by Encolpius, a young teacher who is already tired of working with youngsters who refuse to learn and parents who do not make them study. Encolpius also regrets what he sees as a decline in the arts.[22]

As *Fellini Satryicon* begins, Encolpio (Martin Potter) is looking for Gitone (Max Born) in a large Roman bath, where he believes his sometime lover Ascilto (Hiram Keller) has taken him. A comparison can be made between this scene and the pool sequence in *Caligula*. Ascilto is dark, lithe, and dashing. The fellows fight over Gitone, but remain loyal to each other. They run around in thigh-high belted tunics with a loin cloth, frequently revealed, underneath. This is also the standard costume for young men in *Caligula*. Confronted by Encolpio, Ascilto says he sold him to the comic Vernacchio. Gitone is found on stage during a performance consisting of farting and gross comedy. Generally, elimination was relatively unknown in serious or romantic movies until *Caligula*. Threatened, the actor gives up the boy, and the two seek a cave-like room at the bath. As they climb several levels, they pass by soothsayers, prostitutes, musicians, starving horses, obese and partly naked

1. Divine Metamorphosis

men and women, and mentally and physically impaired people seeking refuge. This is a somewhat different set of unusual people than in *Caligula*, but the idea of displaying those who might be considered the dregs of humanity is similar to the exhibits of sexual perversity Tiberius displays. The bath resembles a huge, dank catacomb. Encolpio and Gitone are comfortable in a cell when Ascilto appears and asks Gitone to go away with him again. After Ascilto and Gitone leave, Encolpio barely escapes an earthquake.

Encolpio, a literate fellow, is browsing in a gallery where he meets a poet named Eumolpo. Amidst figures of beauty — Apollo, Narcissus, and Ganymede — the two complain about the current degradation of art. The poet is a guest of wealthy Trimalchio, who symbolizes how excessive riches can be spent on idiotic pleasures. Eumolpo takes Encolpio along to dinner. The assembly wears elaborate gowns, curled headdresses, heavy make-up, and lavish gold jewelry. In contrast, perspiration-soaked slaves look elegant, youthful, and slender serving the banquet guests. The scene represents gluttony and crude behavior, as the host urinates, threatens to whip his chef, reveals a new mosaic of himself, exhibits his African dancers, has his vomit analyzed for omens, flirts with his pretty nephew, and reads his poetry. Several of these images and ideas are transferred to *Caligula*, especially in clothing and dancing. Eumolpo criticizes his host for poorly copying the work of another poet. As the sequence ends, Eumolpo is about to be thrown into a huge fire pit; instead, the next day the wealthy Trimalchio invites everyone for a rehearsal of his burial at his mausoleum.

In a later sequence Encolpio, Ascilto, and Gitone are captured and taken aboard a ship. The owner is Lichas, an unattractive strongman who collects oddities for Caesar. The handsome blond, Encolpio, wearing a loin cloth, has a sexy wrestling match with Lichas and, unsurprisingly, loses. Lichas takes Encolpio as his husband. The marriage is brief, but the presence of homosexuality lingers, even when armed ships seize Lichas's vessel, and he is beheaded.

A montage of war images pass by and a sequence in which Encolpio, Ascilto, and a thief steal a holy hermaphrodite. The sacred albino dies from too much sun, too little water, and a pitiful traveling sequence.

In another revision of a myth (and in another loin cloth), the lean, good-looking Encolpio has to fight a very tall, muscular man in a minotaur mask, while a crowd of spectators observes from on high. Encolpio pleads for his life: "I will love you, if you spare me." The minotaur accepts his plea, and the crowd, having a good time at the festival for the god of mirth, agrees. The proconsul in charge, however, gives Encolpio another task. In public view he has to satisfy a nymphomaniac, Ariadne. The pathetic woman, lying on a bed in the middle of a sun-drenched arena, is the epitome of consummate desperation. Encolpio is no match for her insatiable desire. Believing himself impotent, Encolpio joins the poet Eumolpo who takes him to the Garden of Delights, where women try remedies, such as spanking him with switches, to restore his prowess. Nothing works.

Another fable is told about an old and ugly wizard who fell in love with a beautiful woman. She spurned him and he extinguished all of the fires in town, saying that the only fire is between her legs, and so her vagina becomes an igniting source. Encolpio and Ascilto seek the woman with the fire. An image in a dreamscape appears, and Encolpio commits his manhood to the unattractive, illusive female phantom, and regains his potency.

Outside, meanwhile, Ascilto has had a fight over money and is mortally wounded. Encolpio finds the poet is dead too, but Eumolpo has invited his friends to eat his flesh if they want to obtain his wealth. Encolpius decides to pass on that invitation and sails away. In a final dissolve, all the characters are preserved in a timeless mosaic.[23]

Significantly, *Fellini Satyricon* was produced in 1968 and distributed worldwide in 1970. Fellini hired unknown actors, except for Capucine, and the film was produced for three million dollars. Costumes and scenery were by Danilo Donati. Donati would design the costumes and scenery for *Caligula*; hence, the two films have a visual resemblance. This was Fellini's departure from autobiographical films; instead, he reenergized and redirected his work. "His preoccupation with the human face has never been explored more graphically," John M. Culkin wrote in *Show*, but Molly Haskell replied, "In a way, the world of Satyricon is one Fellini has always yearned for — a world free of the crippling taboos, moral repressions and cultural defenses imposed by Christianity."[24] *Satyricon* shows a bankrupt world without basic human decency. Its writer Petronius, after serving and observing the evil Nero, committed suicide.

With an exciting concept — marrying traditional and sexually explicit adult movies, with an abundance of talent in Europe and the United States, and with vastly more money than had ever been invested in such a unique film, Bob Guccione had a gift from the gods — an opportunity to make cinema history on a grand scale.

Going All the Way

In 1969, hardcore movies appeared in cinemas. Nudity was already on stage in some large cities and hardcore films accompanied couples performing live sex acts. Gerard Damiano's comedy *Deep Throat* (1972), shot for $25,000, gave permission to the general public to see explicit sex on the screen. Previously, men who felt guilty doing so could now put away their stereotypical disguise, a raincoat and dark glasses. *Deep Throat* is about a young woman (Linda Lovelace, 1949–2002) who cannot get satisfaction from vaginal intercourse. So she consults a loopy psychiatrist (Harry Reems) who suggests that the therapy she needs may be fellatio because her clitoris is in her throat. Entertainment publishers crowned this curious social phenomenon "porno chic." It was essential viewing for socialites and culturally astute moviegoers. Everyone from New York critic Judith Crist to *Screw* magazine's Jim Buckley reviewed it; thus, *Deep Throat* became one of the top grossing pictures of all time, estimated at $600 million (*Newsweek*). This enormous popularity of an adult feature and its unexpected profits quickly attracted major organized-crime families that took over most of the young pornographic film industry.[25]

The Mitchell brothers' *Behind the Green Door* (1973) is a much darker film, and is difficult to understand, as was its star Marilyn Chambers, who was on the cusp of having fame and fortune in more legitimate enterprises, but gave them up for a multi-partnered, multiracial sexual indoctrination. Continuing the interest in sex films with traditional values, almost everyone could empathize with Georgina Spelvin's character in *The Devil in Miss Jones* (1972), who said it would be unfair to sentence her to damnation if she was not guilty of the sexual depravity she was alleged to have indulged in. These films created an atmosphere that stimulated experimentation in pornographic filmmaking, so long as financial backing was available. Perhaps a dozen relatively lavish, story-oriented, vigorously performed, and well-directed sexually explicit adult films constituted what was referred to as the "golden age" of the pornographic film, lasting from about 1968 to 1976. The inference was that, in addition to violence, traditional movies would benefit from encouraging more mature themes, more realistic (and perhaps cruder) language, and more explicit sex scenes.

The softcore pornographic picture was a kind of middle ground where some of the most beautiful pictures were produced. Radley Metzger's adult work in the 1970s revealed his ability to shoot erotic scenes that enabled his cinematic eye to mix a traditional narrative and softcore intimacy, as in *The Lickerish Quartet* (1970), *Score,* and *The Opening of Misty Beethoven* (1975). In *Score,* for instance, Metzger comments on a currently popular activity — partner swapping. In a sun-drenched village, an experienced twentysomething couple, Elvira and Jack, practice seducing other couples. They invite Betsy and Eddie for dinner, alcohol, amyl nitrate, and sex. The women quickly go upstairs where they engage in lesbian caresses, while Eddie and Jack pursue each other in the den. Shots are well composed, the scenes are lighted for mood and intense color, the cinematography is smooth, and the editing parallels the progress of the women with that of the men. Near climax, Eddie mentally substitutes his wife's image with Jack's until the moment of release. Simple special effects create flowing wavy mirrored images that reveal the women having a liquid romantic experience, while the men have a more direct encounter. Sexual intercourse is revealed by reaction close-ups and by gliding past or peeking around carefully composed legs, arms, and torsos. Sometimes, Metzger used perfectly matched body parts for explicit scenes. By the mid–1970s, the techniques for combining traditional and adult softcore scenes beautifully, as in *Score,* were already a practiced art. In 1974, Jan-Michael Vincent was the first big-name American actor to shock audiences with full frontal male nudity in the mainstream film *Buster and Billie.* Male nudity began to appear more frequently after 1980.[26]

In England, writer Derek Jarman (1942–1994) and Paul Humfress codirected a stunning initial softcore film, *Sebastiane,* in 1976. *Sebastiane* takes place in A.D. 303, under the rule of Diocletian. The opening scene is a feast in which a dancing clown, painted in white and wearing a white loincloth, protrudes huge, bright-red lips; he is similar to the clown in Caligula's orgy scene. Sebastiane, a beautiful nobleman from Narbonne in Gaul, commands a company of the Praetorian guards and is clearly the favorite of the emperor. Then Sebastiane tells Diocletian he is a Christian. The emperor urges him to return to Roman gods, but he refuses. The subtitled narrative, told in poetic Latin and beautifully composed scenes, shows a Roman officer and a small band of men sent to one of the deserted prison islands. The officer in charge lusts after Sebastiane, who does not submit himself mentally or physically. The prisoners, mostly nude, try to find ways to amuse themselves in the relentless sun and heat, and the exile quickly deteriorates from playful, erotic homosexual games to extreme trivia — watching beetle races. The torture of eternal nothingless is imminent. Sebastiane is martyred for his faith in God. Legend says Sebastiane was executed by being bound to a stake and shot by arrows until dead. In the Jarman version he is staked to the desert floor to die from exposure. In the legend he is believed dead, but found alive and returns to Diocletian's palace to plead for his friends and against Diocletian's intolerance. He is taken to the arena, clubbed to death, and his body is thrown into the great sewer. It was discovered and buried in the catacombs at the feet of Peter and Paul.

The adult sex film industry self-rated its films as X, a designation shared with the traditional industry, which usually meant some themes, perhaps nudity, and language might be objectionable to families with young viewers. Double XX signaled at least softcore content, and triple XXX referred to hardcore sexually explicit scenes. Newspapers, general publications, and malls began to disallow advertising from the sex film industry; and thus, in the 1990s the traditional motion-picture industry changed its "X" rating to "NC-

17," supposedly prohibiting children seventeen and under from seeing the picture, but enabling adults to screen mature subjects.

During the so-called "golden age" of the pornographic film, the 1970 *Report to the Presidential Commission on Obscenity and Pornography*, which the Johnson administration initiated and the Nixon administration rejected, was widely circulated. After two years of study and two million dollars the report found that pornography might be a nuisance, but that it did little harm to adults. After years of formulation, the tenets of a guideline for determining obscenity were issued by the Supreme Court in the ruling on *Marvin Miller v. California*, 1973. A work is obscene (1) if it depicts or describes sexual conduct specifically defined by state law, (2) if, taken as a whole, it appeals to the prurient interests in sex, (3) if it portrays sexual conduct in a patently offensive way, and (4) if, taken as a whole, it does not have serious literary, artistic, political, or scientific value. As diverse as the nation was, that meant a jury would have to decide whether a film was obscene based on local, not national, standards.

Usually obscenity meant sexual relations with beasts, or in unspecified extremely revolting situations, or with minor children; these acts were relatively easy to judge. The wide range of sexual activity the public was willing to view or let other adults see became increasingly difficult for juries to determine. During the 1970s conservative areas of the country agreed with the prosecution, but the decision was often reversed on appeal. In time the juries, even in conservative jurisdictions, came to recognize that broader freedoms were at stake and agreed with the defense. Cases of alleged pornographic films flooded the calendars of courts across the nation, keeping judges, prosecutors, defense lawyers, "expert" witnesses, and a multitude of generally low-paid sex-parlor and bookstore employees occupied. The decade that led up to big-budget adult productions like *Caligula* quickly reversed direction. As the 1970s ended with some less-than-successful investments in elaborate sex films, the industry, largely run by profit-oriented criminal interests, returned to its main formula for trade productions—explicit, fast, cheap, hardcore action.

In 1960, about twenty cinemas played adult films exclusively; by 1970 that number had jumped to 750. Watching adult films had become an obsession for many viewers. Just as Bob Guccione began publishing *Penthouse* in England, rough and kinky sex films appealing to those who liked bizarre and violent behavior began to replace semen with blood. Many films illustrated the struggle between sex and violence. Over time, erotic pleasure became repetitious, and so it took more inventiveness to interest viewers. The market for the pornographic film industry remained targeted on the pubescent boy or young adult who wanted immediate sexual relief, but potential buyers included a far greater demographic range. Consequently, for the adult picture business to expand it had to have films and products that appealed to every taste.

Since most sex takes place in the mind, viewers sought more adventuresome ways to engage in fantasy to achieve satisfaction. Multiple partners, group sex, and bestiality became early adult-film genres. Images of torture, weird contacts with humans, freaks, and animals, multiple penetration, masochism and sadism followed. This increased intensity and insatiable demand for a variety of partners and experiences seemed to be in concert with an addictive continuum that eventually signals death. This continuum, woven into the *Caligula* narrative, accounts for the profusion of violence over sex, instead of, as viewers might expect from Guccione, the dominance of sex over violence. The substitution of violence for sex had become a reliable palliative for American audiences that shunned nudity. Latent guilt over sex still was dominant, but viewers could enjoy bloody massacres, desecration, and other intense behavior. Sounds of whipping, screams, bizarre noises, and some vulgar language also contributed to the effect.

In an adult picture, a viewer could typically expect ejaculation on the face, back, or stomach of a woman or man. This usually demonstrates dominance over them, or surrender, or ecstatic joy for the partners, depending on what has transpired previously. Naturally internal ejaculation does not do this for viewers. The visual stimulus must be there. Often observed pleasure resonates with nonparticipants in the scene. In *Caligula*, the long lesbian scene illustrates this difficulty. When violence and sex are combined in a film, death may follow, but not necessarily. To experience death before death has a maximum, dangerous, impact. For instance, some believe orgasm is intensified if a person combines it with near death from some form of strangulation. Of course, the emotional and psychological depth of sexual quality is experienced in the mind and cannot be shared with another person. The ultimate turn-on some said, was death itself, thus the so-called "snuff" film, wherein a person is supposedly killed on camera, alleged to be a hoax. In 1976, Nagisa Oshima's *In the Realm of the Senses* (*Ai No Corrida*), already banned, was released after scenes were cut. Based on a 1936 criminal case in which a married man and a geisha retreat into a world of extreme sexual fantasy, they engage in the ultimate orgasm, she strangles him and castrates him. The theme deals with the relationship of death and eroticism so important to *Caligula*. The practice of prolonged execution is cruel and sadistic, but to an obsessed person, witnessing it may entail sexual ecstasy. These films and many more experimental variations with sex and violence came before—and were reflected in—*Caligula*. Methods of successfully filming them were explored during the sixties and seventies. *Caligula* attempted to bring this dimension of sex and violence within the scope of a traditional motion picture.

In order to merge sex and violence, the producer, the director, and the writer needed to be working toward the same vision. Usually this vision is defined by the director. Bob Guccione and his large talent pool had a great many options to choose from by the time *Caligula* was given the green light. In this case, however, *Caligula* was personally financed by the producer who had an agenda that included featuring Penthouse Pets, making a traditional film with explicit sex scenes to advance freedom in the arts, avoiding the use of his famous stars in a hardcore context, and keeping his film legal enough so a that he could get domestic and international releases. This proved to be a daunting task.

The BBC's Surprise

I, Claudius, produced in time for a 1976 release while Tinto Brass was shooting *Caligula* in Italy, was the second attempt by the British to use the novels of Robert Graves to tell the story of the Julio-Claudian family from Augustus through the early years of the reign of Claudius. The result was thirteen episodes lasting about fifty minutes each, for a total of approximately 740 minutes. An epic undertaking, this stunning production was broadcast as a mini-series under the aegis of the hugely successful *Masterpiece Theatre*, originally aired on PBS on 10 January 1971 and hosted by Alistair Cooke. Each night an elderly Claudius (Derek Jacobi) would tell about the incredible manipulations of the family members as they sought power. The most relentless murderers were the women, notably Caligula's grandmother Livia (Sian Phillips), who would do anything to make her son Tiberius (George Baker) emperor, according to Graves's novel.

By now, Graves had translated Suetonius's *The Twelve Caesars*, a widely praised scholarly work. The BBC meticulously developed its production in cooperation with London Films. It had just the right mix of sex, violence, and authenticity for an American public that was not well acquainted with the British cast. Certainly the actors were not nearly as well known as Bob Guccione's acting ensemble. Written by Jack Pullman and directed by Herbert Wise, everyone could be proud of this masterwork.

In Episode 6, Caligula (John Hurt) appears as a pretty little, curly-haired blond child present at the death of his heralded father, Germanicus, who has been poisoned in Syria. Governor Piso is framed for the murder, but Agrippina (Fiona Walker), Germanicus's wife, blames Tiberius. Livia, however, entertains a prominent expert on poisons, Martina (Patsy Byrne), to learn that she blames Caligula for his father's death. Episode 7 is mainly devoted to getting rid of contenders who might be in Livia's way to make Tiberius emperor. The women, obsessed with attaining power through their husbands and sons, are portrayed as even more vicious and permissive than the men, and this enables Tiberius to destroy them and their lovers.

By Episode 8, Livia is dead and Tiberius, freed from his mother at last, establishes his headquarters on Capri. His main henchman is Sejanus (Patrick Stewart), who has managed to get rid of most of the alleged threats to the emperor. Meanwhile, Caligula is invited to Capri where Tiberius accepts some advice from the strange youth. No one thinks about Claudius as a threat because of his physical and presumed mental impairments. Tiberius, who is constantly afraid of a conspiracy to kill him, arranges a plot to eliminate Sejanus. Caligula suggests Macro (John Rhy-Davies) as his replacement and offers to identify Sejanus's allies. A bloodbath follows.

In Episode 9, Caligula becomes emperor after Tiberius rallies and Macro kills him. The senate expects Caligula to lead Rome into a "golden age"; therefore, he is given extraordinary power. Almost immediately Caligula is plagued with extreme mental duress. He has headaches, visions of the dead, and various torments. His demands are excessive, and soon he has taken ill. He seems to be near death, but survives, and claims he has become a god. Claudius says he always knew he was a god. Caligula demands that the heads of statues be replaced with his own, but after his sister Drusilla says she is to have his baby — the child of Zeus Caligula — he is afraid. Caligula attempts to deliver the child by cutting it out of Drusilla's womb.

In a well-written compilation of Caligula's deeds, Episode 10 has Caligula raise money through a palace brothel, go to fight on the German frontier, and quarrel with Neptune, resulting in a treasure trove of seashells. Meanwhile, his wife Caesonia presents him with a child. By now, Macro has been replaced by Cassius Chaerea (Sam Dastor), whom Caligula continually demeans by implying he is a homosexual. In a surprising scene, Caligula appears as a goddess and dances with a man. The small audience he has assembled praises him for his performance; and he follows it with the unexpected marriage of Claudius to Messalina (Shiela White). At the wedding Caligula includes his horse, Incitatus, as a guest.

Simultaneously, Cassius plans to separate Caligula's mercenary German bodyguard from him and assassinate him in a narrow hallway at midday, when Caligula leaves the arena games for lunch. Caligula does not want to leave, but Cassius says a troupe of young male ballet dancers want to perform for him. The ruse works. Caligula, his wife, and child are killed by soldiers under Cassius's instructions. Claudius, hiding in the palace, is pressed into service as the next emperor, for the soldiers believe he will benefit them. The remaining episodes enact the life of Claudius as emperor, but not in detail nor to the completion of his term. The violent and sexual action in this production is not as explicit as that in the film being shot for Guccione that same year; he must take it the rest of the way. Neither production seems to have had any impact on the other.

If anything, *I Claudius* is less likely to be purchased or viewed in recent years because of its length and cost. Then, too, some program directors say its violence and sexual content are not welcome as reruns on some PBS stations with conservative viewers and donors. *Caligula,* on the other hand, is "still alive."

In 1980, David Freedman, president of the Adult Film Association of America and a leading producer-distributor, estimated adult film sales at $12 to $14 million, which represented only 10 to 15 percent of the income from legitimate titles. Rampant piracy of adult films was partly blamed; but on the positive side, recent court decisions had given "obscene material" copyright protection.[27] What could be sweeter?

2

TABLETS AND PARCHMENT

Ancient Rome was a city of about one million inhabitants when Caligula ruled in the first century. As recently as 2004 the people of Rome celebrated the city's founding on 21 April 753 B.C. Legend has it that Rome was established by the twin sons of Mars, the god of war, Romulus and Remus. The mortal princess, who bore the brothers illicitly, was imprisoned and the babies were set adrift. A she-wolf discovered and suckled them until they were old enough to be cared for by a shepherd. They are believed to have eventually settled near Palatine Hill. In 2006 this site, perhaps one hundred fifty feet from the apartments of Tiberius and Livia, was being carefully excavated.

Looking north from atop Palatine Hill, where the emperors resided, the emperors could see the temples of the gods, the center of government, and the marketplace encircled by mostly wooden, five-story apartment buildings and low-rise private homes, notable for their blank walls that shut out the squalor and dangers known to ordinary people. By day, the people conducted their business in the dirty streets and alleys that wound their way through the fabled Seven Hills or wandered to the tributaries of the Tiber River, into which large sewers emptied. Sanitation varied from huge public bathhouses and latrines to open cesspools and piss pots, the contents of which were sometimes dumped from overhead windows on unsuspecting passersby. Malaria and other diseases helped to keep the average age of the population under thirty.[1] By night, the dark streets concealed perils, dangerous humans and uncontrolled animals. No one was safe. The homeless protected themselves as well as they could from robbers and thieves, and everyone feared the constant threat of fires, which were frequent.

Rome consisted of the extremely rich—the 2 percent who are shown in most movies—and the subsidized poor. Slaves made up about one-third of the population. Humanely treated, they often could buy—or were given—their freedom after age eighteen. Although a multitude of tongues was heard, the language was primarily Latin; however, Greek was familiar to the better educated 10 to 20 percent of adult men, who depended on tutors.

Top: Romulus and Remus, Rome's founders, may have had a domus on this newly excavated site on Palatine Hill. *Bottom:* Interior of the Romulus and Remus site consists of large stone blocks built around living spaces.

44 Caligula and the Fight for Artistic Freedom

Tiberius lived in an apartment next to his mother Livia. It is about 150 feet from the Romulus and Remus site.

Hellenic influence was strong. Most children were home-schooled in reading, writing, and arithmetic; public education was deemed a failure.[2] Beyond the five square miles of teeming urban life, where East met West in the center of the explored world, and past the encirclement of crowded urban dwellings was a vast, rolling, rural landscape that could be very hot in summer and cold in winter. Much of the land consisted of large estates owned by wealthy senators and businessmen, and these were at the mercy of raiders.

Researching the Story

Pagan Rome was just reaching its zenith as Caligula came to power.[3] The rulers had religious functions to perform but none of the Caesars were religious zealots. The polytheistic religion that was largely adapted from the Greeks was encountering numerous new ideas from Egypt and the Near East. While Roman leaders prayed to the gods for favors and privilege, their interest in serving the public wavered. Many people were not Roman citizens. The city was inundated with people from all races and ethnic groups, some of whom were fleeing oppression. Rome had no way of prohibiting immigration, and leaders found that helping the poor became increasingly expensive.

The Roman army defended the city, but the frontiers of the empire had to be secured by fewer and fewer Roman soldiers in charge of a growing number of mercenaries.

A major way for the emperor to gain favor with the public was to put on grand events. The Greeks presented plays that challenged the mind, but the Roman public much preferred visual spectaculars, such as gladiatorial contests. Although the Coliseum did not open until A.D. 80, on the south side of Palatine Hill are the spacious ruins of the Circus Maximus, where Caligula initiated the practice of having twenty-four horse races in a single day.[4] The best seats for such an event were reserved for men; women and slaves were relegated to the upper levels of the stadium.

Wealthy men ran the society in a highly competitive environment; but women had the right of inheritance that made some of them very rich. Slaves did the work, and because they were regarded as property, they often had sex at the pleasure of their owners. Adultery was quite common, and same- and opposite sex-relationships were acceptable so long as the encounter involved those of unequal status. Men of position were not supposed to have sex with those of equal status or age. Having sex was regarded as a joyful, natural experience, and was not considered degrading or shameful. There were plenty of brothels.

Generally, a happy marriage was the preferred way of life. The ceremonies consisted of announcements, celebrations with friends, and the symbolic use of rings. Having children was considered a duty, although young men were frequently unconvinced. The mortality rate was high for mothers and children, so a big family was desirable. Divorces were easy to declare so long as the parties involved made it clear that the marriage had ended and the woman had a sufficient dowry to attract another husband.

While some of the events in the movie are less well-documented and may vary from what most scholars believe to be true, *Caligula* for the most part is historically accurate.

The Epic Tale

There are some claims that *Caligula* is an epic; mainly because the word is used casually as an advertising ploy today. Homer's *The Iliad* and *The Odyssey* are epic adventures. These stories are based on the extraordinary feats of men who have or seemed to have supernatural powers or contacts with the gods. Caligula tried to claim such powers, but he had few people who recognized his claims and achievements. Whether Achilles, Hector, and Odysseus ever existed is uncertain, but they do live as characters in Homer's writings. Cities once thought mythic, such as Troy, Ithaca, and Knossos, seem to have been uncovered after relentless research. Archaeologists constantly seek verification for their findings as they apply new scientific technology. During most previous centuries, however, humankind depended on imaginative accounts of history based on personal hopes and fears represented by mythic creatures. The centaur, which first appeared in art about 900 B.C., is such a creature. J. Michael Padgett of Princeton University Art Museum has written that the centaur "straddled two worlds, between the rough freedom of nature and the reasoned ascent of human culture. He is the beast within the man."[5]

Caligula's life also illustrates the beast within the man. His story is about a young man who wants power before he is ready for it. Unfortunately, he had few advisors he could trust and he was evidently not blessed with extraordinary gifts. Even so, he inherited an empire, the often-told story of the fellow who has to deal with too much too soon. One's real life, as Virgil wrote, is the life one does not lead.

The epic heroes from the Trojan War are guided by gods. In Virgil's *The Aeneid*, the goddess Venus is the mother of the hero, Aeneas. Aeneas knows what is expected of him. He is one of those heroes who, like Odysseus, lives after the Trojan War to fulfill his destiny. Venus guides him to Carthage, a city ruled by Queen Dido. Dido is protected by Venus's adversary, Juno, Jupiter's wife. Dido falls in love with the gallant Aeneas and they have a brief romance. When the time comes for them to part, she cannot bear to see him sail away and she commits suicide. Aeneas had been told he must go to Latinus, a land located along the Tiber River, so he went there, and he and his men engage in conflicts with his rival, Turnus, who wants to marry King Evander's daughter, Lavinia, and gain the throne.

In the struggle that ensues, Aeneas is told in a dream that with the help of King Evander he will establish within his kingdom a new city on Seven Hills. To protect Aeneas, Venus gives him a shield forged by Vulcan. Battles rage, killing Trojans, Latins, and Arcadians. After the death of Evander's son Pallas, Jupiter commands Juno to end the war. Juno agrees so long as the Trojans speak Latin and have a distinct culture. Aeneas meets Turnus in a personal battle, strikes him down, and sacrifices the body to the shade of Pallas. With these heroic deeds completed, Aeneas is free to marry Lavinia, build the new city of Rome, center of the nation that will become the Roman Empire.

Aeneas is chosen by the gods for great things; he cannot deny his destiny. The magnitude of the hero's challenge and his link to divine power are essential to an epic drama. They provide the spiritual motivation for the character's obsession for distinction. Regardless of promotional claims, Caligula was not destined to be a hero—thus the movie is not an epic.

The Caesars

There were three Caesars before Caligula, a blood descendent of the Julio-Claudian line: Gaius Julius Caesar (100–44 B.C.), Gaius Julius Caesar Octavianus, renamed Augustus in 27 B.C. (63 B.C.–A.D. 14), and Tiberius Claudius Nero (42 B.C.–A.D. 37). The latter two established a line of emperors. Augustus reigned over the Roman Empire from 27 B.C. to A.D. 14. He was followed by Tiberius, who was emperor from A.D. 14 to 37. Gaius Caesar, referred to as Caligula, was born in A.D. 12, and ruled less than four years from A.D. 37 until his assassination in A.D. 41.

Piecing together Caligula's life, fragment by fragment, from damaged records scattered all over the Roman Empire of his day, is at best a fascinating puzzle that depends upon intelligent speculation as much as it does on facts. Several ancient historians described persons and events before, during, and after Caligula. Philo Judaeus, 30 B.C.–A.D. 45, was an Alexandrian Jewish philosopher; Lucius Seneca, the younger, 4 B.C.–A.D. 65, was a philosopher, dramatist, and statesman; Pliny, the elder, A.D. 23–79, was a scholar; and Flavius Josephus, A.D. 37–100, was a Jewish general and historian. They actually lived during Caligula's lifetime. Publius Tacitus, A.D. 55–118, an ora-

Casa di Livia, currently being renovated, runs vertically down the hillside. It has a garden at the top. Caligula lived with his great-grandmother when he was a teenager.

tor and historian, claimed that histories written during the lifetime of the emperors were fictional. Pliny, the younger, A.D. 62–110, was a Roman consul and author. Gaius Suetonius Tranquillus, circa 69–130, and Cassius Dio, circa 163–285, a government official and historian, wrote extensively about the emperors, but much of their work is incomplete. These writers brought their own prejudices into their accounts. Coins, statues, and earthenware fragments add visual documentation. During the 20th century new translations of these works and extensive additional research have contributed significantly to satisfying an insatiable interest in ancient times. In Italy, tourism related to learning about ancient rulers is a major industry. Palatine Hill is being continuously excavated, including places where Caligula spent much of his life; the adjacent apartments of Tiberius, Livia, and Augustus are being made more accessible, as are sites dating back to Romulus and Remus. Augustus's tomb is about to be renovated. It may hold the remains of Caligula and answers to other unresolved questions. Gaius Suetonius Tranquillus's *The Twelve Caesars,* translated by Robert Graves (1957) and revised by Michael Grant in 1979, is referred to frequently, and recent scholarship such as Anthony A. Barrett's *Caligula: The Corruption of Power* (1989) help to put the man and the period in detailed context. Numerous films and videos have added a substantial dimension, as international scholars discuss the latest discoveries and show actual sites. Both Gore Vidal and actor Malcolm McDowell complained about the modest amount of information that existed concerning Caligula the man and the times in which he lived. Their views and the movies seem to have prompted interest in both the personalities and the period.

The Julio-Claudian Heritage

The first three Caesars were alike in many ways. They were continuously waging battles on behalf of Rome. They had many friends and disposed of many enemies. They were trained more or less on the job as military officers, public servants and politicians. They collected a great deal of money and spent it. They married often, usually for political and financial gain, and had affairs with married and unmarried, ambitious, outspoken women, and sometimes with men. When a minor, according to Cicero, Julius Caesar had sex with Augustus. If true, these encounters were brief encounters for favors or political gains and did not make them homosexuals. Regardless, they cared for and about their families, but did not hesitate to punish severely any member who turned against them. They were very popular with the people and the military, particularly early in their careers, and sometimes bribed people for votes in elections, favors, and support. Like today, they lived during stress-

2. Tablets and Parchment

Domus Augustana, a huge palace nearby, is where Augustus resided and carried on public events. The walls were covered with paintings and sculptures; the floors were mosaics. Caligula is believed to have lived here at various times with his grandmother Antonia.

ful, insecure times. Many in the senate and throughout the empire disliked them.

The three Caesars were nice-looking, arrogant, and suffered from some mental problems (epilepsy, severe headaches, seizures), but overall were rarely ill for more than a month and each lived to relatively old age — Gaius Julius Caesar was assassinated at fifty-six, Augustus and Tiberius died at seventy-six and seventy-eight respectively, perhaps from natural causes or murder. They sought total power, often at great personal risk in military battles and/or in a continuous adversarial relationship with the members of the senate. Yet, they were afraid of some natural phenomena like thunder and lightning. They were polytheistic but not strongly religious, and observed the rituals required by their office, and they held strict moral beliefs regarding conduct. They were superstitious, consulted oracles, studied astrology, and were interested in Egyptian and Eastern deities. They considered deification as the ultimate recognition of divine lineage, if it was offered and confirmed by mere mortals in the senate. According to custom, they were cremated. Of this foursome, the three Caesars and Caligula, Julius and Augustus were deified.

Julius Caesar was a dictator, who might be described as a conqueror: "I

The Circus Maximus, now an oval dirt track, is seen below Palatine Hill. Caligula held horse races here.

came, I saw, I conquered." He defined the borders of the Roman Empire. Augustus was a builder within the empire. He developed government institutions and public works. Tiberius, adopted stepson of Augustus, was a dutiful public servant who did everything Rome asked of him, and did it well. In later life he became a reclusive realist, who tried to balance the state's requirements and his own overwhelming psychological needs. Julius Caesar was assassinated on the Ides of March (15 March) and his prominence has been preserved by having high school students read William Shakespeare's play, *Julius Caesar*. At thirty-two, Augustus, said to be handsome but not as physically robust as the others, became Rome's first emperor after the battle of Actium in 31 B.C. He was a wise and generous man, so long as his beliefs of duty and morality were followed. He took advantage of the enormous influx of money that flowed into Rome from 130 B.C. to 30 B.C. He ruled for forty-five years before dying from ill health on 19 August A.D. 14. His achievements in building and organizing life in Rome were splendid accomplishments. Augustus's wife, Scribonia, gave birth to Julia the elder, who had Agrippina. Agrippina married Germanicus, grandson of Augustus's sister Octavia, and they gave birth to Caligula, among other children. Caligula was the great-grandson of both Augustus and Marc Antony. Tiberius likewise had a long and impressive lineage, and he would become Caligula's grandfather by adoption. Tiberius did not become emperor until he was fifty-five, and so his enthusiasm was largely exhausted. Even so, he ruled for twenty-three years, and died in March A.D. 37.[6]

Caligula's young life was glamorous. He was born on 31 August A.D. 12, probably in Antium. As an infant he was cared for in the palace of Emperor Augustus on Palatine Hill. When he became two, Augustus allowed him and a doctor to travel north to the German front to be with his mother and father, who was commander. Disenchanted with wars, capable Roman recruits were more difficult to obtain, as the young men wanted to follow private lives of pleasure and becoming rich. The northern frontier still remained a "field of honor" for Caligula's ancestors. In A.D. 9, three Roman legions and their commander, Publius Quintilius Varus, had died in defeat. Augustus was deeply concerned not only for the loss of the soldiers but because he thought that the enemy might invade the empire and even attack Rome. "There were no able-bodied citizens of any fighting capacity left in reserve, and the allied forces, such as were of any value, had suffered heavy losses," Cassius Dio wrote. Augustus was forced to introduce conscription. "Finally, since even then a great many men would not respond, he had a number put to death. He then selected by lot as many as possible from those who had already completed their military service and from the freshmen, and after enrolling them in the army, he ordered them with all speed to the province of Germany to join Tiberius."[7] Tiberius and Germanicus alternated as commanders at the front. "Germanicus" was a title of honor bestowed on Caligula's grandfather, and Germanicus and Tiberius, like brothers, served repeatedly at the pleasure of Augustus, the senate and the Roman people. Gaius was barely up north when Augustus died on 19 August A.D. 14; he was removed then from the front for his own safety. When the people heard about this, they were contrite, pleading that they were ashamed of their behavior. Tiberius took over as emperor, and Germanicus returned in triumph and glory.

Then capricious fate stepped in. On 10 October A.D. 19, Caligula's illustrious father died, and all too soon his mother and two brothers would go to their graves under a reversal of circumstances. With his family deceased Caligula had to live with his great-grandmother Livia and his grandmother Antonia. In A.D. 30 Emperor Tiberius, living in absentia, commanded Caligula to come to Capri, and there Caligula was exposed to a life of political intrigue and overwhelming fear that may have been so stressful as to cause or contribute to a mental breakdown or nervous disorder about six months after Caligula began his own reign.

What twenty-something today would not be in danger of turning to drugs, alcohol, criminal behavior, or suicide under these circumstances? How

Villa Jovis, Capri, viewed from a steep, winding walkway, is in the distance. Caligula was summoned there just prior to assuming manhood.

could Caligula, with such an impressive family legacy, start out with so much and end up with so little?

When they were young, Tiberius and Germanicus fought in the northern campaigns just as Germanicus's grandfather had done, but the battles had become more difficult since Varus and his legions were tricked and defeated. Distinguished by their bravery, Germanicus and Tiberius differed in style. Tiberius was a rigorous disciplinarian, while Germanicus led his soldiers by means of his popularity. Germanicus was handsome, with physical and moral excellence, courageous, kind-hearted, educated in Greek and Latin, and won the respect of friends and foes, including those he conquered, because he was tolerant toward his enemies. By bringing young Gaius (Caligula) to the front a second time, Germanicus strengthened the family tradition of protecting Rome; thus, when he returned to Rome with Caligula by his side, he hinted at a future emperor. The Praetorian Guard and the people of Rome greeted Germanicus as a celebrity, a memory that an older Caligula may have appreciated and may have tried to recreate in later years. The mention of Germanicus suggested the possibility of succession. Some scholars have debated his popularity and compared it to that of President John F. Kennedy.[8] Soon he was scheduled for another important government mission.

Overwhelming ambition drove the emperors; their personal lives changed as they became hardened rulers. According to Suetonius, Tiberius married the woman he loved, Vispania, and they had a child, Drusus. Tiberius hoped his son would succeed him. He was forced to divorce Vispania to gain political favor with Augustus, and he regretted this decision all of his life.[9] Such background is often omitted from *Caligula;* consequently, the narrative is occasionally difficult to understand.

Tiberius was a tall, strong, rigid advocate of following the rules, who detested flattery and ignored unattractive slanderous remarks. Eventually his face was overcast by an obstinate countenance of misery and fear. For his second wife he married Julia, Augustus's daughter, whom he detested because she was repeatedly unfaithful. Though touted as second only to Augustus in succession, Tiberius felt insecure for Augustus had two grandsons. Yielding to the probability that one of them might become emperor, and discouraged in his marriage to Julia, Tiberius decided to retire to the island of Rhodes.

Over the next seven years, fortunes greatly changed. Tiberius absorbed Greek life, its attitudes toward human beings regarding their needs and priorities, and he retained his status by accepting distinguished visitors who paid their respects. He grew weary of retirement, however. Augustus's grandsons died and Julia was banished for adultery, so Tiberius asked Augustus permission to return to Rome. Once again he served as a military officer, litigator, and government administrator. He hoped to gradually receive recognition as heir by being adopted by Augustus. In his will Augustus reluctantly named Tiberius his principal heir; therefore, he established him as his successor, a role Tiberius seemed to have earned after years of public service, personal risk and sacrifice, and meeting the obligations of leadership. Augustus's wife, Antonia, was influential in this decision, according to Tacitus, but the popular belief is that Livia arranged the succession for her son through devious means, as dramatized in *I, Claudius.*[10]

In A.D. 14, at age fifty-five, the senate confirmed Tiberius as emperor, and he efficiently carried out his responsibilities. He knew the treachery of political life and the capricious nature of the public. Older, stern, bald, round-shouldered, and with a dour look, Tacitus speculated that his appearance, as well as his cruelty and lust, may have caused his withdrawal from public life in Rome. Tiberius answered to no one and had little taste for public relations, increasing the wealth of senators, or getting involved in public works. Instead, he chose a miserly path of fiscal management for the state and for himself by accruing substantial wealth. After twelve years (A.D. 14–26) of carrying out the empire's priorities, including the restoration of some liberties, and suffering the death of his only son Drusus, he opted to govern the empire from Capri (Capraea), the island Augustus had purchased years before. In A.D. 26, Tiberius finally left, never to return to Rome until his death in A.D. 37. Living in comparative safety and far from his mother Livia's taunting and the criticism and intrigues of Rome, he reduced the potential for assassination by isolating himself and carefully selecting the persons and issues he wanted to support, and procrastinated on the rest. He liked persons of accomplishment and invited many of them for visits; but he avoided those who sought personal gain through flattery. As time passed his popularity decreased, in part because he abolished foreign cults, particularly Egyptian and Jewish religions; yet, he sustained his interest in astrology and forms of prognostication. He remained in power by maintaining the loyalty of Prefect Lucius Sejanus and the military, whose welfare and services he improved for the benefit of himself and the citizens. Meanwhile, Sejanus saw potential for marrying into the royal family through Livilla, Tiberius's daughter-in-law. Tiberius also kept a reliable network of informants who detailed activities of major figures in Rome and flashed messages by means of the lighthouse built near Villa Jovis.

Capri is a beautiful five-square-mile island, much of which is sheer rock surrounded by deep water. Located south of Naples, off the tip of the Amalfi Coast, its midwinter temperature of about fifty degrees Fahrenheit rises to about eighty degrees in midsummer. Its one tiny beach could only be reached by boat. Augustus had twelve villas and a staff there. He called it the "Land of Do-nothings."[11] Tiberius ruled the world one thousand feet above the sea in the largest palace — Palazzo di Tibero, or Villa Jovis (House of Jupiter).

The palace is not easy to reach. The path is narrow, winding, and steep.

Villa Jovis entrance map. Villa Jovis is a major tourist site.

The palace buildings surrounded four huge cisterns, center, that caught and circulated cold and hot water.

In places vegetation is thick. Excavated in 1937, Villa Jovis is over seven thousand square feet. By utilizing the terraced natural cliffs, the living quarters surrounded four huge cisterns that captured and distributed water. To the north and east was a magnificent view of the Gulf of Naples and the coast as the sun rose in the morning in the imperial quarters. On the west was the servants' area, and to the south were the heated baths. Here Tiberius could conduct his secret life far from prying eyes and wagging tongues. Here he could pretend to be young again by watching beautiful adolescents play. Nestled among the rocks, plants, and trees were convenient places where boys and girls could copulate in groups of two or three and engage in aberrant behavior.[12] It is said the cliffs were used literally as drop-off points for executions. If a captive did not die from the fall, soldiers killed him after he hit the rocks below. As old age took its toll, Tiberius reluctantly faced reality and had to think about the prospects of succession, and in A.D. 30 he summoned the eighteen-year-old Caligula to Capri. This is when the screenplay begins.

Caligula's Early Life

Gaius Caesar, born in A.D. 12, was the youngest male child of Germanicus and his wife, Agrippina. Germanicus was the son of Marc Antony and

Augustus's sister Octavia. Agrippina's bloodline could be traced to Augustus, also. They had nine children, of whom three girls and three boys lived. The other boys—Nero and Drusus—were five or six years older than Caligula, and the girls—Agrippina Minor, Drusilla, and Livilla—were three to five years younger than Gaius. Of these children, Gaius became emperor and Agrippina Minor became the mother of a later emperor—Nero, who should not be confused with their brother Nero. (Many family names are repeated.) Germanicus, on duty along the German frontier, allowed Caligula to visit. The cute little boy entertained the troops by dancing in a military uniform and by wearing hobnailed military boots. The dance must have been amusing relief and Gaius was nicknamed "Little Boots," *caliga* being the Latin word for boot. (When he got older, he did not like either "Gaius" or "Caligula.") He probably liked the attention his father gave him when he dressed up and performed for the troops. Showing off provided a basis for Danilo Donati's elaborate costumes for the emperor.

In A.D. 17, Tiberius recalled Germanicus from the front to Rome to accept honors of triumph, while Tiberius's son Drusus replaced him. Drusus and Germanicus were close friends. Battle scenes were reconstructed for the people to view and Tiberius gave away money in jubilation, while Germanicus

Thick stone walls were built to take advantage of the steep terrain. Over the centuries they have been dismantled by robbers seeking building materials. Looking beyond the baths, a summer rain storm approaches from the south.

and his five children, including Gaius, acknowledged accolades from a chariot. So long as his father lived, Caligula was a pampered child.

In the winter of A.D. 18–19 Caligula went to Egypt with Germanicus, where — an impressionable boy — he found a strange land with a fascinating culture. He developed a fondness for Egyptian ways, such as accepting Alexander the Great as a god and allowing brothers and sisters to marry. Caligula would have been in Alexandria when it was a center of advanced learning, with the first great library and the first lecture halls. It was founded about 300 B.C., and about four hundred thousand of its papyrus scrolls were destroyed in 48 B.C. By 30 B.C., Augustus had moved the center of learning to Rome. In 2004 the library site, built under the Ptolemaic Dynasty, was rediscovered. Caligula liked the traditional heroes, too. Hercules, the son of Zeus, was not only the strongest man physically, he could apply his mind to solve whatever problem was presented to him. His eventual reward was marriage to Hera, daughter of Hebe and goddess of eternal youth. Naturally, Romulus and Remus, Hercules, and Alexander the Great were the foremost heroes; they had ascended into heaven, Tiberius told mourners at the time of Augustus's funeral.

Soon Germanicus was sent by the senate on official business to Syria, and he took his wife and some children, including Gaius. On 10 October A.D.

The lighthouse, damaged by an earthquake, is located on a steep cliff beyond the trees.

19, when Caligula was seven, his father died in Antioch. Some thought Emperor Tiberius was involved, but most of the blame fell on Gnaeus Piso, the governor of Syria with whom Germanicus had violent disagreements. No one knows what actually happened. In *I, Claudius,* Caligula is alleged to have poisoned his father. At seven, why? In any case, the public was in deep sorrow over the death of this thirty-three-year-old leader. His wife openly blamed Tiberius. Agrippina, Caligula, and a sister returned to Rome with the urn holding Germanicus's remains. A huge outpouring of public grief met them, and this foreshadowed the enthusiastic public reception Caligula would receive when he became emperor. The principal figures of the Julio-Claudian families—Tiberius, Livia, and Antonia—did not attend the funeral, however, and current opinion was that Agrippina and her children were in danger. This likelihood was enhanced by the rapid rise to power of Sejanus, who was prefect of the Praetorian Guard. He had substantial influence on Tiberius.

In A.D. 29, Agrippina's accusations, together with Sejanus's sinister advice to Tiberius that one of her sons, Nero or Drusus, might try to become emperor, resulted in Agrippina being banished to Pontia, a small island off the coast of Campania. There she starved to death. Likewise both of her sons met with disaster that same year. Nero was held on Pandateria, another prison island, where he starved to death, as did Drusus, who was imprisoned on Palatine Hill.

Orphaned under the circumstances, Caligula was cared for by his great-grandmother Livia, who Tacitus thought may have poisoned possible successors to Augustus; she was obsessed with enabling her son Tiberius to become emperor. Caligula, an incorrigible youth who had no father to look out for his interests or teach him his responsibilities to the empire, received a haphazard education. It was the opposite of what Philip of Macedon gave Alexander: distinguished tutors, a cadre of male friends, training in horseback riding, martial arts, and wilderness survival skills. Perhaps this was fortunate for him. If Caligula had been properly schooled for leadership, he might have been considered a possible danger to Tiberius by some who might theorize that he wanted to be emperor. Instead, he moved through the ranks of leadership without notice. He married Junia Claudilla while still a teenager, and he was promoted to the priesthood as the replacement for his deceased brother and in recognition of his exemplary behavior. During his mid-teens, Caligula lived with Grandmother Livia on Palatine Hill. Soon, Junia died in childbirth and his sister Drusilla may have been there to console him. When Livia died at eighty-six, Caligula moved in with his grandmother Antonia, two sisters, and some distant male relatives, the sons of a murdered king, who had fled from the East. They were young contemporaries who would assume prominent roles in the future.

Of his sisters, Caligula was especially fond of Drusilla. Some ancient historians such as Josephus suggest that he may have had sex with her while they were perhaps seventeen or eighteen, but Anthony Barrett says this is unlikely.[14] Drusilla was married the first time to Lucius Cassius Longinus in A.D. 33; but two years later she was married to Caligula's friend and occasional lover Marcus Lepidus. It looked like Lepidus might be planning to get in line for emperor through marriage, but Caligula rejected that idea. When he was ill during his first year in office, he designated Drusilla his sole heir. Marriage was the standard of respectability; adultery, though common, was not looked upon favorably if it jeopardized the family. In Egypt, however, about 20 percent of brothers and sisters married, an idea that reinforced Caligula's notion of someday moving to Egypt where he could marry Drusilla.[15] Of course, this is speculation in lieu of facts. As mentioned earlier, divorces were prompted for political or business advantages, but incest had the advantage of drawing strength from an existing leadership pool. Romans were virtually obsessed with having sex with beautiful people, and they displayed their fantasies in painting, mosaics, sculptures, and crafts; they surrounded themselves, especially in their private summer homes, with what would be described as lewd pictures, rather like people who view sex films today.

As Caligula's family succumbed to alleged conspiracies, health hazards, and wars, few relatives remained. Securing the empire for the Julio-Claudian heirs was a risky but necessary task that a ruler as duty-bound as Tiberius was compelled to do. With so many losses even in large families, paternal heads of households adopted male heirs. Just as Augustus had adopted his stepson Tiberius, Tiberius adopted his great-nephew Caligula to share in his estate with his blood grandson, Gemellus. Little is known about Gemellus, born in A.D. 18, and immature for his age. Perhaps he fit well with the innocents Tiberius had living at the palace. Tiberius again maintained a wait-and-see approach. Overlooked as a potential successor was Germanicus's unattractive other brother, Claudius, who was considered incapable of holding high office. A deformed person was believed to be cursed by the gods. In any case, the choice Tiberius had to make was as bitter and difficult for him as the one Augustus made previously. Would any reigning leader think his or her successor would be as wise as he had been?

By fall of A.D. 31, Tiberius, in a coup, replaced Sejanus with the brutal Quintus Naevius Macro as prefect of the Pretorians. Looking out for himself, Macro realized that his future might be longer with young Caligula than the elderly Tiberius, and so he supported him in conversations with the emperor. Soon after the death of Junia, Caligula's first wife, Macro was said to have ordered his own wife, Ennia Thrasylla, to make herself available for Caligula's pleasure. This was about the time Caligula was recognized as an adult in a ceremony called the *toga virilis*. This transition is playfully carried out in two scenes in the movie. In truth, Caligula remained careful in his relationship with Macro, because he was no doubt aware of how skillful Tiberius had to be to get rid of his predecessor, Sejanus. So Caligula, appreciating to some degree how important and powerful the head of the Praetorian Guard was to him, remained cautious.

On Capri he seemed to enjoy the excesses in food, sex, and the grotesque that the emperor offered. How could a young adult adjust to the bizarre exhibitions and opportunities that were thrust upon him? There is no indication that Caligula was anything more than a spectator. His later actions as emperor suggest that he despised the sexual activity or perhaps he gained a conflicted view of the innocents at play. Caligula had learned from experts how to be deceptive. He may have seen himself assuming different roles: an entertaining child for the troops, a pleasant son for his grandmothers, a young man on the brink of leadership for his grandfather. He seemed to appreciate that, despite the environment, Tiberius was fluent in Latin and Greek, an educated, experienced man, who cleverly ruled Rome through military power and the public's fear of his unprovoked rages resulting in death.

Still, Caligula had little to do as a virtual prisoner-in-residence on Capri. Barely formed as an adult himself, how could he in his period of youthful invincibility interpret the creeping miseries of an old man's late years when beauty and virility are gone and joy only a faded memory? Fortunately, in the film, two brilliant actors played these contrasting roles of the young man and the old man with considerable exuberance. Tiberius had become the ultimate voyeur. He enjoyed sadistic acts, such as slowly allowing a man to bleed to death by means of tiny cuts on his body rather than a single mortal wound. Suetonius wrote that he had a man's genitalia tied to prevent urination while excessive amounts of wine were poured down his throat. Later, similar methods of torture were attributed to Caligula.[17] Tiberius was an oddly moral man in a pagan world where age was blurred. He liked to observe sex acts performed by the gorgeous and the grotesque, who were recruited throughout the empire. He took special pleasure in surrounding himself with youngsters of beauty, charm, innocence, and breeding. His "minnows," whom he favored, would be invited to nibble at his withered, diseased, and insensitive skin to reassure himself he was still alive, or they would scamper around the palace as pans, creatures with human form except for goat's legs, horns, and ears, or nymphs, beautiful young girls similarly representing fantasies associated with woods, streams, and unspoiled natural rural environments. For Tiberius and Caligula their mirrors were the profuse compliments of their sweet, devoted subjects who accepted them without question.

One such youth, Aulus Vitellius, two years younger than Caligula, spent much of his life on Capri. It was said that he gave himself to a man when he was a youth so that his father could gain a better job. Due to a fall he had a limp, but he compensated for it by serving as an agreeable homosexual, one of the *spintriae*, who specialized in vice and entertainment.[18] Vitellius was a favorite of three emperors: Caligula admired him for chariot racing, Claudius for playing dice, and Nero for rigging lute contests so that he would win. (He had a brief, vicious, sadistic reign as emperor in A.D. 68.) Whatever homosexual acts Caligula witnessed on Capri and whatever stories he may have heard about homosexual experiences that may have taken place between Julius Caesar or Augustus with others, those two were not homosexuals and neither was Caligula. They were perhaps meaningless experiments or more likely joyful trysts eliciting some kind of advantage, political or personal, an acceptable act in a pagan civilization.

Caligula's companions were not exclusively lascivious. His first wife visited him. He had the companionship of a long-time older friend who had similar extravagant views, Julius, usually called Herod, Agrippa.[19] Agrippa, grandson of Herod the Great, remained close to Caligula throughout his lifetime. Agrippa was an opportunist. He learned from his own struggles for survival in Judea, and by cultivating beguiling skills that Caligula and his grandmothers found entertaining. More significant were his family credentials that dated to the time of Jesus. Born in 10 B.C., Agrippa was taken to Rome as a baby to stay with Antonia, Caligula's grandmother. Agrippa's mother was Berenice, daughter of Salomé, whose legendary dance cost John the Baptist his life. Berenice became a cherished friend of Antonia and Livia. This association would benefit him handsomely when Agrippa fell from Tiberius's favor because he failed to pay his debts. Agrippa was clever and deceptive, always looking out for himself. He became a trusted member of the family, even though he was twenty years older than Caligula. Agrippa had shared a history of violence and fears of treason.[20] Caligula liked his thoughtfulness on the one hand and his extravagance on the other. Agrippa made money wherever he could by developing skills as a diplomat and as an avid supporter of his own people.

When his debts defeated him on another occasion, he returned to a land south of Judea where he was received by a relative building a new city, Tiberias, along Hellenistic lines. He stayed a while, then journeyed to Syria; and just as life became uncomfortable, usually through extravagance, he moved on. Back to Rome in A.D. 36, his debts, having been paid by Antonia, made him a welcome visitor at Tiberius's palace. Tiberius wanted him to tutor Gemellus, but Agrippa, like Macro, saw greater opportunity in a relationship with Caligula, whose friendship he kept until the emperor's death. Who can say whether Agrippa encouraged Caligula's pursuit of divine status or whether he told Caligula the impossible might be possible by referencing stories of miracles he had heard from his relatives?

With his son Drusus dead, Tiberius wanted his grandson Gemellus, born from suspected adultery that he did not condone, to succeed him. Josephus tells the story that Tiberius, who was known to rely on astrology and divination, hesitated in making the decision without some kind of divine sign. The day before his final choice he asked Gemellus's tutor to bring to him the child who would be waiting for him in the morning. The tutor brought Gaius, who was waiting for his breakfast. "As soon as Tiberius saw Gaius, and not before, he reflected on the power of God, and how the ability of bestowing the government on whom he would was entirely taken away from him.[21] He gradually reconciled himself to the bitter conclusion that Caligula, who was seven years older and stronger, would be the next emperor. Words like "viper" and lines predicting that Caligula would kill Gemellus were taken directly from ancient histories. Tiberius feared Caligula would kill Gemellus one day. Even so, in A.D. 35 he announced that Caligula and Gemellus would be joint heirs to the imperial throne, which would have been impractical if not impossible. Already maneuvered in line for succession by Macro, two years later Caligula was cheered as Rome's new head of state. Caligula was popular with the masses.

Caligula as Emperor

Caligula may have hastened Tiberius's demise by grabbing the imperial ring from Tiberius's finger as he lay dying, but such details are not without dispute. Tacitus wrote that Tiberius appeared dead, then rallied, and that Macro had him suffocated under a pile of bedclothes. This makes a dramatic highlight for the movie. The varied accounts of ancient historians are the essence of interpretation. Tiberius frequently sailed up and down the coast of the mainland, but never went into Rome. In A.D. 37 he became ill while traveling in Campania, the land opposite Capri. He apparently was dying according Charicles, a nearby resident who was a doctor. Tiberius stopped to rest at one of the many villas, where he put on his best appearance right up to the end, as a leader of his caliber would do. His death probably happened from natural causes. Accounts do vary. Such vagaries may be the reason the movie does not identify specific locations.

The people were delighted that the old tyrant was dead. They shouted for his body to be thrown into the Tiber, a sign of disrespect and disapproval. Instead, Caligula, the likely candidate for emperor, but not yet confirmed by the senate, took about a month to sail to the prison islands to retrieve the ashes of his mother and brother and to return their urns to Rome for proper

Mausoleo di Augusto, Rome, may still contain the ashes of Caligula and some relatives.

burial, perhaps in the tomb of Augustus. Tiberius was also buried with dignity. Lurking in the background Macro saw to it that everything went smoothly. After paying his respects, Caligula was hailed as emperor by the senate and the Roman people. They were overjoyed, believing that a new era of decisive leadership and prosperity had arrived.

The weak senate consisted of about six hundred citizens representing a population that ranged from the middle class to the wealthy. The members held rank. At the low end were quaestors who dealt with finances, aediles who were municipal administrators, tribunes who protected the plebeians, praetors who handled legal matters, and a few well-connected consuls who communicated with or were members of the imperial family. Under capable rulers, the system had the power to make improvements for the common good and for the benefit of the commerce of the country. Frequently, these privileged few would find ways to profit from such projects; it was just as likely that the very wealthy would not approve such projects if there was no clear monetary incentive.

The central government, not having a systematic approach to obtaining money by taxation, depended on reaping it from foreign conquests and from client kings, heads of provinces under Rome's control. After Augustus died public welfare programs came to a halt; Tiberius had little interest in them.

Exterior, Mausoleum of Augustus in 2006. Adjacent to the Ara Pacis, it is expected to be restored, but is presently off-limits to tourists.

The senators got richer from their business deals and slave trade; they were disinclined to do more. Tiberius managed to keep the battlefront far away and to maintain the Roman legions. He saved a lot of money for his own benefit and kept it under his direct control so that he would not have to ask the senate to approve spending it.

Caligula inherited this money and he was hugely popular for about a year from the public's admiration of Germanicus's son and because he gave money to those who seemed loyal, abolished some taxes, paid some relatives' debts, drove out the homosexuals (Tiberius's *spintriae*), restored more freedom in publishing, and presented lavish public entertainments, such as gladiatorial contests and horse races. He named Claudius his fellow consul and Gemellus as Prince of Youth. These things the senate and the Roman people enthusiastically agreed to. About the only thing they resisted but approved was his proclamation that allegiances must be sworn to him and his sisters, which placed duties to them above their own families. Josephus wrote that Gaius "managed public affairs with great magnanimity during the first and second year...."[22] His opinion is otherwise disputed.

Within the first six months of his reign, however, Caligula fell ill, causing widespread concern about the malady and its impact. In the movie, a plague of some sort is prevalent in the city; this mysterious sickness is reminiscent of the pervasive plague in Visconti's *Death in Venice*. Historians have speculated that Caligula may have had a nervous breakdown, a brain-damaging disease, or something else. He had a history of epilepsy. Rather than having the disease target Caligula, the movie suggests it may have been a virus widespread in the population. Thinking he was going to die, Caligula willed the Roman Empire and his personal fortune to Drusilla. The malady lasted from about mid–October to mid–November A.D. 37. Afterward, he recovered, and believing he had overcome death, felt he was invincible. At twenty-five Caligula thought he had fought with death and won. He was master of the Roman world.

A near-death experience almost always causes a reappraisal of one's self and one's relationship with the universe. It is common for one to believe one has something important to accomplish with one's life. But no historian reported that a deity appeared to Caligula in a dream to proclaim his destiny. Instead, perhaps equally valid, Caligula concluded that he could do no wrong, and the violent demons that he had experienced his entire life emerged in full force. Looking at the history of the Julio-Claudian family, it can be seen that peculiar, violent behavior was not uncommon. Obsessive fear, insomnia, nightmares, over-abundant sexual activity, wars and executions were not necessarily counterbalanced by joyful times, good intellectual judgment or experience. Caligula needed the sound advice of the late Augustus who believed afflictions of the body also affected the soul. There is no difference between them, he claimed. "The truth is that there are many ailments which affect both men's minds—however disembodied they may be—and their bodies, and that these often possess elements in common. Thus the mind may experience a sense of contraction through fear, and of excessive swelling through passion: pain may on occasion make it seem to shrivel up, and arrogance make it grow with conceit. And so, since the divergence of experience between minds and bodies is comparatively small, they require treatment of a similar kind." He went on to say that speech may appease the enraged, "just as a harsh word will rouse to fury another who has been thoroughly composed, while the granting of forgiveness will cause the most arrogant temper to melt, just as punishment will incense the most easy-going of men." "Acts of violence," Augustus observed, "however strongly justified, will always provoke men, while considerate treatment will calm them."[23] What impact might such wisdom have had on Caligula? Instead Caligula struggled onward, advised by his own observations of the passing human parade.

Whether Caligula, through a sense of hubris and privilege, may have been unable or unwilling to control his excesses, is unclear; but they led to uncontrollable expenses that became outrageous to those advising him. Like

Tiberius, he used fear and excess as shields of protection. It did not take long for him to locate places where he sought security and escape from the pressures of being emperor. He had vacation spots near Rome. He liked to stay in Ostia, for six hundred years Rome's main port, a place that is well preserved today, due in part to its having been covered in silt and not exposed to the air. It is a major tourist attraction, although it must have been a rough shanty town in the first century. Like Troy, the relationship of the land to the sea has changed, for Ostia is about three miles inland from where it used to be, and no relics typical of a seaport have been discovered, although mosaics in floors of homes depict the kinds of ships that may have carried cargo.

South of Rome, villas, some family-owned, served as retreats for those who could afford to own one overlooking the sea. The cliffs of Campania that overlook the Bay of Naples were popular. From Misenum in the north to Surrentum in the south, breath-taking views and beaches were plentiful. Much of this lovely country was founded by the Etruscans and developed by the Greeks and Romans. Caligula may have relaxed in the sexual pleasure palaces offered in Pompeii, a city of twenty thousand people located near Mt. Vesuvius, a volcano which destroyed the city in A.D. 79. A cluster of some of the most elegant villas were located three miles south of Pompeii at Stabiae. These homes had spacious atria and peristyles, lush gardens, broad walkways, libraries, and picture galleries. For members of the senatorial class and their

Pliny the Younger described the eruption of Mt. Vesuvius destroying Pompeii in A.D. 79.

families, numbering a few hundred, these places allowed them to get away from work in Rome; but for another ten thousand rich residents these homes were used as conference centers for forging business decisions. Cicero had three villas, one at Puteoli and another near Pompeii where he could work in solitude.[24]

One of Caligula's most elaborate hideaways was an elegant vessel built on tiny Lake Nemi, about six miles to the southeast of Rome. The volcanic, dark blue lake, at times shrouded in mist and mysticism, harbored on its forested shore a small temple to Diana, and welcomed Caligula like Capri protected Tiberius from Rome's whispers and criticism. He had two ships built. One ship, over two hundred thirty feet long and about sixty-five feet wide, was a splendid example of naval construction, having meticulously finished matched wood, bronze castings of satyrs, fauns, and nymphs, inlaid tiles, colorful paintings, and a remarkable system of pipes that carried hot water to baths. The details and the technology for distributing the water are reminiscent of Villa Jovis. The precise purpose of these ships, with the prow of a gracefully carved bird, is open to speculation for they had no outlet to the sea.

After the ships were discovered in 1928, Benito Mussolini, in his desire to restore the legacy of ancient Rome, had Lake Nemi drained so that the hulls could be removed from a depth of sixty feet and housed in a museum on the lakeshore. There they served as a testament to the glory of Rome for fifteen years. Caligula's distinct imprimatur—Gaius Caesar Augustus Germanicus—was recovered at the site. These treasures of antiquity were burned by the retreating Nazis as World War II ended. The drawings and charred remains may have inspired Danilo Donati's bordello constructed in the form of a ship's skeleton for the huge orgy scene in *Caligula*.[25]

With the lack of dependable funding resources, Caligula was unable to adequately maintain the central government. This prompted extraordinary and undesirable fundraising schemes. For instance, Caligula confiscated the property of the wealthy by exterminating them for alleged conspiracies and crimes against Rome. Challenges against the charges of the emperor were presented in court, but not won. Caligula continuously devised plans to liquidate entire families if he was sufficiently displeased. The senators overlooked these casualties so long as it did not involve them. Caligula could be upset by trivial details that might result in the accused opening his veins, the usual approach to suicide. Caligula's reaction to causing these deaths was defended with interesting logic in Albert Camus' play: there Caligula says that he had been responsible for far fewer deaths than would be lost in the briefest war.

Caligula liked to entertain, as well as be entertained. He fancied himself a public speaker, for he liked the sound of his voice: "Even Gaius' mental disorder did not weaken his vigorous speech," Tacitus wrote.[26] A well-known member of the court was Seneca the Elder, who came from Spain with his son. It was rumored that Caligula considered putting him to death because of his excellent oratorical abilities; but when he learned that Seneca was ill and would die soon, he changed his mind. Seneca the Younger (4 B.C.–A.D. 65) was educated in literature and philosophy. He became a prominent member of Caligula's court as a speaker and playwright. His plays were written to be recited rather than acted out on the stage. They are based on works of the great writers, such as Euripides, known for *The Trojan Women*. Seneca was criticized for excessive violence, thought to be realistic, in his adaptations of *Phaedre, Medea,* and *Mad Hercules*. While the Greeks kept violence offstage, Seneca brought it into the readings. The killing of Medea's children, for instance, was a chilling reminder of the temper of the times and of the deplorable, but not unusual, bloodthirsty circumstances that engulfed their lives. In A.D. 41, Seneca became involved with Julia, Claudius's niece, and it was believed that he was exiled to Corsica, where he may have spent time writing his tragedies. In A.D. 49 he was recalled by Agrippina, Caligula's sister, who had become empress of Rome. She wanted Seneca to tutor her son Nero, the future emperor of Rome.

Most deaths were caused by Caligula's nagging fear of being overthrown, that is, of someone wanting his job. The more one reads about his competition, the more one gets the impression that emperors were correct in being constantly terrorized by this possibility. The usual suspects were family members or powerful military leaders. In the movie, Caligula mentions Gemellus as a competitor, Drusilla counters that Macro is a greater threat. In fact, Caligula got rid of both of them. With Macro's help he disposed of Gemellus in A.D. 37; Gemellus was accused of an unproven charge of conspiracy. The next year he disposed of Macro, because of his growing concern that Macro was more powerful than the emperor himself. Either person could have been set up for execution based on few facts and mere suspicion. Macro seemed to have been loyal. It is unknown why he and his wife were forced to commit suicide. Barrett points out that thereafter the leadership of the Praetorian Guard was assigned to more than one person. Gemellus, on the other hand, was doomed from the start. He seems totally incapable of planning any conspiracy on his own. Who would have enticed him into such a role is open to speculation. These scenes are appropriately integrated into the narrative for *Caligula*, and both recognize the depth of the fear that supported a conspiracy theory.

Suetonius mentions the idea that Gemellus regularly took medicine. In the film, Caligula accuses him of taking it as an antidote for poison that could be attributed to Caligula. The scene plays well enough. He was forced to commit suicide early in the year. Caligula's erratic conduct extended in many directions and included behavior toward kings governing countries outside of Rome.

On 10 June A.D. 38, Caligula's favorite sister, Drusilla, who is shown from the beginning of the film in a romantic incestuous relationship with him, may have died in childbirth. In *I, Claudius* the baby is supposedly attributed to Caligula and he is said to have cut the fetus from her womb so that he could apply his divine powers to restore her body. This act could have ranked among the top horrors in *Caligula*; instead, no such dramatization occurs. After appealing to Isis without success, Drusilla dies. This event seems to be ultimate proof that he had no divine powers, was not a god, and was not favored by the gods.

How much value was placed on human life in pagan times comes into question. Natural causes and suicides seem to destroy numerous lives; of course, the suicides are mainly attributed to wealthy people caught in complex political circumstances. Caligula is devastated with grief after his sister's death, but in fact went on a tour, appearing at gambling parlors and public events to assuage his sadness. The public was confused, yielding a mixed response to her death and the period of mourning. While many people might withdraw from life to contemplate their grief in solitude, the theory goes, Caligula went out to redirect his grief by surrounding himself with those who were having a good time. Would this technique have improved his disposition? This seems to have been Tiberius's view. He surrounded himself with youth and beauty. The movie takes somewhat longer to stabilize Caligula's disposition.

The Responsibilities of Caligula

Caligula's most important job was providing an heir. Rumor had it that he might be impotent. This would have been ironic because of the long line of female and male lovers he'd had in addition to his wives. His male lovers were often linked to the performing arts. He admired the voice of the actor Apelles and the dancing and acting of Mnester. While he pursued the beautiful people, his own attributes began to fail him. Particularly annoying was his tendency to lose his hair; few men want to lose their hair, especially when they are only in their twenties. When under extraordinary stress, this is a fairly common occurrence even today. The presidents of the United States show the impact of the office: they often lose hair and become remarkably gray.

He must have been thought of as a good catch, and he certainly tried to find someone compatible. Augustus did not complain that young men were permissive. He complained that they did not want to take on the responsibilities for raising families. What a burden it must have been for Caligula to find it difficult to produce a living child. For his second wife, Caligula married Livia Orestilla, who was supposed to marry Gaius Piso; after a few days he divorced her and prohibited her from marrying Piso. Shortly after mourning the death of Drusilla, Caligula married for the third time. Despite his third wife's vast wealth, his wedding to Lollia Paulina did not last. Already overloaded with the burdens of office, finding a compatible wife who would produce an heir intensified. In A.D. 38, these concerns exploded in the form of a serious confrontation with the senate as a scapegoat for his misadventures and as a complacent body he could abuse. The ominous predicament may have prompted the line from the poet Accius: "Let them hate provided they fear."[27] It will be remembered that this technique for governing was effectively used by Tiberius, but he was financially secure and independent from the senate.

In A.D. 39, Caligula took the first of three consulships that showed his proactive efforts in leading the government. Admittedly they were short. Most of his major attempts ran into trouble. At considerable expense he built a bridge at Baiae, endangering his position with the army he had to replace the general at the German front, and weighing its importance to him and to Rome, he had to decide whether to invade Britain. The bridge at Baiae, a village near Misenum, was located at one end of an inlet. The notion of spanning the tiny bay may have been prompted by a prophecy that Caligula would not truly become emperor until he crossed the water as if it were dry land. On a previous challenge he had been asked to have a horse race extended over water, and he instantly took to the idea of placing boats covered with earth and arranged side-by-side in a double line so that they provided a kind of road for his chariot and extensive entourage. For two days Caligula (dressed as Alexander the Great), his retinue, and the townspeople raced back and forth. It must have been a dreamy, drunken, surreal parade. As night fell, torches were lit in the hills and at the points of crossing at Baiae and Puteoli, merging their twinkling lights like stars from the sky reflecting into the sea.[28] To the public that appreciated Caligula's extravagant theatrical events, this expensive spectacle was promoted in the grand tradition that would become centuries later the trademarks of P. T. Barnum and Cecil B. De Mille.

Apparently after the show at Baiae, Caligula embarked on a long journey to Upper Germany. He went to relieve Cornelius Lentius Gaetulicus of his command because he was accused of being lax in the discipline required for the security of his legions. This was an unpopular task made possible by his eager replacement, Savicus Sulpicius Galba. Caligula's efforts to secure the

German front at the Rhine River were serious attempts, but unlike his ancestors he had no battlefield experience. Taking a large retinue, he traveled at the rate of about twenty miles a day, which meant that his excursion would take months. Anyway, it was better to have Galba, who went on ahead, to have replaced Gaetulicus before he arrived. Caligula, perhaps with Caesonia, headquartered in much safer territory at Lyons, where the Rhone and Saône rivers joined in east central Gaul (France). It will be remembered that Germanicus was so elated with the progress of his legions that he wanted to extend the empire to the Elbe River, when the wiser strategist, Tiberius, told him to come home and enjoy his triumph. The Roman generals had increasing difficulty in maintaining the German front at the Rhine River; therefore, when Caligula finally arrived, he staged a careful and brief excursion into enemy territory, mostly for self-promotional value.

If the insurgencies in Germany had been quelled by early A.D. 40, Caligula might have invaded Britain; but they remained tentative. At one point it was said he had assembled over two hundred thousand troops on the shores of northwestern Gaul, evidently near Boulogne, overlooking the Strait of Dover, just south of today's channel tunnel at Calais, for a possible invasion. He had to evaluate the situation carefully. The weather was bad and an invasion by crossing the English Channel appeared treacherous. In the past the Roman fleet had been battered on the shores of the British Isles. The biggest factor was that he could not take on a war in the West without having a secure border on the East. This trip would serve as a preliminary assessment for a later invasion.

Instead, he settled for the symbolic surrender of the banished son of an English king, supposedly by meeting him on a trireme at sea or maybe it was a more comfortable place on shore.[29] He marked the occasion by building a lighthouse to aid shipping, and commanded his soldiers to collect seashells for display in Rome. While this may seem odd, like politicians today Caligula apparently understood the value of visual images. As he traveled homeward, to his surprise he learned he was a celebrity. Cities wanted to host him and his entourage, and the people were willing to purchase anything they could get from imperial Rome. His welcome was so rewarding that he sent messages to Rome to supply him with more items he could sell.

Returning to the capital, he displayed his spoils—the trireme, seashells, and few tall Gauls posing as captives. He also brought back several Germans who served as his bodyguard because they were identified in a prophecy. None of these decisions suggest that Caligula was insane, as the movie implies. To the contrary, they were thoughtful judgments. Upon his return to Rome he was greeted with a modest and disappointing welcome. He had been away about six months. His flamboyant entrance to reveal his display of riches in the film's banquet scene is appropriately exaggerated — he was trying to excite a blasé Roman hierarchy. The film's abrupt transition from the orgy in the galley to an unexplained gathering of papyrus (not seashells) by naked soldiers may reinforce the notion that Caligula was crazy. These actions have little merit and are essentially inaccurate, according to historians.

There was no lack of conspiracy theories in Rome. Earlier Caligula had learned that his occasional lover, Marcus Lepidus, had been sleeping with his remaining two sisters, which could be interpreted as an effort to obtain power. So Lepidus was executed for conspiracy, and the sisters were banished. Then Caligula married for the fourth time. The bride was Melonia Caesonia, a well-known, promiscuous, divorced mother of three girls. She was born in A.D. 5, and even though she was said to be unattractive and older, she quickly presented him with a daughter, an important birth because questions had arisen about whether he could produce an heir.[30]

For many years the Roman emperors had difficulty bringing North Africa under their control. Wide stretches of the continent were almost impossible to effectively manage. In A.D. 39, with the northern regions of Germany erupting from time to time, the southern countries from the Atlantic to the Nile posed additional military problems. The huge territory of Mauretania had been colonized by Augustus and made a client kingdom. Augustus took its most promising leader, Juba, to be brought up in his own household, and then he returned him to rule over his ancestral land by marrying Cleopatra's daughter, Selene, abiding in Hellenistic traditions. Their son was Ptolemy, who shared power with his father about A.D. 23, when despite receiving honors and recognition, Ptolemy's leadership crumbled. By A.D. 39, Caligula decided to end Ptolemy's ineffective reign by inviting him to Rome as an honored guest, only to have him killed in A.D. 40, after Caligula returned from his trip to Germany and Gaul. Other than his wealth, historians are at a loss to account for what prompted Ptolemy's death. Other kings who had not lived up to expectations retired in comfort. There may have been conspiracy links to Caligula's sisters or Gaetulicus, who knew Ptolemy. Still, the complicated political commingling of those in power with those ambitious enough to connive for power repeatedly produced changes as unexpected as the decisions of the goddess Fortuna herself.

Caligula as a God

Little proof survives that suggests Caligula met his alleged goal of being recognized as a god. Barrett discusses this matter at length because it goes to the heart of the question as to whether Caligula was sane or insane, especially during A.D. 40 and after. Discussion among the ancient writers is inconclusive, partly because some writers favored him and others were critical. Objective histories are not common. Prejudice depends on the relationship between the writer and the sources. Attempts by Caligula to impose his statue as a god, like Jupiter, or to replace gods in temples scattered around the empire, or to establish a cult that supported Caligula as a god, either did not happen or failed. There is the notion that himself as a god was just role-playing. Other emperors and distinguished persons have been recognized for extraordinary qualities, much as they are recognized today as gods of beauty, athletic strength, or mental genius. Barrett concludes: "Whatever the precise form of the worship of his genius or of himself, it is clear that he did not impose it on the Romans."[31]

The most notable case arose when Gaius sent Petronius to the Middle East to place his statue in the Temple of the Jews at Jerusalem. The Jews were furious; they threatened to revolt. So, Herod Agrippa, according to Josephus, gave a sumptuous dinner for Gaius. The emperor was no fool; he knew he wanted something of unusual value, perhaps a kingdom. Outrageously perilous extravagant affairs, which he knew he could not pay for, excited Caligula, and that is what he liked about Agrippa. Risking his life, Agrippa asked Gaius not to install his statue in the Jewish temple, which was against God's commandments according to their faith. Gaius was not expecting a request of this nature for it did not personally benefit Agrippa; however, he was in too delicate a position politically to deny it. He wrote to Petronius saying that if the statue had not already been installed, he did not want him to do so, and then, under threat of death, he changed his mind. The letters were delayed in reaching Petronius, who did not want to install the statue or establish a god cult. When they did arrive, Gaius was dead, and Agrippa was assisting Claudius in becoming emperor.

As previously discussed, Albert Camus used Caligula as a vehicle for his intellectual exploration of Caligula's passion for the impossible, such as attaining and preserving his independence, or becoming a god, or simply dealing with contradictions. By the end of the play Caligula has killed those close to him, including Caesonia, and awaits the "perfect suicide," being killed by Chaerea, a destiny he knows is unavoidable. Caligula admits that he was wrong in the way he conducted his life, but who believes him in this gigantic reversal? What is he looking for—forgiveness? Caligula discovers in his last moments that "nothing lasts," which yields yet another reversal with his final breath, "I'm still alive." And he was right. Considering that Caligula is being written about two thousand years after he walked the earth, his desire for godlike immortality seems to have been attained. This amusing irony in the play allows its contemplation long after the curtain has fallen.[32]

Having lived a life of conspiracies generated by those around him and perpetrated on someone else, Caligula's fear of a conspiracy against his own life proved accurate. While he did away with Gemellus and Macro, many other less-well-defined conspiracies may indeed have been formed about him. During the last six months of his reign a conspiracy developed that was successful. In Rome, Caligula continued to embarrass and anger senators. He goaded the senators to act against him. One by one he carried out heinous crimes of torture, even killing children in front of their parents. The notion of a united senate eluded them, and therefore, senate members were destroyed individually. Nearly everyone who ever knew Caligula was a suspect at one time in a conspiracy against him, including his wife Caesonia. Imagine what one's life would be like if one could not trust any of those around. Of course, Caligula's companions learned not to trust him. Paid mercenaries seemed to be the only security he had, and, after all, they could be bought.

Within his own household he could not prevent mounting distrust. Caligula had replaced Macro with Cassius Chaerea, who remained loyal and carried out Caligula's wretched tasks. Josephus, in a long and detailed narrative, describes the conspiracy and death of Caligula.[33] Caligula persisted in embarrassing Chaerea with homosexual inferences that Josephus mentions. Even if Chaerea were not as masculine as other men in the army, why would that matter? This was the pagan era for Rome, but Josephus was heavily influenced by moral values established in the Old Testament and how issues were interpreted as God's will. Perhaps other reasons concerning his job performance, sympathy for some of those being punished, and secret support from senators who would profit from Caligula's death were explanations.

Indecisive sources say it was the last week in January, probably 24 January A.D. 41, with bad omens and gossip in abundance, that Caligula, in high spirits, attended the horse races at the Hippodrome for the final time. At least three separate conspiracies were in progress, according to Josephus. As usual, at midday Caligula left for a bath and lunch using narrow corridors that reduced his German bodyguard, and left him vulnerable to Chaerea and his men who were resolute in assassinating him. Chaerea struck the first, nonlethal blow, and then his soldiers stabbed him thirty more times. Caligula's body was removed to the palace where Caesonia and her daughter, Drusilla, mourned over it. The tribune Lupus was assigned to kill them. Caesonia accepted her fate quickly, and it is said her daughter's head was smashed against a wall. The reign of Gaius Caesar Augustus Germanicus was at an end.

Central to the screenplay is a study of the forces that molded the complex personality of Caligula himself, who found he was the unchallenged leader of a vast world bordering the Mediterranean Sea and even beyond. Poorly trained in the fundamentals of governing, he had to depend on whatever survival abilities he could muster. As a young leader and a human being,

Entrance to the Mausoleum of Augustus, 2006.

he was a work-in-progress with few reliable friends or associates to guide him. He must have felt desperately alone when he learned about his tremendous responsibilities. As public popularity grew, his sense of self-confidence rose, and perhaps this led to the hunger for power many politicians crave and to an ego that deluded him into believing he was chosen by the gods for greatness and eventual divinity.

Once Caligula was dead, Caligula's long-time friend and shrewd politician Herod Agrippa saw the advantages Claudius had for preserving the empire. Claudius was found hiding behind a drape, quivering in terror. Some influential people wanted the monarchy to continue; therefore, they seized upon him, after Caesonia, whom some believed urged Caligula's evil deeds, and their daughter were slain.[34] Caligula's body was partially burned in Campus Martius and his remains disappeared. They may be in the tomb of Augustus that has yet to be excavated. The names of Agrippina, Caligula's mother, and Drusus, his brother, whose ashes Caligula brought from banishment, appear on a tablet outside the tomb. By the end of Caligula's reign the monarchy had been firmly established.

Within twenty-four hours, Claudius (10 B.C.–A.D. 54), brother of Germanicus and Caligula's uncle, was being prepared to become the fourth emperor, depending on all the usual attributes, such as support from a strong military believing in turn that he would support it, the senate remaining complacent, and the public approving of Claudius as emperor. After Claudius had reigned eleven years (A.D. 41–54), Caligula's sister, Agrippina Minor, who was Claudius's wife by then, may have poisoned him so that her son Nero could become emperor. Nero was more vicious than Caligula and is believed to have been responsible for the burning of Rome in A.D. 64, which he blamed on the Christians. He did this partly so that he could build his Domus Aurea (Golden House), a magnificent palace near Palatine Hill and the Coliseum. After he committed suicide, the structure was buried so that no reminders were left of Nero's cruel reign. In 2005 the site was rediscovered, preserved under two thousand years of debris.[35]

3

A Movie Marriage

Robert Charles Joseph Edward Sabatini Guccione is the son of Anthony and Nina Guccione. The Sagittarian was born on 17 December 1930 and raised in New Jersey. His Catholic family of Sicillian ancestry encouraged the former altar boy to become a priest, but that pursuit ended in 1949 when he married. The couple had a daughter, Tonina. Soon the marriage ended and he went to Rome to become a painter. Only in his twenties, he sustained himself and gained experience doing various small jobs. He traveled to North Africa, where, like Camus, he met a group of expatriates, and Muriel Hudson, a British singer, whom he married in 1956.

They moved to London, where he sought employment writing, acting, or drawing cartoons; in addition, his family increased by four children: Robert, Jr., Nina, Anthony, and Nicholas. His first important, but brief, job was on the staff of the *London American,* a weekly that shut down after he became the managing editor. His leadership prompted the staff to resign en masse. This experience identified two of Guccione's characteristics: he was not easy to work for and he was tenacious once he found what he wanted. Again, his father helped him out financially. Guccione had paid close attention to what magazines were selling at newsstands; and he took a particular interest in men's magazines that featured women. The long tradition established by *The Police Gazette* and *Esquire* had been reinvigorated by *Playboy,* which first appeared in 1953. A decade later, just as the social turmoil of new self-awareness was underway, he met Kathy Keeton, who was studying ballet in London, but was also a known stripper. They were highly compatible, both being interested in the arts and ascribing to progressive concepts regarding sexuality, such as open marriage. Guccione had difficulty finding backers for a slightly more spicy version of *Playboy.* He sent out a promotional brochure to interested subscribers, but he sent it to the wrong London demographic and found himself in legal trouble that actually gave his fledgling *Penthouse* magazine, first published in March 1965, a great deal of unexpected public attention. His initial one hundred twenty thousand copies sold out.

In his effort to launch and sustain *Penthouse,* Guccione worked incessantly. His interests skewed toward the artistic and editorial side and Kathy Keeton took on the financial aspects. His second wife found that his preoccupation with the magazine, the bevy of *Penthouse* beauties, and his lack of availability at home with the family put too much strain on the marriage, and so she took the children and left him. After a successful three-year run with the magazine in London, Guccione and Keeton moved to New York to declare war on *Playboy.*

The Publisher-Producer

The content of *Penthouse* was purposefully similar to *Playboy. Playboy* publisher Hugh Hefner had pioneered the role of the ultimate playboy, stated in his philosophy concerning individual rights, obscenity, censorship, repression, casual sex, homosexuality, and religious truth. Hefner wrote: "We believe in a society based upon reason. A man should use his intellect to create an ever more perfect, productive, comfortable, fulfilling, happy, healthy and rational society." He also emphasized the benefits of diversity, a culture that accepts, respects, and nurtures differences. "Our American democracy," he clearly stated in *Playboy,* "is based not on the will of the majority but on the protection of the will of the minority. And the smallest minority in society is the individual."[1] Hefner described a suave, wealthy, urbanite, a man sensitive to the needs of women, a metrosexual. In earlier decades a playboy was a rich young fellow who could devote much of his time chasing after pretty girls who were on the stage in New York; that is, a "stage-door Johnny," who did not have such noble intentions in mind. Hefner extended his influence beyond the magazine through strong visual elements: the Playboy mansion, an airplane, music festivals,

Bob Guccione was coproducer and financier of ***Caligula***. Courtesy Photofest.

television shows, and Playboy clubs that were symbolized by women dressed as bunnies—warm, cuddly, procreative—in tight, low-cut one-piece white costumes resembling bathing suits, and by wearing rabbit ears and cottontails. The bunny logo was stamped on everything he touched. Despite 1950s conservatism and 1960s turbulence, his highly publicized lifestyle defined what it was to be a carefree bachelor or married swinger living the good life.

In 1969, after Americans had survived assassinations, riots in large cities, and were still in the midst of the Vietnam War, Bob Guccione brought *Penthouse* to the United States from England. Applying a somewhat more macho male perspective and perverse outlook toward lifestyle and political issues, Guccione's *Penthouse* combined beautiful photographs of nude or partially nude women in racier poses, articles reflecting his viewpoint, fiction by famous writers, advice columns, cartoons, and numerous trend-setting male-oriented advertisements. Guccione claimed to initiate pictures showing pubic hair, full frontal nudity, the complete clitoris, and liberalization of laws regarding freedom of expression in media. Much of the magazine was headed by female editors and it took a woman-friendly attitude in its organization.[2] The differences between *Penthouse* and *Playboy* were measured in subtleties of taste, wherein writing was a key factor. Guccione was involved in every detail of his empire and so was Hefner; but Hefner's accessible, gregarious personality, uncanny eye for exciting people, and items that would have enduring cultural impact always gave him the edge in publicity.

The Great Society envisioned by President Lyndon Johnson held promise for reforms; and the sexual revolution, enhanced by the birth control pill (1960) and the women's rights movement, accelerated a sexual revolution already in progress. Guccione's various interests progressed rapidly in the United States and England, and he became very wealthy. Guccione's expertise concentrated on the magazine's content and Keeton's attention stayed with the business aspects of an international corporation. They also had to sell the premise that sex is beautiful and should be enjoyed. They had to create attractive products that prompted fantasies of pleasure. This was key to giving a hesitant, puritanical society permission to view and to accept sexually explicit content without feeling shame or guilt.

By summer 1974, a third adult magazine entered the marketplace, *Hustler*. Publisher Larry Flynt sought a particular reader. His formula included more explicit photographs, featuring models from his nightclubs, and he, like Guccione and Hefner, added his personality to the magazine: "From the outset, *Hustler* made people uncomfortable and at times apoplectic. Without a doubt, *Hustler* is the most reviled of the mass-circulation porn magazines, and I have been the most hated of publishers," Flynt would eventually boast.[3] Competition became intense and fear rippled through the Penthouse organization, as Guccione attempted to bind employees, under threat of dismissal, to a lifetime agreement that prohibited them from discussing with outsiders and the media what the company was planning to do next.[4] To some, these restrictions seemed contrary to free speech espoused by *Penthouse* and the adult publishing industry. Secrecy was a common business practice. The objective was for *Penthouse* to retain a niche between *Playboy*'s less explicit and *Hustler*'s more explicit sexual material. *Penthouse* met the challenge by increasing its monthly distribution from over one million copies in 1971 to rival *Playboy* at 4.7 million by the end of the decade.[5]

During the 1970s, many adult publishers and film producers were trying to promote adult businesses as valuable, healthy, and stimulating ways to energize adult society. They claimed with increasing vigor that there was nothing wrong with enjoying sex; it was not simply for procreation. It should be celebrated and not subdued. The sexual revolution had just begun. The all-night dance club — with drugs; hypnotizing, mirrored, revolving balls; and endless, high-decibel, throbbing music — was perfect for the reintroduction of Priapus, the ancient god promising fertility and financial prosperity in the pages of *Penthouse*. The growing adult industry diligently sought to combine freedom of expression with acceptance. Print publications and clubs increased and so did filmmaking. Since the late 1960s filmmaking had become sexually explicit; yet hardcore action had not penetrated the legitimate cinema world. To gain legitimacy for adult media, a sexually explicit, aesthetically and intellectually pleasing feature picture representing a substantial investment was a likely prospect.

Thirty-two-year-old Bernardo Bertolucci had convinced Marlon Brando, then fifty and out of shape, to play the lead in *Last Tango in Paris* (1972), shot in Italy as *Ultimo Tango a Parigi* with Maria Schneider. The film is an emotional outpouring of Brando's own life, with some lines Brando ad-libbed at Bertolucci's encouragement. Two people meet just for sex — without names, without love — in a vacant Parisian apartment. Italian censors said the movie was "obscene, indecent, and catering to the lowest instincts of the libido." No scenes are explicitly shot, Brando is always clothed. Pauline Kael referred to it as "the most powerful erotic movie ever made ... and the most liberating." *Last Tango in Paris* became a world box-office hit. Magazines and early adult movies cheaply made and minimal in concept were not enough for crossover recognition by the general public.

Guccione had a brief involvement in movies, appearing as a pornographer in *The Magnificent Seven Deadly Sins* (1971). That same year Playboy Enterprises produced its first film, Roman Polanski's *Macbeth*. The picture appeared just two years after Polanski's wife, Sharon Tate, and four others

3. A Movie Marriage   81

were brutally murdered in their Hollywood home by the so-called Manson family. *Variety* said *Macbeth* was "rugged in its telling, raw in its motivated violence, and rich in its appropriate physical trappings."[6] The Manson murders predate Stanley Kubrick's *A Clockwork Orange* (1971), which shows youths (led by Malcolm McDowell as Alex), on a rampage, violating a woman and her husband in their remote luxurious home.

An implied challenge was open to Guccione. When Polanski decided to direct *Chinatown*, 1974, Guccione invested in it. The political mystery involving incest — and starring Jack Nicholson, Faye Dunaway, and John Huston — was a huge critical and commercial success. As Guccione explained in his documentary on the making of *Caligula*, he wanted to show that traditional and adult films could be comparable in quality, though appealing to the particular segment of the mainstream adult audience that would tolerate, if not enjoy, sexually explicit scenes on screen.[7] Applying this concept, *Caligula* would have to have a universal theme, wide scope in its cinematography, depth in its characters, and a fascinating narrative. The film needed to excel in these attributes, if violence, sex and nudity were to evolve naturally and be accepted by the mainstream public as essential to telling the story. The "fusion" film, meaning a merger of established and underground techniques, took eighteen months to setup and shoot in Dear Studios, Italy, known for *Ben-Hur* and *Cleopatra*.

Violence has always been accepted as part of life and a dependable marketing staple of American cinema, although many viewers in America and Europe thought movie violence was also obscene. During the late 1960s, film violence became more graphic in such releases as Arthur Penn's *Bonnie and Clyde* (1967), in which gangsters are riddled with bullets in slow motion, and *Little Big Man* (1970), in which helpless Indian families are slaughtered by American soldiers, leading to the deaths of General George A. Custer and 264 cavalrymen at Little Bighorn, Montana, in 1876. Francis Ford Coppola's *Godfather* series (1972, 1974, 1990), revealing ruthless assassinations of rival Mafia families, and *Apocalypse Now* (1979), showing the murder of schoolchildren to clear an area of Viet Cong in order to stage a surfing demonstration, probe the depths of endless evil.

Since silent movie days, the principles that guided Paramount's movie moguls — Jesse Lasky, Adolph Zukor, and Cecil B. De Mille — still applied in the 1970s. The four bankable criteria were major stars, an A-list director, a well-written script, and high production values. As an independent producer, perhaps bravely, perhaps foolishly, Guccione set out to meet these same criteria, as any major studio would. He had the money and drew upon his knowledge of Rome and London to determine the direction of his movie project. "But I promised to produce a blockbuster, a landmark film. I promised that

Caligula would fundamentally change the theatergoing public's perception of motion pictures. I said that it would foment changes within the industry itself."[8]

Sagittarius is a changeable fiery sign ruled by Jupiter. A Sagittarian has a strong intellect, curiosity, mental energy that may be applied to philosophical matters, and is likely to be restless, adventuresome, and a traveler. Guccione's birthday is mid–December, and the influences of Capricorn are present. This earthly sign is ruled by Saturn, depicted as a dour figure, solemn, tenacious, and one with an interest in the past. He wants to control his life and the lives of others. But who believes in astrology?

The Coproducer

The competitive but private Bob Guccione, who built a secluded world of his own displayed in the voyeuristic pages of *Penthouse* and surrounded by attractive Penthouse Pets, was complemented by his coproducer, the gregarious and well-connected Franco Rossellini (1935–1992). Born in Rome, Franco Rossellini was the son of Renzo Rossellini (1908–1982), who scored many of the films of his brother, the renowned director Roberto Rossellini (1906–1977). Roberto Rossellini's cinematic work emerged from the ashes of war-torn Italy in the mid–1940s. Often using citizens who were not professional actors, available settings amidst the rubble, stock newsreel footage, and raw film stock in short supply, Roberto Rossellini was a pioneer of the widely influential cinematic movement known as neorealism. Franco was his nephew.

Franco Rossellini, being a generation younger, was a knowledgeable cinema insider who began as a twenty-two-year-old actor in Antonio Pietrangeli's *Nata di marzo* (1957) and Federico Fellini's *La dolce vita* (1960). As producer, he worked with Pier Paolo Pasolini on *Teorema* (1968), *Medea* (1970), and *The Decameron* (1971). In 1970, he and Gore Vidal were in discussions about adapting *Jim Now*, a screenplay based on Vidal's 1948 novel *The City and the Pillar*; however, funding proved to be insufficient even for a low-budget version. When Guccione's interests turned to filmmaking, Franco Rossellini offered him *Caligula,* based on a treatment by Roberto Rossellini. Originally budgeted at four million dollars, that amount was increased to nine million, and finally stabilized at sixteen million. When Gore Vidal entered the picture, the cost rose to $17.5 million, and later, when interest on a loan was figured in, Guccione estimated the total budget at about $22 million. In the summer of 1975, Franco Rossellini's Felix Cinematografica and Bob Guccione, in a joint venture, asked Gore Vidal to write the screenplay. Rossellini signed Vidal for $225,000 dollars and

10 percent of the gross, potentially a very high salary, to write *Gore Vidal's Caligula*.[9]

This project was to be funded by Bob Guccione himself. Later, he would say that the original Vidal script would have cost thirty to forty million to produce. "Franco was the line producer on *Caligula*. He assembled most of the players, artists, and craftsmen, handled the money, and effectively ran the day-to-day operations of the company," Guccione said. A charming and handsome facilitator, Franco Rossellini understood the Italian film industry and knew many of the rich and famous Americans who visited Rome, such as Elizabeth Taylor, Doris Duke, and Andy Warhol. Franco's contribution was similar to that of Diaghilev rather than the great ballet dancer Nijinsky: "A ringmaster," Guccione said, "with an impeccable nose for public taste." "Franco is a window dresser; fussy, temperamental but very insightful, creating clever relationships with the right alchemy of people and talent and then dealing with them as one deals with a classroom full of unruly, temperamental and spoiled children." Guccione's praise of Franco Rossellini has been unwavering.

Franco Rossellini continued to make raunchy, quick films in Italy, such as *Messalina, Messalina* (1977), using the discarded sets and materials from *Caligula*. Guccione hired him as associate publisher for the international distribution of *Penthouse*—and *Omni* when it debuted in 1978—and he distributed the Italian edition of *Io, Caligola* (1984) after a lawsuit with Tinto Brass was settled. Rossellini died of AIDS in 1992.

The Screenwriter

Gore Vidal, born in West Point, New York, in 1925, began a prolific writing career after World War II. His interests are writing and liberal politics. He is the grandson of Senator T. P. Gore of Oklahoma, which helped to give him recognition on the national scene even before his third novel drew attention. *The City and the Pillar* (1948) is a romantic tale about two young men in a homosexual relationship at a time when the subject was avoided in society. Controversy and his tireless wit have garnered Vidal and his work a great deal of recognition. Over twenty-five novels, among them *The Best Man* (1970), and numerous essays such as "A Thirsty Evil" (1956), followed and often combined history, sex, politics, and Hollywood. Obsessive in his work and fast in output, he became an acclaimed writer of live television dramas (*Visit to a Small Planet*, 1955) and movies (an uncredited rewrite of *Ben-Hur*, 1959). Although he had homes on the East Coast and in Ravello, Italy, he traveled constantly on the speaker's circuit and even ran for U.S. Congress from New York in 1960 and California in 1982. He has received many awards, especially for books on criticism, and an honorary doctorate from Brown University.

With expectations high, Vidal wrote the screenplay for *Gore Vidal's Caligula* in his usual realistic style during 1975–1976. He claims that director Tinto Brass agreed to a realistic style for the production. "No Fellini," insisted Vidal, who had appeared as himself in *Fellini's Roma* (1972). In the documentary on the making of *Gore Vidal's Caligula* Vidal says that Rome has only three industries—the government, the church, and the movies—and that each is a "dream-dispenser."[10] Fellini similarly considered it a city of illusions and myths. Often Fellini directed from inspiration he found on location. He loved to discover unexpected images of fleeting beauty and unusual, expressive faces. Vidal, however, did not believe that Fellini's style was appropriate for what was touted as "the 'Ben-Hur' of porn" (*Playboy*). In any case, from the outset, Vidal and Brass began to disagree, as the film seemed to abandon realism for sexual fantasy and violence. Guccione complained that Vidal's description of Roman society was intensely homosexual; however true that may be, Guccione wanted to see his movie mainly viewed by a straight audience. Vidal's complaints about Brass grew because Vidal believed that the writer, not the director, is the principal figure in filmmaking. Of course, it could be said without a script there would be no film. Many directors only shoot pictures they have written, but most of them depend on screenplays from others.

Gore Vidal was principal screenwriter for *Caligula*. Courtesy Photofest.

Gore Vidal's contract should have included more writer authority if he wanted more power over the production. Typically, the original screenwriter, once the script is finished, has no further input or power over the completed work, unless it is specified in the contract. The original screenwriter finishes a version, and the producer passes it along to other writers, and indeed to the director, for revisions. Brass says that Vidal rewrote it seven times, but they could not agree on a shooting version. In summer 1976, Vidal returned to Rome eager for the initial shooting to begin, only to find that he was not welcome on the closed set. Journalists were not allowed on the set either, largely to enhance publicity. Rumors became rampant. "I believe they are using a good part of *my* script, but to what effect? The film is full of improvisation of a particularly loathsome kind — women blowing horses, that kind of thing," he told *The Advocate*.[11] "Whether he likes it or not, he's the author of the original screenplay," Guccione insisted over the years.[12]

When Vidal finally saw the movie, he was bitterly disappointed. In 1979, he sued to have his name removed from the film. The settlement allowed his name to be removed from the title, but it was retained as screenwriter in the credits. Usually, the Screen Writer's Guild arbitrated credits, just as it did when it gave credit to Karl Tunberg for *Ben-Hur*, but acknowledged Christopher Fry, Gore Vidal, Maxwell Anderson, and S. N. Behrman as contributors.[13] Vidal's lawsuit cost him 10 percent of the gross profits and attorney fees.

The film's cultural value might have benefited substantially, if Vidal's political concerns for America had been clearly expressed in *Caligula*. "For years I have been warning my countrymen that the dictator, when he comes, will not be some crazy little man like Hitler or some pompous asshole like Douglas MacArthur, but somebody terribly warm and folksy and good on television who looks like Arthur Godfrey."[14] Parallels between American and Roman politics at this vulnerable time in American history (the resignation of President Nixon) were ignored despite the prominent place politics already occupied in *Penthouse*. The Caesars ruthlessly destroyed their political opponents in any way they could. Political paranoia, assassinations, alleged conspiracies, lying and deception of all kinds, buying votes, cronyism, squandering money, and dispensing favors were the price of doing business in Rome. Trust was minimal and corruption was rampant. As long as senators, the military, and the wealthy continued to profit under the emperor, the emperor remained in power.

Vidal's theme for *Caligula*, reported in Fred Kaplan's biography *Gore Vidal*, was that America and Britain must be vigilant because, as he told the London *Times*, "Freedom and liberalism are aberrations in the history of the world."[15] If this troubling theme had been expressed in the final cut, it would have enhanced the universality of the story and helped to make it an important, as well as a benchmark, adult mainstream picture. If Vidal, Brass, and McDowell could have agreed on Caligula's raison d'être, the narrative would have had cohesion. Was he an anarchist? Brass thought so. Was he a madman? Vidal wondered what it would mean to a young, inexperienced adult — who had lost his family to executions and feared that his own life would fall to a conspiracy — to lead the Roman Empire.

As for Guccione, his concerns were of little help because he wanted to produce a significant adult feature picture *and* to benefit from the marketing advantages the film would provide the Penthouse conglomerate of magazines, clubs, and audiovisual products. Many others in adult businesses were moving in this same direction, but they were hastily producing films for a few thousand dollars. They were in it for fast profits; they made no claims on history. The initial budget of nine million was typical for an average traditional feature by 1976. George Lucas's *Star Wars* (1977) cost eight million to produce. At twice the cost, *Caligula* had a good chance of meeting its creative goals. If *Caligula* were the breakthrough adult picture with a blend of serious content, sexually explicit scenes, exquisite production values, and appropriate public appeal similar to the best traditional films, it would be poised to have an enduring place in the history of cinema. At the very least, this was an admirable, pioneering gamble for Bob Guccione to assume, in the context of the 1970s, when freedom of choice in adult media was a hard-fought emotional issue.

Gore Vidal was no stranger to the difficulties of having his work produced for the screen. Like many authors who have charged Hollywood with ruining the intention and content of their novels and scripts, Vidal experienced his 1968 novel *Myra Breckinridge* become, in his words, "another bad joke movie." *Myra Breckinridge* (1970) has a minimal plot about a young man who has a sex-change operation, changing him from Myron (Rex Reed) to Myra (Rachael Welch). The operation allows Myra to have bisexual roles, although she would be tormented by sexual and psychological instability. "Deeply anti–Christian, the novel attacked a civilization that had forced many people to be at lifelong war with themselves."[16] The film story is made unnecessarily confusing by frequent inserts of sight gags from old movies. The most memorable gag was the appearance of 1930s sex icon Mae West. As a talent agent, West's role is extraneous to the plot but enabled West to make a comeback at age seventy-eight. West intended to play the character she believed she had become to her audiences—"the embodiment of campy, lusty, predatory sexuality." The blonde queen of sexual innuendos, diamonds, and musclemen was on tour in *Diamond Lil*, her original Broadway triumph in 1928, during the late 1940s and 1950s. *Myra Breckenbridge* was a literary experiment that enabled Vidal to express through fictional characters his personal view, but the screen version ran into serious arguments between the cast members and an inexperienced director.[17] Director Michael Sarne was "very difficult," Mae West told *Take One*. "He wanted desperately to be Fellini with that picture. During the shooting he kept running over to see *Satyricon* at a theatre in Beverly Hills. I think he wanted to have his name over the title, too," as Fellini did.[18]

The commercialization of *Caligula* similarly involved other writers, mentioned later, although the principal story is attributed to Gore Vidal, who tried to legally withdraw his name from the film. A principal disagreement was over the characterization of Caligula. Brass saw him as "a big baby," an anarchist, but Vidal did not consent to this interpretation. Brass, therefore, was concerned that Vidal might undermine the production if he were expressing contrary opinions on the set. Brass claims that Vidal would do annoying things that were intended to discredit him. Brass's credits were not well known and some members of the cast were creating an unpleasant working environment. Once principal photography began, Tinto Brass dominated the production and Gore Vidal's input ended. This was unfortunate because a movie needs as much encouragement as it can get from everyone associated with it. The point is that there were no innocent participants in making *Caligula*. Guccione's intention was to hire experienced people, and he did that. How well he used them and how much they contributed to the quality of the film remains to be seen.

The Directors

While the 1970s showed an increase in the quality of films made for adults, traditional movie box-office receipts indicated that the public was attending en masse the ten or so very expensive and compelling films Hollywood produced annually, but it was only going to lower-budget pictures sporadically. This meant audiences were no longer habitually attending movies as they did in previous decades. To draw the twelve- to thirty-five-year-old audience that saw 75 percent of the movies, the major film companies introduced the "blockbuster" concept: spend a lot more money on a single film to make a lot more money at the box office. "The average cost of producing a feature film rose from $1 million in 1972 to more than $14 million by the mid–1980s, making the small film financed, made, and distributed outside of the major studios all but obsolete," Thomas W. Bohn and Richard L. Stromgren, wrote in *Light and Shadows*.[19] Guccione was wealthy enough to play a long shot, knowing that the odds were against him.

Jaws (1975) illustrated the transition that was taking place in Hollywood. The picture, about a giant shark terrorizing bathers off the New England coast, captured the wave of perfect timing. News stories about the rare attacks reinforced public imagination. *Jaws,* produced for $11 million, returned over $130 million in North American rentals, and the products with which it was associated were an additional marketing bonanza. To many, the summer release was the benchmark for the beginning of the Hollywood blockbuster era. Steven Spielberg, a director of note early in his career, overcame numerous problems to make *Jaws* profitable for Universal.[20]

The director's job is to take the printed pages of a screenplay and translate them into sounds and pictures that amaze and excite viewers from the first to the last frame. This is a decidedly different task from that of the screenwriter. By the mid-1970s, time was taking its toll on the numerous strong, imaginative, unique Italian auteurs who each had made at least one brilliant, sexy masterpiece, and ventured into unexplored realms of cinema. Five died in the decade: Luchino Visconti (1906–1976), Roberto Rossellini (1906–1977), Vittorio De Sica (1902–1974), Pietro Germi (1914–1974), and Pier Paolo Pasolini (1922–1975). Michelangelo Antonioni, Giuseppe De Santis, and Franco Zefferelli carried on. Neorealism, influential during the forties and fifties, yielded to greater escapist influences from Frederico Fellini (1922–1994) and Bernardo Bertolucci (1940–). Particularly noteworthy was Bertolucci who received international acclaim for *Last Tango in Paris*. He extended the grand period for Italian directors beyond the seventies.

Hiring a distinguished director was not out of the question, but it was not easy. Guccione, having invested in *Chinatown*, asked one of its leading actors, John Huston, seventy, who had directed Rudyard Kipling's epic *The Man Who Would Be King* (1975), but his price was too high. Huston had directed an eclectic group of pictures since his debut as director of *The Maltese Falcon* in 1940. An eccentric, Huston directed scripts that showed survival, victory over adversity; he had faith in humanity rising above adverse circumstances; he liked new adventures and work outside rather than inside studios. His characters dictated a strong masculine style. He preferred meaningful spectacle and avoided the use of gimmicks. He usually found humor in the characters and story. Huston reveled in the filmmaking process. For him it was the journey, not just the result.[21] Guccione had discussed the picture with native Roman Lina Wertmuller, who got her start as an assistant director on Fellini's *8½* (1963) and was in a successful, four-year directing period culminating in *Seven Beauties* (1976), for

Tinto Brass is credited unofficially as director and officially as principal cinematographer for *Caligula*. Courtesy Photofest.

which she became the first woman nominated for an Academy Award in directing. To that date, however, the flamboyant, spontaneous director, known for comedies and a high shooting to screen ratio, had written all of her screenplays and wanted to do her own version of *Caligula*. Gore Vidal suggested the British director Nicholas Roeg, who was cinematographer on David Lean's sweeping Academy Award winner *Lawrence of Arabia* (1969), and whose directing debut was *Performance* (1970), starring Mick Jagger. The latter is a study in hedonism, perversion, and decadence that sat gathering dust while studio executives tried to figure out whether to sue Roeg or release it. Its successful release rocketed his name to among those at the top of the list of promising new directors. His nonlinear editing style consisted of shifting planes, intercuts of past, present, and future time, including fast-forward shots; his work seemed fragmented and improvised on location. "You can say things visually, immediately, and that's where, I believe, film is going. It's not a pictorial example of a published work, it's transference of thought," Roeg told *American Film*.[22] From this selection it is clear that Guccione's choice would probably be one of compromise, and his time for making such a decision was short.

Over lunch, Bob Guccione hired Tinto Brass to direct *Caligula*. Brass was born in Milan, Italy, in 1933. He had a tormented relationship with his father, who believed Brass by his mid-teens "already manifested evident signs of unbalance."[23] He spent his early years completing law studies in Venice before working at Cinémathèque Française, the world-famous film archive, and as assistant editor to Dutch documentary director Joris Ivens. He became an assistant director to Brazilian director Alberto Cavalcanti in 1958, and to Roberto Rossellini during 1958–1959, for whom Brass edited with minimal instructions *India* (1958), and served as assistant director on *General Della Rovere* (1959), which revived favorable distinction for Rossellini. Only thirty, Brass's directing debut was *Il capo al mondo — Chi lavora è perduto* (To the Ends of the Earth — He Who Works Is Lost) in 1963. He also ventured into making a western and a thriller before he made his first erotic film, *Black on White*, in 1967, and won a Venice Film Festival award for *The Vacation*, which enabled him to examine favorite themes concerning madness, repression, and outcasts. He directed about one film a year and gained a reputation for making softcore films. He had been recognized in Paris at the Cinémathèque Française as the best of the outrageous sex filmmakers in the industry.

Guccione's task was to sign a director who could competently film a traditional narrative and who had some experience in the requirements of adult filmmaking. Brass has said he believes in sex as a medium of communication because everybody understands the language of sex. Brass says he is a voyeur, for anybody who looks at the world through a hole is a voyeur. He likes to think of himself as a kind of Russ Meyer (1922–2004), an independent producer famous for featuring big-bottomed women in his nudie-cutie films. "If there was an auteur working in American commercial filmmaking during the Sixties—a man totally in control of every aspect of his work—that had to be Meyer," Roger Ebert contended.[24] Brass has certain ideas about what he was willing to film. For example, sexual transgression is not necessarily pleasureful, and Brass did not intend to film it that way. Brass, being in the neorealist tradition, favored stories emphasizing the welfare of the masses over that of the elite wealthy classes. All directors of the neorealistic period were heavily influenced by Marxist theory. Between his political leanings and his bravado—"I put two big balls and a big cock between the legs of Italian cinema," Brass said—the work of Tinto Brass had been marginalized.[25]

Apparently when Guccione screened *Salon Kitty*, he did not realize that Brass had a passion for underlying themes, and that Brass thought of *Salon Kitty* as his first film in a "trilogy of power." Guccione's offer to make *Caligula*, therefore, fit perfectly into his plans. The *Salon Kitty* story is a Nazi-era tale about a young, loyal socialist determined to gain power within the Third Reich. Brass is deeply convinced that power is immoral. "I must admit that power I hate deeply," he once said. Yet, he admitted that there is such a big amount of energy involved with power that it can also be fascinating. "The monstrosity of power, in fact, is much more comprehensible when it is exemplified by actions of sexual violence."[26] The exploration of power, especially bestowed on the young, is the absorbing theme exploited in *Caligula*, which he regarded as the second part of his trilogy. In addition, Brass, a multitalented man, would direct and shoot much of *Caligula* himself. Frequently, he produced his movies. He'd had French, German, and Italian financing for his just-completed *Salon Kitty*, which aptly depicted his capabilities and interests.

Tinto Brass's *Salon Kitty* (1976) opens in Berlin, but quickly moves to the seclusion of the suburbs. Consumed with gaining greater power within the Third Reich, Lieutenant Wallenberg (Helmut Berger), an SS officer, decides to obtain it through blackmail. He secretly converts an established brothel, run by Madame Kitty (Ingrid Thulin), into a center for recording conversations between prostitutes and German officials who reveal precisely how they really feel about the Nazi government.[27] Thematically, there is a hint of the Watergate tapes and break-in, and the plot borrows ambience from Isherwood's Berlin stories that became *Cabaret* (1972), in that Madame Kitty puts on song-and-dance routines for her champagne-drinking guests. Wallenberg keeps tight control over the whorehouse and becomes enamored with Margherita (Teresa Ann Savoy), a teenager who manages to record his criticisms about the Reich after she learns through recordings that her favorite lover has been executed. The surface of dominance, the Nazi flag, and the prominent swastika signifying a corrupt and evil state are reminiscent of Visconti's *The Damned* (1969), but particularly striking are the characters, scenes, and actors that presage *Caligula*. Wallenberg is a tormented tormentor like Caligula. He rounds up young men and women for an early group-sex scene that even tests women's loyalty by having them copulate with deformed and demented men. It's an eerie projection of life on Capri. There are touches of Pasolini's *Salò* too, in that the young people are rounded up from the best in the country. In the end, Wallenberg, standing stark naked in a bath house, is shot by his successor, who then checks the body by rolling it over, somewhat like the assassination in *Caligula*. The 1930s clothes, especially for Madame Kitty, are stylish, detailed, and decadent. Brass reuses his favorite cinematographer Silvano Ippoliti and actors Teresa Ann Savoy and John Steiner. The dialogue is in Italian, but there is a dubbed English version that includes subtitled scenes for the director's-cut edition. *Salon Kitty* clearly shows that Tinto Brass is a capable filmmaker. The film has a problem typical of Hollywood movies—a fast, formal conclusion, but Brass's preference for full-bottomed women who are strong enough to handle arrogant men allowed him to be categorized as a Russ Meyer adult moviemaker rather than a Penthouse Pets showman.

Caligula is about a youth who inherits power that he misuses because, according to some ancient historians, he is a madman. Immediately, Brass and Malcolm McDowell agreed there had to be a more complex character for him to play. Perhaps Caligula was an anarchist who wanted to deconstruct the society around him. Some would say there were honest disagreements in artistic perspectives about his character. Caligula's character became a work in progress as various writers, McDowell, and Brass added lines not only to assist the development of the character but to provide continuity between scenes. Dramatic situations could be presented on the screen as either sexual or violent. Some examples include slaves who are forced to perform sexual acts for Tiberius, slaves who supply semen to enhance Ennia's appearance, the raping of Livia and Proculus as the wedding couple, the sale of the senators' wives for sexual encounters to raise money for the treasury, the display of grief and consolation upon the death of Drusilla that could be interpreted as necrophilia, and the replacement of the heads of statues of divinities with Caligula's own head (omitted in the final cut). These are acts subject to interpretation.

Although Brass was quite capable of directing the film, he was surrounded by artists who favored telling the story in other ways and styles, such as a later rather than the more realistic earlier neorealistic style. In *Salon*

Kitty, Brass uses newsreel footage of Hitler like Roberto Rossellini did in early neorealistic films. Brass borrows from both styles; he uses Fellini-like faces in *Caligula*, whereas in *Salon Kitty* the cast is very Aryan, very pretty, and very elegant in a display of 1930s costumes. When an artist is provided with more advice than he can use, he must go within himself, as Joseph Conrad so beautifully wrote, "in that lonely region of stress and strife, [where] if he be deserving and fortunate, he finds the terms of his appeal. His appeal is made to our less obvious capacities; to that part of our nature which, because of the warlike conditions of existence, is necessarily kept out of sight within the more resisting and hard qualities—like the vulnerable body within a steel armor."[28] The artist then follows his own vision. This is what led to the disagreements banning Gore Vidal from the set.

Once Brass had the script in his hands, he had to seize control of the production so that everyone understood who was directing the movie. Still, this was difficult. There is general agreement that a film, particularly involving sex and violence, could not be completed unless the cast and crew had total confidence in the director. The production was plagued with human problems. Twenty-four-year-old Maria Schneider, whom Tinto Brass wanted to play Drusilla, decided after she arrived that she did not want to do nude scenes, which she had already done so successfully in *Last Tango in Paris*; Helen Mirren wanted the role, but she was considered too old for it; Teresa Ann Savoy, who had completed *Salon Kitty* for Brass, was young, sweet, reliable and worked to get it. Peter O'Toole was unhappy because about one half of the scenes he had shot were ultimately not used. The dispositions of all of the actors had to be massaged from time to time, but they held strong professional traditions and did what they were asked to do. The British leads of course spoke English, but the other actors spoke Italian. All of the actors knew *Caligula* was to be a sexually explicit and violent film. The film was shot with four cameras zooming in and out most of the time, and the set was often noisy, even after the call for "action." This was intentional for the dialogue was dubbed/looped into English. Brass himself spoke broken English.

No matter how temperamental the cast and crew were during the shooting, they did not pose the crushing, insurmountable dilemma Brass faced as the shooting neared completion. In the United States films are typically edited by crafts people under the supervision of the director. Stories abound about famous films being disastrously edited at the insistence of studio bosses, who wanted a picture the audience would sit through and pay for. Eric von Stroheim's silent classic *Greed* would have run, some said, for fourteen hours, if studio executives had not taken the editing out of his control. At one point von Sternberg cut it to about four hours, but that was still too long.

What Tinto Brass did not anticipate was that Bob Guccione would take

John Gielgud, as Nerva, and Malcolm McDowell, as Caligula, chat between scenes. Photograph courtesy General Media Communications, Inc., and Robert C. Guccione. Used by permission.

the negative away from Brass before he could edit it. Brass doted on the montage, the editing process. This is when the multitude of shot and scene choices are narrowed down to one. For David Lean, Hitchcock, and for Brass editing Roberto Rossellini films, this is the heart of the filmmaking process. Guccione denied Brass his right to edit the footage he had shot; consequently, Brass would not have the final cut. The final cut enables the director to emphasize the main theme of the movie, that underlying force that drives the story and initially motivates the director to endure the rigors of making the picture. "The editing is a magic moment," Brass claims, "in which I attempt to infuse my personal style to every film of mine; I could never entrust it ... to another person."[29] Brass said that some scenes were shot to provide proper context for Caligula's actions, but that they were omitted by other editors, for instance, a scene wherein heads of gods on statues were replaced by Caligula's and another scene where Caligula offends the bureaucracy by sacrificing a high priest rather than an ox. Brass uses a film editing system that was popular during most of the twentieth century "to marry" or conform picture and sound together, so that he can actually handle the strips of film, protected by white gloves, being cut. He thinks of his editing room as a "cathedral," a sacred place. In Brass's opinion, if he does not edited the film, he has not directed it.

Bob Guccione got what he paid for, an experienced filmmaker who competently shot the scenes for *Caligula*, but how he would focus the viewer's attention during the editing process, if given the opportunity, was another critical matter.

Human reactions invaded the process. Hiring Tinto Brass was his biggest mistake, Guccione later told AVN, saying that Brass was a Communist. Guccione claimed that Brass would follow orders when he was present, but in Guccione's absence would reverse himself. When he learned that the director also owned the film under Italian law, Guccione turned to drastic measures. With shooting complete, Guccione fired Brass for allegedly running up huge expenses, casting criminals as Roman senators, and using ugly women instead of Penthouse Pets. The relationship between Guccione and Brass turned nasty.

Brass claims he shot 160,000 meters or about one hundred miles of film; Guccione says it was 120 miles. If true, that would be an extremely high shooting ratio of over ten to one. Approximately 4,000–4,500 meters of film were actually used for the release print.[30] Guccione charged that some sets were built and never used, resulting in further waste. If a director does not have full control over the film, or if he prepares insufficiently, or if there are labor disputes, unexpected expenses typically arise. Some great screen directors preplanned frames precisely — Hitchcock and Peckinpah, for example; and some did not — Fellini and Wertmuller. Brass tended to follow a less precise preplanned approach. Even so, Brass did deliver sufficient picture continuity so that the film editors, of whom he expected to be the main one, could assemble it into a viewable whole. This was not to happen however. Brass was not allowed to edit the film, and he has not certified his role as director of the film to this day. This position was upheld by the Magistrate of Rome in an ordinance on 1 November 1978. This is a sentiment widely held by directors. The art of filmmaking is in the editing, the montage, a position long held by the great Soviet auteurs Sergei Eisenstein and Vsevolod I. Pudovkin. Still, Brass could have claimed directorship, and in fact, he is commonly credited for it in reviews and articles. He needed this rationale to avoid further court liability concerning obscenity. In a long film a director seldom directs every scene. For example, Victor Fleming did not direct all of *Gone with the Wind* or *The Wizard of Oz*, even though he received awards and recognition for them. A director may direct the principal actors, and second-unit people may direct action or special-effects sequences.

When the Italian court ruled that Tinto Brass had the right to do virtually as he pleased in editing and completing the film he shot, Guccione had to recognize that this was not going to be the film he wanted. Brass's thematic concept was not what he wanted and the Penthouse Pets were minimalized in the film. To resolve the problems he perceived with his multi-million dollar venture, he took drastic action. He smuggled the exposed film print out of Rome by wrapping it around the legs of trusted couriers who would edit it in London, once they got it past British customs.[31] The editors, all of whom were more interested in cash than recognition for their work, stayed in a small apartment, working night and day. By day they phoned instructions to Rome, telling Guccione the shots they needed to match the continuity. By night the film was developed and printed at Twickenham Studios. It was particularly difficult to salvage the orgy scene on the galley, a scene lasting nearly eleven minutes. The match/mismatch involved at times using different actors and surroundings inasmuch as the original actors were gone and the scenery was struck. Guccione and Lui repropped the galley set and used about thirty people who worked for the film. They were not necessarily actors, but they restaged part of the action. The extras were scheduled for five or six nights to film pick-up shots and to provide orgy scene continuity. None of this met union or color or professional standards. Guccione could have been exposed at any time. The future of the film was at stake. Further, Guccione and Lui shot two days of Anneka Di Lorenzo and Lori Wagner in their lesbian encounter. These changes, according to Brass were "miserable and laughable," but account for most of the added length to the unrated version. The lesbian scene is not essential to the narrative and instead illustrates the purposes for the film — to complete a unique contribution to cinema and to give prominence to some of the Pets, and significantly promote the Penthouse franchise.

Whether these added scenes are erotic or pornographic depends on the viewer's taste. The result of this bitter clash of personalities, aside from the lawsuits that were about to begin, was that *Caligula* was very close to becoming the significant cinematic benchmark that Bob Guccione and a multitude of viewers wanted it to be.

Brass went to London to claim his right to edit the film, which he had in his Italian contract. The English and American courts did not recognize his claim because Bob Guccione held the registered copyright. After some private showings in the United States and Cannes, *Caligula* had its initial public exhibition in Rome on 14 August 1979, and was shut down within a week by the censor for obscene content. Brass, considered to be the director responsible, had to defend himself in the Honorable Court of Forli at the end of February 1980.[32] His plea was easily understood by many international directors, even though some of them, including Orson Welles, whom Brass admired, did not edit their films. (Robert Wise edited Welles's *Citizen Kane*.) In essence, Brass told the court that he and his crew, a devoted entourage of cameramen with the company, including his long-time associate and director of photography Silvano Ippoliti, did not shoot explicit sex scenes, nor would he have necessarily chosen such footage for inclusion in the editing process, even if they had shot it. Editing is not a mathematical process, it is an aesthetic one; it is qualitative, not quantitative, he insisted. The multitude of choices a director makes in the editing process depends on content and context; that is, what images and sounds have been captured and what purpose they serve in the story. At twenty-four frames per second, editing a movie is not like editing a magazine. The images are fleeting and not controlled by the viewers, who may look at a magazine at their own pace. If Brass had edited the film, he says he would have assumed its authorship as director. [33]

If Brass had been more open about his philosophical basis for *Caligula*, Guccione might have decided that he was incompatible with his own objectives. For Brass, *Caligula* was the second part of a trilogy that began with *Salon Kitty*, illustrating the immorality of power. The third picture probably would have been "Borgia." The monstrosity of power is made "much more comprehensible when it is exemplified by actions of sexual violence," as Brass points out in Mario Gagliardotto's book-length interview.[33] Caligula's character therefore presents himself in three aspects captioned the Logic of Utopia, the Logic of Power, and the Logic of Folly, showing Caligula beginning with his aspirations, being corrupted by power, and destroyed by folly. Applying this premise, the sex scenes are not romantic, they are despicable; the opposite of the erotic exhibitions displayed on the pages of *Penthouse*; therefore, the Penthouse Pets could be interpreted as examples of degrading rather than idolizing women.

The Brass theme and accomplishment is reminiscent of Pasolini's *Salò— The One Hundred Days of Sodom* (1975). In 1976 *Salò* had been refused censorship approval in Italy. Pasolini, a Marxist, had been murdered on 1 November the prior year. Alberto Grimaldi tried to offset adverse connections the press might make over the film, but some reviewers could not be dissuaded from vicious speculation. Producer Grimaldi hoped the international press would be more receptive, more open. The story is based on the book by the Marquis de Sade, which concerns "the organization and execution of orgies." An important addition, however, was that Pasolini updated the story to the 1944 Mussolini fascist era, making it relevant and political. "Every scene attacks, every sensibility is ruthlessly crushed. Every form of sexual, sadistic, and psychopathic depravity is shown, but none of them separates these actions from the everyday.... What we are told here, again and again, is that there is no history, no change, no evolution, and that the human continuity is only a series of variations on the principle of anarchic power application," wrote Gideon Bachmann in *Film Comment*.[34] Usually a film production realist, for this one Pasolini post-synchronized the sound from a script, which is typical of Roman filmmaking, and the actors spoke the lines precisely as written. He tries to create the sense that what we see as horror is normal, part of basic human behavior. He even borrows Dante-like segments labeled as "cycle of mania," "cycle of shit," "cycle of blood," and so forth. Actors did not question the nudity or sado-masochistic acts because of their respect for Pasolini. Pasolini showed the illusion of equality realistically, with those in power reigning over human minds and bodies. The actors believed that they were involved in an enterprise of total respectability. The idea of domination of one person by another is a metaphor for capitalism's treatment of working people. Pasolini was "very good at intellectualizing, after the fact, what he was doing on the screen," Vincent Canby wrote in the *New York Times*.

Salò shows the powerful—a magistrate, a president, a judge, and a bishop—imposing their morality and depravity on the younger generation. The images are difficult to view, as hatred toward those in power heightens. The conclusion is that evil cannot be eliminated, perhaps only controlled. Evil, like good, is indestructible. Brass, like Pasolini, favors the proletariat, antiestablishment themes, relevant sex and violence in his films, and his work would be delayed for reasons of censorship by the courts. The parallel is interesting because *Salò* presumably takes place during the Mussolini era, when Mussolini tried to revive positive aspects of ancient Roman culture.

After a settlement with Tinto Brass, Franco Rossellini's Felix Film and

Penthouse Film International released an Italian-language version, *Io, Caligola,* in 1984. This edition, described as "mad rubbish" by Brass, was at first banned in Italy, but had limited release in France, at first rated "unrated," then "X." Of the several editions of *Caligula* released worldwide, Brass says the edition nearest to what he had in mind is Guccione's unrated version, apart from the rehashing and additions.[35]

The Actors

Bob Guccione preferred British stars as principal actors—Malcolm McDowell, Peter O'Toole, Helen Mirren, and John Gielgud. He believed they were more acceptable in the roles of ancient Romans and they were less expensive than American actors. They were expertly trained professionals who had Shakespearean stage experience and excellent film credits, often including a stint with nudity on screen, and appreciated the salary Guccione offered them.

Malcolm McDowell

Born in Leeds, England, the principal role went to thirty-four-year-old Malcolm McDowell, whose screen career began by playing likable, arrogant, insolent characters with a glint in the eye. The most memorable one was Alex in Stanley Kubrick's *A Clockwork Orange* (1971). Based on the Anthony Burgess novel, Alex spoke a unique but understandable language to his thug companions. They hung out at a decadent milk bar where they hatched cruel entertainments, consisting of attacking unsuspecting citizens. In short, although he was supposed to be an incorrigible kid in high school, he did as he pleased as a captivating and seductive macho man. Arguably, this is the character the public hoped to see again, and one reason Tinto Brass chose him for the part. Alex was cruel and mischievous at the same time; he is a delight to watch doing bad things: the devil with a smirk.

McDowell's early education enabled him to get rid of his Yorkshire dialect and join the Royal Shakespeare Company. His acting career began in the late 1960s when director Lindsay Anderson hired him as the lead in *If* (1968), which shows a young boy becoming a rebel, first in fantasy and then in real life, resulting in a confrontation between school administrators, teachers and parents against young revolutionaries. In another Anderson film, *O Lucky Man* (1973), he met Helen Mirren, and they became kindred spirits dedicated to the theatrical arts and to having fun while pursuing them. When he was called upon to spend a year abroad shooting *Caligula*, for tax purposes, he encouraged the casting of Mirren so that she could join him.

Actors like to think every character they create is different, even though some characters may be similar. A versatile and brilliant actor, McDowell had difficulty portraying the troubled Roman ruler ten years his junior. The focus of his character was elusive and complex, reminiscent of the troubles Charles Laughton had in finding his voice for Claudius. Caligula came from a politically powerful family, but his personal popularity contradicted his status in his intimate circles. His astute cleverness in carrying out his imperial duties, his relationship with his wives and lovers, his growing insular tendencies and arrogance, his increasing fear of conspiracies, and his anxieties about rising to the level of a god so that he could join his ancestors destabilized his already fragile persona. McDowell's experience would enable him to handle the character walking a tightrope between reality and fantasy. Besides Gore Vidal, McDowell, Brass, and T. A. Whitehead added some depth while rewriting or ad-libbing some scenes. For the most part McDowell was on his own. He is in almost every scene and needed whatever support was available. He sought a point of view for the character and a reason for his unnerving actions. Madness and anarchy were decided upon as the principal traits motivating Caligula's character.

In previous interpretations, such as the 1950s biblical films, Jay Robinson relied on Caligula's illness during his first year that some believed caused him to go mad. "Anarchist" is one label that was used to explain his behavior, but Caligula was quite responsible in carrying out the affairs of state. He seemed to absorb Tiberius's administrative responsibilities in stride. "We know very little really about him ... I suppose I see Caligula as the ultimate anarchist," McDowell told Guccione's documentarist.[36] Caligula also was able to set aside the personal tragedies in his own life, expending little emotional capital on them. He did many things people liked, entertaining them, paying old debts, and increasing soldiers' pay. He was a populist and a tyrant at the same time. The movie emphasized his role as tyrant, but ignored the reasons for his playful, theatrical acting, sexual fundraising attempts, and modest military exploits. Caligula could have been a beguiling enigma. Instead, he was mainly labeled an incomprehensible madman. How could one be so charming and yet so evil? The more scholars find out about Caligula, the more his multifaceted nature is evident. Perhaps that disposition can be explained by madness, but the causes may be reaction to the death of his young parents, the terrifying environment in which he lived, and the debauchery he observed when he was with Tiberius. The later reign of Vitellius, who spent his youth on Capri, suggests that he too may have been tainted by the same source, when he said, "Only one thing smells sweeter to me than a dead enemy, and that is a dead fellow-citizen."[37]

Perhaps the most evident clashing element in Caligula's personality, particularly for a contemporary Guccione film, was his penchant for androgynous sex. This would not have been a problem in pagan times. In the opening tease, when he is having an incestuous romp with his sister Drusilla, he shows romantic sexual arousal and playfulness, but he doesn't display such loving tendencies again until he matures into a family man close to the end of the picture. Even when Ennia offers herself to him, Caligula's response is at best mechanical disinterest. His last sequence of happiness of any kind is when he and his family are rehearsing a play near the end of the story. Furthermore, there is no attempt to make Caligula like Alex, a seductive character. His only frontal nude scene is in the storm sequence, when, deeply disturbed, his mind returns to the security of his childhood by repeating the boots dance.

McDowell was kept very busy, working long days and nights. Typical schedules for movie productions are from five or six in the morning to midnight. McDowell changes his costume for nearly every scene. Fortunately, the cast and crew got along well, but the language barrier must have been difficult to overcome. He received a good deal of help from his dialogue coach inasmuch as the dialogue was recorded in English. Brass did not give much personal instruction to his actors. Directors vary on this point. Some of them act out the entire scene, expecting the actor to copy what the director does. Most directors want actors to bring their own special interpretation to the part; if that is inconsistent with what the director has in mind, the director will ask them to modify it. The boots dance was choreographed, and McDowell says that Incitatus was a "splendid animal" who could have seriously hurt him, especially in the bed scene, even though he was drugged. Reminiscent of his line in *Caligula* ("It's just a play"), McDowell says he enjoyed the experience and thinks he did some really good work in the movie. He is still amazed at the lavish production, the huge settings, the extraordinary lighting, and his extensive wardrobe. Nudity he regards as just part of the job.

Today Malcolm McDowell is very prominent in the movies and on television, continuing to play wealthy, arrogant, dominant leaders setting rules and enforcing them. He has the skill to play a character that is mean, ornery, and unlikable or one who is admired and respected. He played the devil in Allen A. Goldstein's *Pact with the Devil*, and is frequently seen on television. Having lived in the United States for years, McDowell says his family comes first; as much as he loves his profession, it is second. In 2006, McDowell was listed in *Entertainment Weekly* as having the lead in two of its "top twenty-five most controversial films of all time": Kubrick's *A Clockwork Orange* came in at Number 2 and Guccione's *Caligula* at Number 24.[38]

Peter O'Toole

Emperor Tiberius, played with enthusiasm by Peter O'Toole, is an excellent portrait of an old man dying, but hardly dead. Tiberius is trying to drain the last drop of power from his office and, like Dracula, is trying to suck the last drop of energy from the young beauties surrounding him. He is complicated and understandably pathetic. Tiberius likes his form of voyeurism for it may be all he has left of faded memories of pleasure.

O'Toole, born in Connemara, Ireland, in 1932, grew up in Leeds, England. He was the third choice to play the lead in David Lean's *Lawrence of Arabia* (1962). When shooting of that film ended, he had suffered from two sprained ankles, a dislocated spine, and had been knocked out twice. Having survived, he became an international star. Richard Burton included him among "the odd few men and women who, once or twice in a lifetime, elevate [acting] into something odd and mystical and deeply disturbing."[39] This time he could not depend on his handsomeness to make the character compelling. By contrast, he is the personification of evil as a shriveled, diseased, miserly, hated deviate, who would have been totally believable if he were not having so much devilish fun playing the part. He gave his role the same high-quality professional attention he gave *Becket* (1964), *Lord Jim* (1965), and *The Lion in Winter* (1968).

It was widely reported that O'Toole was suffering from alcoholism

Peter O'Toole, surrounded by extras in the pool sequence, plays Emperor Tiberius. Photograph courtesy General Media Communications, Inc., and Robert C. Guccione. Used by permission.

throughout the 1970s that led to major surgery in 1979. Guccione complained about keeping him sober, but whatever his health problems or remedies, they did not jeopardize his acting skills in playing Tiberius. He flew from scene to scene with the energy of a young man, and yet expressed thoughtful remorse over the imminent death of Nerva and his concerns for the future of Gemellus. Tiberius must have a larger than life imperial presence without taking the main story away from Caligula. O'Toole was said to be upset because some of his scenes were eliminated. What remains on the screen concentrates on what comes from ancient history. Tiberius, looking dreadfully scaly and untouchable, had disturbing proclivities toward children. In fact, Tiberius was a devoted servant of the Roman Empire for most of his life. Among the range of work admired by his fans, Peter O'Toole's convincing performance as the emperor was included in his acting retrospective when he was given an Academy Award for lifetime achievement in 2003. Accepting the recognition, he said he was still a working actor and wanted to be considered as a competitor. The speech seemed to prompt his role as King Priam in *Troy* (2004), and since then a variety of appearances, including *Venus* (2006), for which he was nominated for another Academy Award.

O'Toole dressed behind drapes as he got in and out of a swimming pool, there was no nudity for him. He engaged in direct violence once when a soldier was being punished for dereliction of duty. This memorable sequence shows a soldier being filled with wine, while his penis is tied off. The soldier is then executed by Tiberius as a routine, dispassionate act, according to Suetonius. The excessive punishment seems to reflect on a tiny leadership group that had the arrogance to believe it was better than most people. Centuries since have given human beings the sense that distinguished leaders are rare and that most of the other leaders are doing the best they can to benefit the masses by helping them more than by suppressing them. Of course, Tiberius's most interesting crime is alleged to be watching young children copulate. It is unclear how young these children might have been or how offensive such an act might have seemed to the Roman people. With barely pubescent youngsters already having children of their own, and with everyone else who was capable having children to preserve the empire, such an act may have been relatively acceptable in pagan times. In any case, history has recorded many occasions when old men and women have imposed bizarre behavior on youth during war and peace. Disgusted historians may have prejudiced their appraisal of Tiberius.

Peter O'Toole was married to Sean Phillips, who was coincidently playing Livia in *I, Claudius* for the BBC. She said: "I was astonished that anyone was making such a silly movie, for so much money." She thought the production was all wrong. They were divorced in 1979 after twenty years of marriage. They had two daughters, and later he had a son. O'Toole has said that there is only one attitude to take and that is to be a pro: "Just do it.... I don't want to be pompous. You know, but whatever the circumstances, the profession should be honored."[40] Whether he is playing a majestic character in a blockbuster classic drama or is portraying the intimate life of an ordinary person, current generations are in awe of Peter O'Toole.

Helen Mirren

Helen Mirren, who plays Caligula's fourth wife, Melonia Caesonia, was just gaining recognition in the United States in the 1970s, but the former "Sex Queen of Stratford" is world famous and very active today. She dropped her top for the delightful British comedy *Calendar Girls* (2003), which is about middle-aged British women who want to raise money for charity in their cash-strapped town by posing nude for a calendar. Helen Mirren's dramatic acting career could hardly have gotten better than her triple sweep in 2006, when she received Emmys for the series *Prime Suspect* and *Elizabeth I*, and an Academy Award for *The Queen*, a portrayal of Elizabeth II as she reacts to the news and funeral of Diana, Princess of Wales. Already a dame of the realm, she says that these are the best of times.

Mirren was born in Leigh-on-Sea, Essex, England, in 1945. Her career gained momentum during the mid–1960s as Cleopatra on the London stage. In 1967, she joined the Royal Shakespeare Company and also made her screen debut in *Herostratus*. Besides Shakespeare, she played a supporting role in Ken Russell's *Savage Messiah* (1972), a drama about a passionate, but platonic, love affair between a young sculptor and his girlfriend before he is killed in World War I. Mirren appears nude as the daughter of a military officer. Some acquaintance with erotic film is common for actors trying to establish themselves early in their careers, when they have the bodies for it. After having three wives, Caligula may not have been enthusiastic about having another one. Melonia Caesonia appears on ancient coins with a large nose and a thick neck.[41] Amusing conclusions are drawn from so little that suggest she was not attractive, but she had a beautiful body that Caligula liked to display at banquets and was fertile enough to deliver three girls before he met her, which was no doubt an attribute because Caligula had no living children at the time.

The role and experience were odd for Mirren, who remained almost silent about *Caligula* since she appeared in it. She contributed no gossip, few quotes, little speculation, which Guccione praised. Nevertheless, her career is referenced frequently by the film. In hindsight she can see the value of *Caligula* to her experience and career. It seemed like a surreal documentary at the time, overflowing with excess, but she loves costume dramas. She sometimes refers to it as being like a fantastical acid trip. She liked Tinto Brass right away because of his passion for the work. "I loved the way he made movies," she said. He had four cameras zooming much of the time, and had a fifth camera mounted on some rooftops. She appreciates the bold move that it was for Guccione to invest in such an anti-establishment picture. Guccione, she found, was a very proud man who had brought together top actors, craftsmen and artisans, and paid them well. She said it was the most money she had ever been paid and she bought her first house with it. She arrived two weeks after John Gielgud departed. She loves to tell that, when she arrived, it was her first experience at night shooting; she was in the middle of a woods, naked. First chance she got, she threw up.

In *Caligula*, she is always seen as a youthful attractive woman, a competitor with any of the Penthouse Pets; yet significantly, Brass never uses her for that purpose. The character is never a siren or a woman of extensive sexual experience as portrayed by historians. She is referred to in that capacity by Drusilla, but she never exhibits it. She is always dignified. She makes no particular effort to interest Caligula. At times, such as in the meeting around Drusilla's pool, she virtually ignores him, although she senses he is a man poorly disguised as a woman. He singles her out, as a second choice, to determine whether she is a sexual fit. Again, she seems passive and tolerant. There is no sense she needs him or wants him. If he decides to rape her, as he does, there is nothing she can do about it. The imposition of power, especially of a man over a woman, is apparent.

Helen Mirren is cast as Caligula's fourth wife, Caesonia. Photograph courtesy General Media Communications, Inc., and Robert C. Guccione. Used by permission.

As the movie progresses, Drusilla becomes less important and Caesonia becomes more significant, not so much for sexual needs as for nurturing and emotional comfort. Drusilla is married anyway, and her sexual abilities seem limited to her being a body in the room. Her advice in quelling his impetuous nature and in conducting his life emerge as more important. After

Drusilla dies, Caesonia comes into her own by attending to Caligula's emotional needs. Mirren standing behind a Roman mask screams through the graphic birth of a live baby, named Julia Drusilla, and he recognizes her through marriage. Caligula's desire to have a boy is nicely established in the film, when he mistakes the baby for a male child, but shows no displeasure when it turns out to be a female.

The historical account denies that much of this really happened because Drusilla died in A.D. 38. Caligula's acquaintance with Caesonia did not begin until the next year, when he must have felt really alone and lonely at times. It could be concluded that he needed her a lot more than she needed him, but so little is actually known about her that no one can say with certainty. Mirren is glimpsed nude during a few dark frames in the bedroom scene, which ends with Caesonia and Drusilla enjoying each other's company more than consoling Caligula. Perhaps the most interesting sequence for Caesonia is her dance at a banquet while she is pregnant. She looks attractive in her heavy Roman wig and bejeweled costume, performs the dance well enough, and she seems to be more of an appropriate promotional accomplishment for the childless Caligula than she is for herself. Her later scenes showing her maternal tendencies toward Caligula are more empathic. The couple grows to appreciate each other, a notion that is not developed in the story, but hints at positive qualities Caligula may have had. The relationship is unexplored.

These character relationships and scenes do not permit explicit sexual scenes that are essential to a movie marriage; but they do reduce or stop sexual activity for instant gratification. In other words, *Caligula* is not a movie one sees for sexual release, it is a picture designed to show sexuality applied as a tool to acquire power.

John Gielgud

Initially John Gielgud was offered the role of Tiberius, which he declined because he thought the script was pornographic. After the seventy-three-year-old received "an outraged letter from Gore Vidal," biographer Sheridan Morley wrote, "saying how impertinent it was of John to refuse the role," he accepted the part of Nerva, supposedly a major advisor to Tiberius. Gielgud was glad to get movie offers: The money was good, his calendar was open for the three-day shoot, and he could work in Rome with actors he knew.[42] Gielgud, an acclaimed Shakespearean stage actor, was highly sought. Delivering his lines in his classic, sonorous, aloof style, Gielgud in one scene gives a brief history of the Caesars, in another reveals his loathing for Caligula, and in his last scene introduces suicide as an acceptable way to end one's life by slitting his wrists and drifting away peacefully in a bath. As Nerva is dying, Caligula tries to determine, unsuccessfully, in a naive inquisition, whether his ancestors are gods, a central question posed in the film.

Though fascinating, the question remained unanswered. Later be would try again. Suicide was a common option for Romans who considered their life futile or complete. Gielgud is clothed in an ankle-length gown for his scenes, even in the bath. He said he was cold, and the scene took several hours to shoot. Ironically, in 1991, for Peter Greenaways' *Prospero's Books*, a version of William Shakespeare's *The Tempest*, Gielgud is naked. "One morning Peter told me to take off all of my clothes and be naked in the bath, and there were all these girls and fat women in the nude, but after a day or two one had completely forgotten. I don't think it offends in the least, except in Japan, where they had to cut out all the genitals."[43] Critics said that *Prospero's Books* was stunning and beautiful. "Sir John Gielgud gives a magisterial performance. 'The Tempest' as viewed through the wide eye of Peter Greenaway," wrote John Anderson in *New York Newsday*. Vincent Canby of the *New York Times*, called it "glorious." It's hard to imagine that Bob Guccione could have chosen four better actors.

Teresa Ann Savoy

In 1976 Teresa Ann Savoy turned twenty. She was a well-known European photographer's model and had appeared in some softcore films, beginning with *Le farò da padre* (1974). Shy, retiring, attractive, and "sweet," she worked very hard to convince Brass she deserved the part. She had just finished a long featured part in *Salon Kitty* (1976), directed by Tinto Brass, when the role of Drusilla became available. The role, as mentioned, was originally offered to Maria Schnieder, but she and Tinto Brass began arguing from the start. The woman Brass had admired so much in *Last Tango in Paris* no longer existed. She did not have the same appearance or interest for him, as she initially did. She would not do nude scenes. How could she top what had already made her world famous? Besides, her lifestyle and temperament seemed to ruin their opportunity to work together. Other actresses were considered, but Savoy campaigned for the part and had done a very respectable job in *Salon Kitty* the previous year. On screen she looked like an innocent teenager. She was lacking in the glamorous finishing touches that are associated with American models and stars. Her teeth looked crooked in close-ups and her vocal range and interpretative acting depth left something to be desired, but she was available and dependable.

So Savoy was Drusilla, one of Caligula's three sisters, who some historians claim had a sexual relationship with Caligula when they were teenagers. Drusilla is played as a loveable and vulnerable character with some influence on the emperor. She is easy to like, for she seems trustworthy and has empathic warmth. Her first-century plain Roman coiffure, often imperfectly arranged, and unremarkable costumes reinforce her soft voice and low-key delivery. She looks and appears to be someone's sister. This unassuming manner suggests that her relationship with Caligula is one of affection and a sister's concern for her brother's welfare more than one who wants to share his bed and his realm. She is always there to support him, although much of the time she disagrees with his decisions. She offers occasional advice, which he may just as often reject. She tries to be a moderating force, mostly to protect him, and she is convincing as the one person who does not want something from him. She has no desire for sex or favors. She accommodates him sexually, but she does not desire him. Savoy offers a reasonable contrast to the other women vying for Caligula's attention.

When he thinks that he might die, Caligula has his will written, with Drusilla as the beneficiary, which historians say really happened, but she seems unprepared to assume any such role, unlike strong, ruthless Roman women such as Livia and Antonia. Although Drusilla and Caligula's romantic relationship is mostly speculation, in the fictional narrative it is an important and logical link. Drusilla seems to sacrifice herself for her brother by nursing him back to health after he contracts the fever that is prominent in the city and may have been the cause of his so-called "madness." In contemporary times it may be difficult to imagine what life would be like without vaccines and structured medical care. Contagious diseases were easy to catch in Roman times, and Drusilla's sacrifice is emotionally impressive from a dramatic perspective. She apparently catches the vaguely described ailment from him and dies. There is no reference to her being pregnant with

Teresa Ann Savoy plays Drusilla, Caligula's devoted sister. Courtesy Photofest.

Caligula's child, which was the basis for a horrible sequence in the *I, Claudius* telecast. Although Drusilla runs around in belted gossamer tunics and her bare buttocks are frequently exposed, she never appears completely nude in a long shot until she dies. Caligula cannot understand why she has died, and he is angry at Isis for not restoring her to life. In a rudimentary animalistic act, Caligula places Drusilla on the bed and licks her body, as we have seen animals do when they demonstrate incomprehensible loss. While necrophilia carries disturbing implications, this scene provides no such thing. It is the mortal wound to his broken heart that cannot be repaired. Callous as Caligula has been previously, his scream to the gods and a universe that does not grant favors is the proper punctuation for this dramatic highpoint in the movie. Drusilla is his last close relative and now he must proceed alone. Of the five leading actors, none has more than a few frames of minimal nudity on-screen, except for Savoy's death scene; and only Caligula and Tiberius enact direct violence on someone, although both consent to violence. The principal actors are lighted and staged with appropriate guarded care, reminiscent of their work in previous theatrical pictures. The arrangement of light to create depth, with a bow to the great German designer Adolph Appia, clusters the emulsion's pixels in a diffuse impressionistic panorama contrasted by the black shadowy reminders of Caravaggio glimpsed in other scenes.

Featured Actors

Twelve actors were cast in supporting roles, most of them Italian. Voices on the soundtrack are looped because most of the editions, though distributed worldwide, are in English. The actors tried to learn English well enough so that they could mouth the words to assist the matching with the English speaking voices. Patrick Allen voiced the role of Macro, played by Guido Mannari. Movies are based largely on visual type casting and so the actors had to appear believable. Mannari is convincing as head of the Praetorian Guard. His allegiance is to Caligula, even though he is supposed to protect Tiberius. He proves to be quiet, a mostly expressionless observer, and deadly. He is good looking and, in the English edition, has a deep voice that never betrays his subservient position. He is tall and trim, what one might anticipate of a respected military officer. He is cautious and never exaggerates his importance; he is well aware that just as he had replaced Sejanus, Caligula, whose mercurial disposition could never be predetermined, might replace him. Macro and his wife Ennia do everything they can to please Caligula, but in the end Caligula could not tolerate the power he believed Macro had. In a scene in which Macro gets a surprise kiss of allegiance from Caligula, it is said that in response, Mannari held his arm over an open flame long enough to be severely burned. Actors are a breed apart, and they sometimes go to extremes to create believability in their characters.

His replacement as Guards Commander is Cassius Chaerea. Here is where thoughtful casting is so important. Macro is lean and hungry, but Chaerea, played by Paolo Bonacelli, has a round face and a somewhat stocky body. He looks strong and capable of serious fighting, but his entire manner is different from that of Macro. There is at times a light-hearted response to Chaerea. He does not seem to be an assassin; a soldier definitely, but an assassin, a plotter, one who would betray his leader's trust, probably not. Ultimately Chaerea would plot the death of Caligula. In fact, historians debate his reasons. He is a pleasant, likable-looking man who exudes more authoritative presence than Macro. Macro worries and seems to have no confidence in himself; Chaerea is confident. Though verbally assailed by Caligula, he seems to appreciate that he holds the power over Caligula. In Chaerea's scenes, Chaerea gives orders; in Macro's scenes, Macro tries to win favor with Caligula.

Chaerea, Macro, and Tiberius are the only identifiable characters who commit murders on-screen, except for Caligula who pushes weakened Nerva under water.

Giancarlo Badessi as Claudius had an interesting part. With his cherubic face and rotund body, he had to gain sufficient attention to be memorable during the film through cutaway shots. Badessi was one of the character actors who had also appeared in *Salon Kitty*. He needed to sustain his presence and show incompetence, knowing however that in the end he has to be acceptable as emperor. Another of Caligula's relatives is Gemellus. Bruno Brive has this part. He looks pathetic as an emaciated teenager who seems to be no threat to Caligula even though Caligula thinks he is. With few lines, he is still a necessary presence. Watching Claudius cast dice to foretell their fortunes is another pervasive touch, as these characters thread their way through the film with minimal reference, although one will die and the other will reign. Gemellus has a haunting presence. Their fortunes seem to be preordained. Tiberius predicts the future for Gemellus and there is nothing he can do to change it.

Adriana Asti as Ennia, Macro's wife, adds an energetic sense of timing. An Italian actress, she was well thought of but had little knowledge of English. When she bursts into Caligula's presence to encourage him to take charge of his own life, the lip sync in medium close-up is more critical than it is later when she is carried out of the large bedroom where she is seen on a long shot. She is most notable, perhaps, for being the center of attention while some young men actually ejaculate over her to provide semen that was thought to preserve one's youth and beauty. The regenerative powers of sperm were thought to be virtually unlimited in the pagan world. This treatment is a substitute for the milk bath shown in the earlier Cecil B. De Mille film, *The Sign of the Cross*. Self-assured and beautifully dressed, Ennia moves toward becoming Caligula's wife, an engagement promised to her in writing by Caligula.

Other members of Caligula's entourage include John Steiner, another actor retained from *Salon Kitty*, who plays Longinus, Caligula's financial advisor and lawyer. He has a long, narrow, memorable face and bald head. Charicles, the doctor, played by Leopoldo Trieste, hovers around in the background, coming forth at key times to announce Tiberius's weakening condition and confirming that he did not give Gemellus an antidote for the plague in the city. Here again is a well-chosen actor, this time one of relatively nondescript middle age, who could play an undistinguished role essential to the story while not competing for attention.

Mirella Dangelo as Livia and Donato Placido as Proculus, the betrothed virgins, perhaps provide the most wrenching sequence. Completely credible, the romantic couple is the perfect contrast to Caligula's aggressive advances on their wedding day. Some scenes were partly extemporized because it is not always possible to envision the details until the characters are on location. The emperor's blessing turns out to be an androgynous comment on equal rights for the sexes during the seventies. Who would have expected it to be so graphically illustrated? It was explicit enough to rape the bride and check her virginity and then to fist her fiancé, a touch suggested by Franco Rossellini. McDowell has said that Donato Placido particularly objected to the flower Caligula placed atop the glob of grease on his rearend, used to lubricate his fisting humiliation. To fist a heterosexual man is the epitome of degradation; however, Caligula was not finished with the torture he planned for Proculus. It is said that Caligula's motivation was his jealousy of Proculus's thick head of hair, while he was losing his; but the psychology of his torture must have gone deeper, as it concluded in an intense, sadistic death scene. These events were known to the intimate elite circle that Caligula dominated. Intensification of the viewer's hatred toward Caligula was not difficult; what the movie was unable to explain was Caligula's popularity with the people.

Richard Parets as the actor Mnester and Paula Mitchell as the Sudura Singer are vaguely identifiable in cameo appearances. Emerging from a jail cell late in the narrative, as if the part were written for him, is the strongman Giant, Osiride Pevarello. He does not speak English well, but Tinto Brass referred to him amusingly as *his* bodyguard.

A noticeable job scarcity for English and Italian workers was evident during the making of *Caligula*. This contributed to a willingness to meet the unusual and rigorous job requirements. There were few occasions of labor tension—most people were just glad to have the work.

Penthouse Pets

Bob Guccione had flown in thirteen Penthouse Pets to be in the movie. Anneka Di Lorenzo and Lori Wagner were featured players, but they had no assigned parts like the ones identified in the cast credit list. Group scenes with the Pets are the galley orgy and the meeting of the Isis cult. The women look stunning in the isolated setting at Drusilla's villa. They are enjoying themselves bathing nude in a shallow pool sprinkled with rose petals. Surrounding them is a circle of sheer drapes and columns supported by niches, where eunuchs sit. In this gorgeous setting Drusilla gives Caligula over to Caesonia in an adjacent space where there is an altar to goddess Isis. Oddly, the setting was built in isolation without any architectural connection to a house or, therefore, to reality.

The Pets appear discreetly from time to time throughout the film. They are shown as slaves, somewhat humorously running down a hallway in Tiberius's palace on Capri and later on a street with their bare breasts flapping up and down. Some of them might be noticed in large gatherings at banquets and as extras at Tiberius's palace. They are always an attractive addition.

The most talked-about sequence is approximately three minutes of hardcore lesbian activity between Lorenzo and Wagner. The reason timing is important is because it measures just how fleeting the explicit sex moments really are. Often they flash by in a world of confusion and activity, rendering them almost invisible. This sequence is an excellent example of integrating an explicit sex scene into the narrative, even though there is no rationale for it except that Guccione had promised the women screen time and he delivered on his promise. He realized that what they did on-screen was the kind of scene his *Penthouse* readers would expect to see in the movie. So, he accomplished two purposes here. The women were vaguely identified as Agrippina and Messalina, two very prominent women in the lives of Caligula and Claudius. An uncharacteristic, brief, pointless, transitional homosexual scene was even more laughable because the men kept fumbling around for their objects of desire and were not connected to the film within the two minutes they were on the screen.

The Penthouse Pets are also involved in the main sex scene, the orgy that takes place on Caligula's faux galley. What viewers expect to see are gorgeous women and virile men having fun. Here the editing really counts. In the long sequence for the unrated edition, the guests do not seem to be having enough fun. The sex looks like hard work, for there is no romantic foreplay to prime viewers to the joy of the climactic moments. The men and women are largely unidentified. Few faces are shown and so the shots reveal dissociated body parts in which there is no emotional investment. The galley sequence runs about eleven minutes in the unrated edition, with about five minutes of explicit sex, mostly fellatio. The final twenty seconds ends in ejaculation, but who cares? This is not a typical arrangement for a pornographic movie, and the action is far more discreet than in the usual adult film. The R-rated version of the orgy scene is cut to five minutes and forty-eight seconds; therefore, nothing is explicit. Most nudity, sex, and violence are relegated to featured players and extras, some of whom are Penthouse Pets.

The Production Staff

Guccione's artisans and crew who staged the film were as much a part of the marriage of traditional and adult values as any other element. They were charged with creating the settings in which the actors would be able to work comfortably. Designers and builders contributed their interpretative skills to the project. The pride and passion that most of them put into this work is amazing. Three-time Academy Award winner Danilo Donati (1926–2001) was greatly admired and respected by Guccione. Donati, who could be exceedingly temperamental, was passionate about what he did. He found a life of satisfaction and accomplishment by remaining in Italy. He was constantly in touch with the appropriate Italian providers when a multitude of costumes or shoes or headdresses were required. He could rely on his network of artisans and artists. Donati was responsible for creating the style and look of the production; as art director this included the designs for scenery and costumes. He began as a costume designer for Mario Monicelli's *The Great War* (1952), and continued his career by working with distinguished directors like Franco Zefferelli, Federico Fellini, and Pier Paolo Pasolini for over thirty years. In the De Mille tradition, Donati liked the big show. He served the production well as the general supervisor. He boasted about authenticity in sixty-four sets, many of which utilized actual moldings of ancient statues and artifacts, a three-hundred-foot galley, and an open arena three football fields long and 150 feet wide that could accommodate his killing-machine invention. In addition, there were the properties: jewels, crowns, armor, writing instruments, dinnerware, paintings, and, of course, hundreds of costumes, many of which were original, and all of which had to be maintained during a long production period. As production supervisor, the look of the production was his responsibility; every item in a film frame was subject to his approval. The task of sewing and replicating about thirty-six hundred costumes and five thousand boots was delegated to many trusted workers.

Importantly, Danilo Donati was the coordinating director for the production of *Fellini Satyricon* about six years earlier. He was particularly skilled

3. A Movie Marriage   113

The Villa Jovis grotto was shot in a multi-level setting. Photograph courtesy General Media Communications, Inc., and Robert C. Guccione. Used by permission.

Top: Under construction is a skeleton of a Roman galley about 300 feet long. It served as a brothel that resembles one of Caligula's actual pleasure ships. Courtesy Photofest.
Bottom: Danilo Donati, art director, visits with John Gielgud. Courtesy Photofest.

3. A Movie Marriage

at designing in-studio movies at Cinecittà with relatively few scenes shot on location. *Caligula* required huge sets inside Dear Studios, where *Cleopatra* was filmed in 1963, and some open-air facilities on the edge of the city. The fanciful *Satyricon* is light, hot, and expansive because of its exteriors, while *Caligula* is dark, oppressive, and claustrophobic. Much of the design expense centered on Tiberius's palace, a multipurpose open arena, and the galley. Various interiors for bedrooms, meeting places, dining halls, government buildings, and the main exterior for the invasion of Britain are less challenging. This does not mean they were less detailed; Donati may have spent too much time on demanding detritus at the expense of the whole setting for these areas. Donati was a wizard at staging multi-use interiors using drapes, painted backdrops, and three-dimensional set pieces, such as meticulously painted columns, arranged with intensely lighted areas to obtain an illusion of space and depth, apparently dwarfing the characters in immense surroundings. Tiberius's palace resembles the staging in an early sequence from *Satyricon*, where multilevels were used to enable the characters to go from the pool to the ground floor to the upper-level exhibition of sexual displays. One versatile interior was Caligula's bedroom with the adjacent courtyard, and the simplest small set was the elegant atrium in Drusilla's villa.

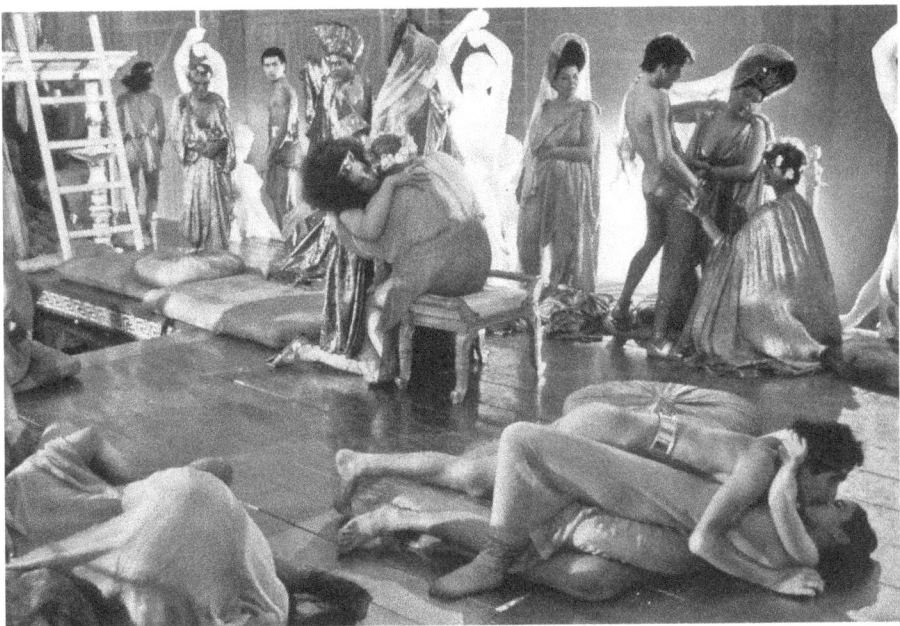

The galley was so complicated and crowded that camera set-ups were difficult to position. Courtesy Photofest.

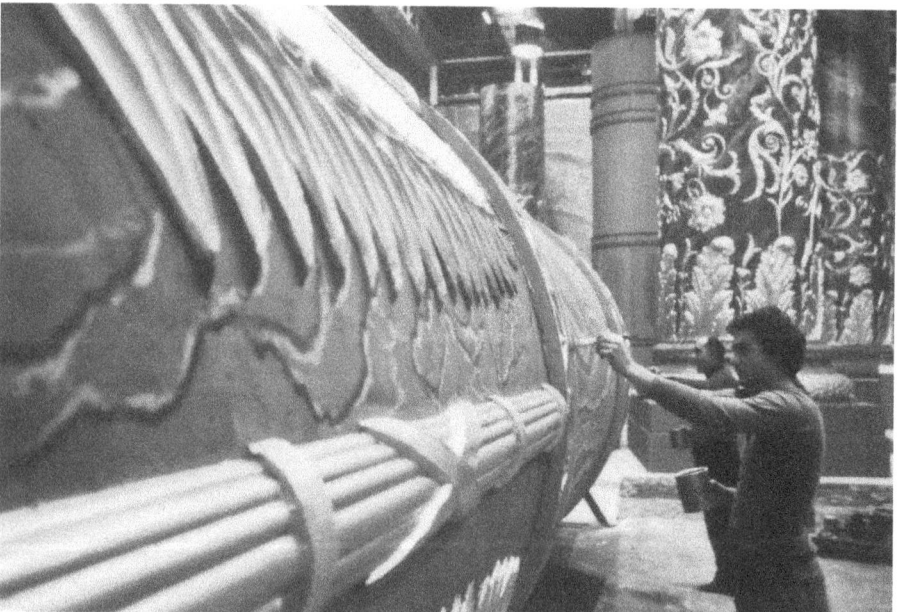

Top: Several scenes required large columns that emphasized space and grandeur. Courtesy Photofest. *Bottom:* A skilled craftsman details a column. Courtesy Photofest.

The most versatile large set was the arena. An odd piece of undocumented machinery was supposedly used to decapitate Macro, who actually died from suicide. It appears expensive and out of place. De Mille's gladiators always were watchable human beings. Viewers cared about them. If the muscled combatants were not sexually virile enough, then naked pugilists fighting hand to hand with animals, or female Amazons, or other empire oddities exemplifying the diversity of the proletariat could have illustrated raw oppression with greater emotional impact. This large arena space allowed for Caligula's entertainments and executions, a small stage for the Caligula family play, and the grand stairway where Caligula and his family were slaughtered. The staircase had to be well lighted to follow the action and to maximize the high contrast of the white marble background and spotless clothing with the bloody murders. It seems odd that Donati chose to construct the skeleton of a galley rather than having the bordello on his luxury ship anchored in Lake Nemi or at his palace, where the fundraiser really happened. The late scenes—in the brothel, the galley, and the invasion—weaken the narrative. They are less plausible and lack the authenticity exhibited in earlier scenes.[44]

Like the cutaways showing Claudius and Gemellus rolling dice, several moments are inserted to pander to superstitions and supernatural power in the form of animals and birds. The blackbird seems continuously threatening, but the appearance of Incitatus, Caligula's white horse, is a symbol of a free spirit. They illustrate that considerable thought went into these atmospheric touches. McDowell fed oats to Incitatus daily to maintain their relationship. The blackbird is imprisoned in a mesh, while the horse is set free in the arena in the closing seconds. Incitatus, present at most of Caligula's moments of triumph, becomes metamorphic as Caligula's spirit gallops into the future.

Like some settings, the costumes for *Caligula* are reminiscent of designs for *Satyricon*. The crotch-high tunic and thong underwear for young men and ankle-length tunics and togas for older characters are typical, and so is the standard helmet, short tunic, leather body armor, and boots for soldiers. Multicolored sheer fabrics, white tunics, and scanty, jeweled girdles clothed the women, some of whom had elegant, heavy period wigs. Malcolm McDowell wore a different costume in almost every scene. The colors and fabrics varied from draped white tunics and togas to an oddly skirted net tunic, which stuck out rather like a ballet dancer's tutu. Overall the often gold and silver costumes were elegant as well as utilitarian, but these outfits stray from any semblance to realism, even if Caligula were a clothes fanatic. What the clothes really do not do is make Caligula sexy. The young men in *Satyricon* are always hot and sexy; but in *Caligula* clothing exhibits the ostentation of power.

A moving arena wall designed as a decapitation machine uses a spinning five-blade scythe to sever heads. Courtesy Photofest.

Guccione had done so many things well. What he needed later in the fall of 1976 was a course adjustment. He needed to clearly state his somewhat revised vision of the purposes of the film: to marry adult and traditional scenes in a single movie in such a way that it would be marketable to traditional and adult viewers, to promote *Penthouse* and the Pets, and to expand freedom of expression and artistry in the motion picture industry. He could have made some critical adjustments, particularly in the scenes involving sex, to achieve these objectives. Most good adult sequences have precise expectations—to establish the relationship of the characters in a long shot, to show them physically related to each other, to reveal well-lighted body parts, including genitalia and faces, in close-up. The facial expectation of what actors are supposed to be experiencing—moments of entry, of position, of action and so forth—must flow smoothly so that they satisfy the enjoyment of the performers and spectators simultaneously with a complete climax of pleasureful release and a caring romantic-follow through with an embrace or other gesture. These scenes are not easy to shoot; hence, too often adult movies are visual failures.

3. A Movie Marriage

The outdoor arena is constructed from a scaffold above ground. When complete, the below-ground spaces will be covered with a sand floor that is flexible enough to allow for shooting the beheading sequence. Photograph courtesy General Media Communications, Inc., and Robert C. Guccione. Used by permission.

Guccione had such a fine cast and such a talented staff and crew that he was in a position to apply his managerial skills to adjust, reinvigorate, and point them in the right direction. He needed to exercise his authority as producer, just as David O. Selznik did for *Gone with the Wind*, regardless of who was directing. Guccione had demonstrated his business acumen and his artistic percipience. He was a masterful and knowledgeable entrepreneur of the design, style, beauty, and details of *Penthouse*, and this same kind of investment had to be applied to the final weeks of shooting *Caligula*. He was on the threshold of creating not only a benchmark adult film but an aesthetically important crossover picture. If he failed to do so, the public and the movie industry would be the loser, for this was the turning point in cinema history from the discreet, romantic old days of Hollywood to the beginning of the bold, raucous, new era of in-your-face sex, violence, nudity, language, and preemptive challenges. This was the period of the Cold War's ending, the Contra scandal, the Meese Commission, and the prelude to hot wars in the Middle East. This was the transition to the eighties.

4

EDITIONS OF *CALIGULA*

Seldom are there three different editions of the same motion picture, designed for different audiences, available for comparison. *Caligula* is one of those pictures. A scene-by-scene analysis of the pictures and sounds as they are presented on the screen provides the answers to whether Bob Guccione reached his cinematic objectives and to what degree he was successful. If Guccione's unrated and rated editions of *Caligula* and Franco Rossellini's *Io, Caligola* are closely compared, the comparisons reveal qualitative and quantitative answers. Guccione's unrated edition tells its story in 51 scenes lasting 156 minutes with credits; the rated version plays 39 scenes and credits in 102 minutes; and *Io, Caligola* shows 45 scenes with credits in 124 minutes. European PAL editions play somewhat faster. Do they tell the same story?

Guccione said that his objectives were to expand artistic freedom, to marry adult and traditional scenes, and to promote the Penthouse organization; these goals could reasonably be expected to elicit strong praise and opposition. The first half of this chapter deals with the narrative in the unrated edition and the second half discusses the changes that were made to the three editions, so that they would conform to acceptable standards as they were distributed and exhibited throughout the world. In other words, this chapter is an evaluation of the narrative and its censorship.

For decades producers had tried to include nudity and some strong language in movies, but most filmic nudity was European (e.g., *Ecstasy*, 1933), and most language was limited to the likes of "damn," a breakthrough in *Gone with the Wind* (1939). Frontal nudity was not allowed in mainstream motion-picture distribution. During the 1950s, as human rights movements and Supreme Court legal opinions favored greater artistic expansion for films, explicit shots and actions were still kept within the context of underground films having a limited adults-only distribution. Even *Deep Throat* (1972) was shown as a daring, porno-chic oddity without ever being classified as a traditional film. Guccione sought world distribution of *Caligula* to those adults who wanted to screen it. Such an accomplishment would be a cinema-industry triumph in the 1970s when the viewing of *Deep Throat* was being fought in courtrooms across the country.

In Pursuit of Artistic Freedom

Many traditional films had made gains, becoming racy and daring by expanding degrees of sex and violence, but none achieved what *Caligula* was going to attempt — explicit sex and graphic violence. The underground films of pop artist and cinéma vérité filmmaker Andy Warhol did not include explicit sex, but his collaboration with Paul Morrissey produced commercial films that came as close as any to being hardcore traditional pictures. They were not hardcore, however, because they did not show penetration and they were not "wet." Produced in 1976, *Caligula* would take up this challenge by presenting hardcore sex and violence in a traditional film context. After several editing refinements, much litigation, and a few previews, *Caligula* opened in Rome in August 1979. Within a week it was withdrawn for reasons of censorship, exactly what Guccione was trying to resist. Nevertheless one of Bob Guccione's dominant personality traits rose to the occasion. While the Italian version remained in limbo, he released the full length and even more explicit edition in Los Angeles in October 1979 and in New York City in February 1980. He continued to be tenacious, showing the unrated version wherever possible, while allowing local distributors to satisfy legal and other restraints in their countries. This resulted in a multitude of variations in exhibitions. In other words, it was uncertain where the artist's challenge would meet the businessman's compromise to get international distribution.

The call for artistic freedom echoed through the 1970s, as it was repeated by many adult stars and traditional directors, who were trying to prevent television companies from reediting their films for television distribution. Of course, in the United States it has always been about the money; therefore, the directors lost their fight over cutting their films and occasionally colorizing them. The integrity of their work came up against the refusal of various business interests to show traditional movies that had content or timing difficulties when presented on television. Long films, running well over two hours in cinemas, were cut to ninety minutes so that commercials would share whatever screen time remained of the picture. That cause has even greater impact today as some large DVD distributors and cable television companies sell films that have been edited to accommodate a PG-13 rating. Smaller film retailers may have an adult section where a miscellany of soft and hardcore films may be rented or purchased. Viewing or purchasing adult films carries a higher price as well as a warning label. By the end of the seventies the adult movies were segregated in newsstands and bookstores, just as the traditional newspapers were refusing to run advertisements for excellent adult live or filmed shows. What advertising *was* done was limited to special readerships like New York's *Village Voice*.

Shooting for *Caligula* ended in early 1977, after Guccione and Lui quickly finished photographing some additional scenes. The editing concurrently took place in London for the unrated edition. Then the lawsuits from Gore Vidal and Tinto Brass followed, with Vidal's ending rather quickly, but Brass's cases lingering well into the eighties, for he had to respond to charges of obscenity in the Italian courts in addition to dealing with his own suit in the British courts over copyright violations before finally reaching settlements. The settlements were mainly agreed upon in financial terms, but to the artist the pain of what was intended in the film, of what might have been, never goes away.

To resolve the artistic freedom issue during the 1970s, a producer had to be very wealthy — justice is expensive — and determined. Bob Guccione proved he was both. He also used the lawsuits to keep *Caligula* in the news so that the public would be conditioned to greater acceptance of adult cinema and continuously reminded that *Caligula* was going to open soon. Three years is a long wait, and public interest can be very short. Catholic Italy was an excellent test environment, for standards of morality run high but parameters of forgiveness through interpretation may be broad indeed. As might be expected, the Italian censor objected to a few frames here and there. In Scenes 5 and 6, Tiberius's tour of his speaking statues and violent execution of a soldier, the rated version only suggests the sex acts and the soldier's punishment is eliminated. By contrast, in Scene 11, the morning after a night of debauchery, the *Io, Caligola* film cuts these moments less severely than might be expected. Scenes 16 and 27, the Guccione-Lui explicit additions, are omitted from both the rated edition and *Io, Caligola*. A few scenes, never really a part of the final cut of the unrated edition, showing particularly heinous acts, were eliminated because of public objections and time constraints.

Judgments had to be made not only regarding morality, but as to whether the public would be turned away from viewing the film if the producers had exceeded reasonable parameters in either content or running time. Two hours and thirty-eight minutes is a long time for an audience to watch sex and violence, and in the 1970s the general public was just coming to understand that there was more to sex on-screen than the missionary position and that violence could mean desecrating a human being depicted by the film as a good person. The freedom to be offensive, especially within the context of making an artistic work, is essential to expanding an appreciation of human life. Bob Guccione pushed the limitations of artistic endeavor in filmmaking at a time when restraint was intensely debated. The initial release of *Caligula* gave Guccione a hint at what controversy was to come.

A Movie Marriage

Guccione's second principal issue was the integration of sexually explicit frames in an otherwise traditional film. Though *Caligula* was explicitly violent, American films had exploited violence without retribution. Nudity had long been considered taboo in American films, however. The blacked out scenes of presumed sexual intercourse from, say, *The Outlaw* (1943), to *Henry and June* (1990), are examples of American censorship by omission. *Caligula* had to show explicit sex scenes as well as violent ones. Is it more acceptable to show a soldier's genitalia cut off (Scene 35), than it is to show fellatio (Scene 44)? What justification is there for such scenes? During the 1970s, jury trials tried to determine community standards of acceptance. How tolerant was the mass public? In trials it was learned that most jurors had little or no knowledge of complex sexual or violent acts on film; therefore, such scenes were both enlightening and disturbing to most adults. Upon reflection, however, the discomfort vanished. Once they had seen such films, adult jury panels were always ready to meet their responsibilities and opted to make their own judgments about such matters rather than having censorship boards, the government, or other bureaucracies make decisions for them. The decade was the perfect time to test the public's conscience.

An abundance of nudity may be overwhelming to an American audience, just as a nude beach may be a location for snickering or patrolling in America but a place for enjoyment in the sun on the golden beaches of France or Spain. In *Caligula* the cast is either nude or semi-nude for most scenes. In Scene 5, at Tiberius's pool, presumably the young actors are of age for American and British viewing, but who is to say? The extras look very young and the inference of pederasty is clear. To see so much nudity assembled in one place tends to distract from continuity, just as the violent moments in the same scenes may conjure up thoughts of revulsion. On a filmmaker's palette, nudity is like a color. An artist wants to be able to choose from all the available colors. At times nudity in *Caligula* is overwhelming and gratuitous. Male extras serving as workers or soldiers in Scenes 2 and 45 need not be naked. This decision goes to the larger question of whether *Caligula* was intended to be realistic or fantasy?

Nudity, of course, does not mean sex necessarily. In Scenes 6 and 44 it does, however. The clothed characters personify power and the nude figures are slaves showing the immorality of power. Explicit sex acts are being performed, and the viewers see only fleeting glimpses of whatever is going on.

Why have speaking statues? Ancient sources mention that Tiberius liked watching men and women copulate. They are images of invention; pederasty was evidently not enough. The activities are reminders of freak shows at carnivals decades ago, only with less variety and concentrating on a sexual smorgasbord. Tiberius is having a serious conversation with Caligula about the necessity of nymphs and satyrs as they pass a collection of extras posing as obsessed participants in rather common acts largely used to stimulate impotent men, perhaps someone as elderly as Tiberius. If viewers can separate themselves from the intriguing erect penises and snakes for a moment to listen to a teenager discuss sexual proclivities with his grandfather, the scene becomes amusing as well as rather troubling.

Caligula lives in an isolated community with the wealthy; he does not know any other life. He accepts routinely the rituals of morality shared by those in power, knowing that the sexual and even the violent acts are dominated by the mundane business of government — stamping approved documents. At the end of the day Tiberius and Caligula are papyrus stampers. How humbling is that? Further, the old man is infected by disease and the young man fears he will not live long enough to have an heir. Basic human desires preempt the importance of the environment. It is difficult to imagine the swimming pool activity en masse, as depicted in the film happening at Villa Jovis, because the cisterns seem smaller than the movie set and Tiberius appears to have been continuously engaged in affairs of state rather than affairs of the body.

By adding explicit sex scenes, Bob Guccione expanded the parameters of artistry in motion pictures and he married, at least in the *Caligula* narrative, adult and traditional scenes. How well he achieved his goals requires closer examination. The third objective for Guccione — promoting *Penthouse* magazine and the Penthouse Pets— will be examined in the next chapter.

Caligula *Editions*

For easy reference, detailed scenarios of the three principal editions follow this commentary on the narrative. The titles and scenes presented with the unrated edition first, then the rated, then *Io, Caligola*. Overall the essential story is preserved in continuity, along with the running time of every scene, pointing out how much has been omitted in the rated and *Io, Caligola* editions. A comparison of the unrated and rated versions basically shows how the rated version has been eviscerated to accommodate content for foreign distribution and time constraints for television; most notably, in the R-rated version the reason for Caligula's madness, his metamorphosis, is omitted. *Io, Caligola* shows how much more tolerant the Italians are of explicit shots than the Americans and British seem to be. A multitude of other editions exist; they have been altered by governments allegedly working for the benefit of their people. They are essentially a cross between the unrated and rated versions with frames adjusted in accordance with legal censorship or public taste requirements in each country. While Americans may shy away from three or four seconds of a breast exposed on a television program intended for general audiences, international audiences may disapprove of American violence or politically sensitive subjects. It could be said, for instance, that a determined Caligula coup could have been carried out with just a few zealots who dislike the dictator. Generally, despite criticism, all *Caligula* editions are available in most countries either legally or illegally.

Pagan Rome

Two of the three editions open in disagreement. The rated version is largely an edited copy of the unrated edition. They both open on titles setting the time period — Pagan Rome 37–41 A.D. — using white letters on black. This period runs from just prior to Caligula's reign to his assassination. Drumbeats add a native, ritualistic aura, and a chorus humming reinforces a primitive ambience. The *Io, Caligola* edition opens with credits over a mask of the dead Tiberius. There is no attempt to establish a pagan sensibility, no effort to suggest that there is anything different from contemporary times. For some viewers establishing an ambience distinct from Christian times may be quite useful to understanding the story and to quickly gaining acceptance of pagan rituals and lifestyle. Drumbeats and a chorus humming understates this quiet beginning. "Pagan Rome" refers to pre–Christian Rome, a period less well understood and researched in the 1970s than it is today because of continuous excavations and discoveries on land and under the sea in Italy, Greece, Turkey, Egypt, and elsewhere. As Rome became the center of the civilized world, it became more heavily influenced by Greek, Egyptian, and Middle Eastern cultures. The word "pagan" does not mean people living in those times were uncivilized or godless. To the contrary, their civilizations were sophisticated and they had an abundance of gods.

Within the constraints of the cinematic narrative we see that pagan Roman culture was absorbed from Alexander's triumph over the Greek city-states weakened by wars, as was well told in Charles Freedman's *The Closing of the Western Mind: The Rise of Faith and Fall of Reason*. It was polytheistic and dependent on several gods to bless mortal activities with success. Prayers and sacrifices were part of the common ritual of seeking favors from powers beyond the comprehension of even the most intelligent persons of the day. By 148 B.C., after trade and wars had integrated much of the culture of neighboring regions, the polytheistic beliefs of Greece, Egypt, and the Middle East were absorbed too. The Egyptian goddess of fertility, Isis, was married to Osiris, who personified death and resurrection, self-renewing vitality and fertility of nature. They were favored by Caligula, who visited Egypt in his youth.[1] A substantial number of Greek gods were renamed and adopted by the Romans. These deities, worshiped for centuries, performed the same tasks for the Romans. Zeus, the foremost god of the Olympian pantheon, was renamed Jupiter; love goddess Aphrodite became Venus; and the god of wine and a happy time was Bacchus, formerly Dionysus. Bacchanalian entertainments were part of the regeneration process. Priapus, best known for his protruding penis, was god of fertility and regeneration. These gods, among many others, blessed and protected homes and public places, and those who were fortunate enough to have beautiful, healthy children were considered blessed.[2] At a time when the average life expectancy was only a few decades, the anxieties surrounding copulation, the probability of giving birth, the potential for unhealthy children, and the questionable health of the mother in childbirth were deeply worrisome.[3] Having children is after all a legacy and to some the nearest a human being comes to immortality. Caligula sought the benefits he thought the gods could bestow.

"Ancient Romans would find most of our attitudes toward sex strange, even absurd. The rules we take for granted — rules that regulate what we do or do not do in bed — have nothing in common with the rules the ancient Romans followed," writes John R. Clarke in his beautifully illustrated book, *Roman Sex*.[4] The Romans became acquainted with the practices of the Greeks and absorbed them. Older men often paired with young men, prostitutes, and slaves. They avoided pairing with equals, for this might jeopardize their status. So if one of Vidal's early scripts suggested more homosexual activity, as Guccione complained, the origins of Vidal's comprehension of history are well founded. Upper-class women in this male-dominated society were more restricted in their maternal roles, but at times they could be quite promiscuous. Lesbian sex was well known. Free citizens engaged in lifestyles that placed no shame on engaging in sex with men and women.[5] Satyrs, nymphs, and less-well-known human oddities, such as seers, oracles, astrologers, and hermaphrodites, were part of the complex superstitious beliefs that looked to garner favor from deities for a range of enterprises. These freedoms and constraints, assimilated by rich Romans, are presented in *Caligula*'s opening scenes.

Nudity was relatively common. Men were more inclined to appear nude than women.[6] Intermittently women were completely covered. Those most likely to appear nude were Spartan women, known for their athletic skills.[7] Well-built male and female bodies were admired, just like they are today. Athletes often trained in the nude and in earlier times the Olympic games were played in the nude. The nude form carried no uncomfortable connotation, for it referred to a "balanced, prosperous, confident body," as Kenneth Clark mentions in his well-known book, *The Nude: A Study in Ideal Form*.[8] "Nakedness," the term applied to the unclothed body, is an embarrassment. Homer's *Iliad* refers to the beautiful bodies of fallen warriors with compassion. The concept of blessed and beautiful people was a part of pagan times. "Even today," Clark wrote, "we cannot turn the pages of Petronius or Apuleius without being slightly shocked by the absolute matter-of-factness with which the antique world accepted the body, with all its animal needs...."[9] In *Caligula*, nudity is commonplace at Emperor Tiberius's palace, the meetings of the Vestal Virgins, some dinner parties, games and contests, and celebrations. These occasions give the picture frequent opportunity for sexual activity that is within actual historical parameters but difficult to fully understand in modern times.

Theme and Scenes

A second title appears, a biblical quotation, a reminder of Cecil B. De Mille's moralizing, as he did in *The Ten Commandments* (1923) and *King of Kings* (1927), usually to balance his orgy scenes. When sound arrived, De Mille, who had a fine authoritative voice and was on radio for many years (*Lux Radio Theatre*, 1936–1945) provided his own voice-over perspective. What is also remarkable about pagan life is an acceptance of the credo that life is short and that only lives of citizens were really worth preserving. Of course, even the lives of close family members could be terminated by the emperor without retribution, and there were wars and crimes that killed many other Roman citizens. The lives of slaves, however, were assessed at the price paid for them. Thus, the prevailing attitude was that life was relatively cheap, and that everyone was expendable. For *Caligula*, this second printed title quotes Jesus's words from the Gospel of Mark: "What shall it profit a man if he should gain the whole world and lose his own soul." Presumably, this line adds weight and theme, but if the initial task is to establish a pagan environment, why bring in Christ for support, when Caligula's story is not a Christian one?

SCENE 1 • In Scene 1, Caligula and Drusilla are having an incestuous relationship somewhere in the countryside. Incest is evident but minimalized in *Io, Caligola*. Italians today are less inclined to point out or support the notion that Caligula and Tiberius were into incest or pederasty. Villa Jovis is not described in promotional material as a haven for immoral relations between minor children and the emperor; however, it does mention that Tiberius may have thrown adversaries off the cliff. One of the wonderful things about the tales of two millennia ago is that they are open to interpretation and reassessment as years go by, influenced by new data and changes in public attitude to social issues. Viewers may be struck by the joyful game of catch the two young characters have in their intense romantic romp under the seclusion of shade trees, wearing the film's typical sheer flowing tunics consisting of a front and back panel belted at the waist covering a thong.[10] In the foreground shepherds tend their sheep ("sheep" is what Caligula calls the members of the senate late in the film) and barely noticeable in the background are two white horses. One is Incitatus whose presence punctuates the highs and lows of Caligula's reign, and seems to absorb his spirit in the final sequence, most recognizable in *Io, Caligola*. So in the opening sequence of the unrated and rated films, the beginning and the end of the story are foreshadowed and merged. The addition of this scene was said to be a late decision, but it fits nicely. This exterior sequence has strong lighting that helps to produce clear and lovely pictures, worth mentioning because as the picture progresses, especially in the Italian edition, the visual quality tends to degenerate into what is thought of as a fairly typical 1970s standard, skewing toward rather garish hues that in this case enhance its theatrical look, as in Scene 13 which covers the murder of Tiberius. Some color variations may be caused by different printings.

The titles continue in the first two editions with a profile of Caligula on a gold coin, with blood streaming down his face. In a voice-over, Caligula says that he has existed since the morning of the world and because he does not associate himself with other men nor is he like other men, he concludes that he is a god. His opinion will be deferred until later. This statement makes no sense if it is attributed to Caligula the man; but if he is considered as a kind of human prototype of good and evil, then maybe it does. Perhaps the line can be attributed to Caligula's lunacy because it is recited after his illness. Dwelling on his immortality, and supposedly his ego, will be developed subsequently. *Io, Caligola* opens on the mask of Tiberius (seen also in Scene 14). This is an odd place to begin because Tiberius is very much alive in Scene 2, when the narrative really gets underway. Ultimately, the lack of gold coins is what causes Caligula's anguish as his years in office progress. If he had a means of raising money through taxation, most of his acts of cruelty probably would not have existed. He would not have had to execute wealthy people in the name of Rome to acquire their property for the state. His predecessors, after all, benefited from wars, plunder, and slavery. In any case, *Io, Caligola* omits this sequence, which was not originally intended to start the movie. The production schedule went awry at the outset and this pastoral scene was shot just to get the film rolling.

So, intentionally or not, a clever aesthetic touch would become an unmistakable logo for the movie: Caligula's profile impressed on a gold coin, an image distributed worldwide on posters, tapes, and DVDs.

Undoubtedly, the intensely sweeping romantic music from Aram Khachaturian's *Spartacus* is just what the film needs in its attempt to seem epic, and that is soon followed by the threatening pulsation of Sergei Prokofiev's *Romeo and Juliet*. These sweeping compositions are placed throughout the film to emphasize in a rather saccharine way the bittersweet, ironic, romantic reign and young life lost to darkness.[11] By contrast, the musical score and arrangement for *Io, Caligola* is unimpressive. Paul Clemente is credited with scoring the rated version and Renzo Rossellini with the latter. The differences bring up the so-called modern view of the importance and place of film scoring — keep it dramatic and obvious — versus the older, subdued-background or wallpaper approach. Both have their place.

SCENE 2 • Caligula and Drusilla are rolling around on a large bed in an attractive room somewhere. Geography is often confusing. Perhaps they are in Grandmother Antonia's house in Rome.[12] The room is vaguely defined by sheer drapes that maintain an insubstantial surrounding and require viewers to get used to the idea that the young lovers are seldom alone. Sheer drapes are frequently used for ominous and voyeuristic purposes. Caligula, acting rather playfully by performing a summersault, teases her about her husband. She does not agree with his demeaning assessment and establishes at the beginning that she may be sweet but she has a mind of her own. They look youthful, but Donati's wall-less rooms add to a theatrical rather than a realistic decor. This interior lighting does not favor Caligula with the same dewy appearance he has in Scene 1, and so he looks older than eighteen. Drusilla usually wears long unkempt hair, which is good for this role, because it reinforces her age and nonconformist ways.[13] When the no-nonsense Macro enters, he seems polite, reserved, and respectful. These actors will maintain these character traits throughout the movie. The theatrical setting, a bed surrounded by floor-to-ceiling panels of chiffon that float back and forth with the slightest breeze, provides the principal scenic contrasts: inside them the world is a fantasy, outside them for the most part it is real.

SCENE 3 • Caligula often traveled by sea. Seeing him sail to Capri would have been impressive. A wide shot of the island with Villa Jovis high on a distant cliff and with the lighthouse beckoning would have added scope. They would have seemed remote and threatening, rather like Xanadu in *Citizen Kane*. A screen title announcing "Capri" would have helped, too. None of this is present in the English versions. In *Io, Caligola* there is a brief insert of an unidentified rock island and the sound of waves. This is an improvement, but inconsistent with opening titles.

In Scene 3 a road is under construction somewhere. It sounds like bricks are being split by hammers for a roadway, but there is no evidence this is true. Is Caligula passing a construction project on the mainland or on Capri?

Caligula, carried in a sedan chair, listens to advice from Macro about the emperor's closest advisor, Nerva, whom he does not like. In the background muscular men, either stripped to the waist or wearing tunic skirts and loin cloths, look like they have come from a gym rather than being members of a chain gang. Every element in every scene should contribute to the main story. The dialogue could have been merged with Scene 4, as Caligula is carried up a steep incline toward the palace.

SCENE 4 • This scene could have efficiently shown how difficult it is to get to Villa Jovis, a reality that many tourists flock to daily.[14] Instead, Nerva greets Caligula in a pillared entryway, whose light construction might have served more accurately as a solidly built stone corridor into the palace. Nerva complains that many of his colleagues have been executed in Rome and he knows this was done on Tiberius' orders. There is no point in discussing it with Caligula, except to reinforce Nerva's failure to influence Tiberius in a positive way. Tiberius executed those he suspected of questioning his authority; he was wise enough to look out for himself. Without reference, whipping and screams are faintly heard; there is no obvious place for a prison at Villa Jovis.

SCENE 5 • Caligula descends to a large pool. The setting is dark and cavernous, a difficult construction out of a rock cliff. Other than using the dark space to suggest weird sexual activity, there is no reason to have Tiberius in gloomy quarters. In fact, he lived in marble rooms above the bath areas. The only large pools were cisterns for rain water. It is a summer's day. This occasion could have been one of those visual moments for Vidal or Guccione to compare the decadent life of wealthy Romans to that of Hollywood's superrich. Villa Jovis is about seven thousand square feet, not vast by today's ostentatious standards. Excavations record that the living, reception, and service rooms were organized around four cisterns. Variations in the ground levels would have allowed visitors to walk up an

In Scene 5a, Tiberius (Peter O'Toole), elderly and diseased, rises from the pool with a spring in his step. Photograph courtesy General Media Communications, Inc., and Robert C. Guccione. Used by permission.

incline past the baths. East views were of the mainland from the private imperial residence and the great reception hall. The west side housed Tiberius's entourage living in a continuous central compound. The architecture of the palace indicates that it was an attractive place of light marble. Villa Jovis was not a miserable place. Tiberius enjoyed pagan decadence, which is part of his sinister charm.

In any case, this is not an attempt to engage in reconstructing what might have been done. That is futile. It is an effort to hint at the range of options every artist has in constructing a fictional recreation of actual people and events.

In the movie, scores of nude young men and women, referred to by Suetonius as "minnows," playfully swim around Emperor Tiberius, who rises dramatically from a dark pool. Tiberius is energized by the presence of the youngsters, even though his pale, reddened, scaly complexion reveals that he is in declining health. In general, the extras are not identifiable. There is no sexual activity, but there are many quick shots of genitalia, sometimes in close-up. Faces are not memorably linked to these body parts. Around the pool are many mothers suckling their babies, teenagers of both sexes, a few human oddities, and guards. A wide shot of the ensemble resembles a tableau in a Las Vegas revue, rich in colors and sparkling minimal costumes.

The nude images may be rather overpowering at first, but the actors move casually without any awkwardness whatever. Tiberius demands that Caligula perform the dance he did for soldiers at the German front when he was two years old. This is humiliating for Caligula, not yet recognized as a man, but it shows that Tiberius is still very much in charge and his whims are to be obeyed. In the final scenes of the movie Caligula's whims are obeyed.

Tiberius greets Caligula. "Why do you say such monstrous things about me in Rome? I hear you pray for my death." "I don't, lord, ever," is Caligula's wide-eyed, unconvincing response. Viewers don't know whether he is lying, but he is under suspicion. Tiberius retorts, and an environment of hatred, deceit and terror is established. No one is safe, especially Rome's leadership. The constant threat of a conspiracy isolates Tiberius from most associates. He despises the senate, and expresses his hatred to Caligula, who becomes an unlikely ally through birthright. Tiberius is seeking understanding and sympathy. He asks Nerva to help mold Caligula into an emperor, for the time has come for Tiberius to identify a successor. Gemellus is his younger grandson by blood and Caligula is his grandson by adoption. Like Augustus at the time he adopted Tiberius, Tiberius is not pleased with either option. Tiberius's brother Claudius is thought to be mentally and physically incapable, and so he is passed over. Tiberius dresses quickly behind a drape held up by his servants and ascends to an upper chamber. Caligula dumps Claudius into the

In Scene 5b, "Grandfather" Tiberius (O'Toole, right) greets Caligula (Malcolm McDowell) with trepidation. Photograph courtesy General Media Communications, Inc., and Robert C. Guccione. Used by permission.

pool to the laughter of bystanders, as they leave. The hatred between them will increase.

SCENE 6 • A soldier who was drunk on his watch is being punished, as Tiberius and Caligula rush by.[15] Macro has tied off the soldier's penis with his bootlace, while a bladder of wine is poured down his throat. A wide shot reveals that designer Danilo Donati has replicated the basic multi-level background that he used for *Fellini Satyricon*. If this were a grotto along the shore where the sun's rays reflect shimmering images on craggy wails and white sands, it would create another dramatic transition for Tiberius. Instead, he crosses the face of the dark rock-like scenery to reach a higher chamber. With his white toga flying, Tiberius makes this ascent with great energy that lifts the pace of the scene.

Layered in this scene is a collection of attractive adults and more human oddities, such as one with extra body parts. They come from throughout the Roman Empire, also mentioned in *Satyricon*. Most of the "speaking statues" are performing sex acts—masturbation, snake fetish, intercourse, and anal penetration—in individual displays, again rather like the cave whorehouses in *Satyricon*. Tiberius and Caligula hurry by them as if touring a diorama of

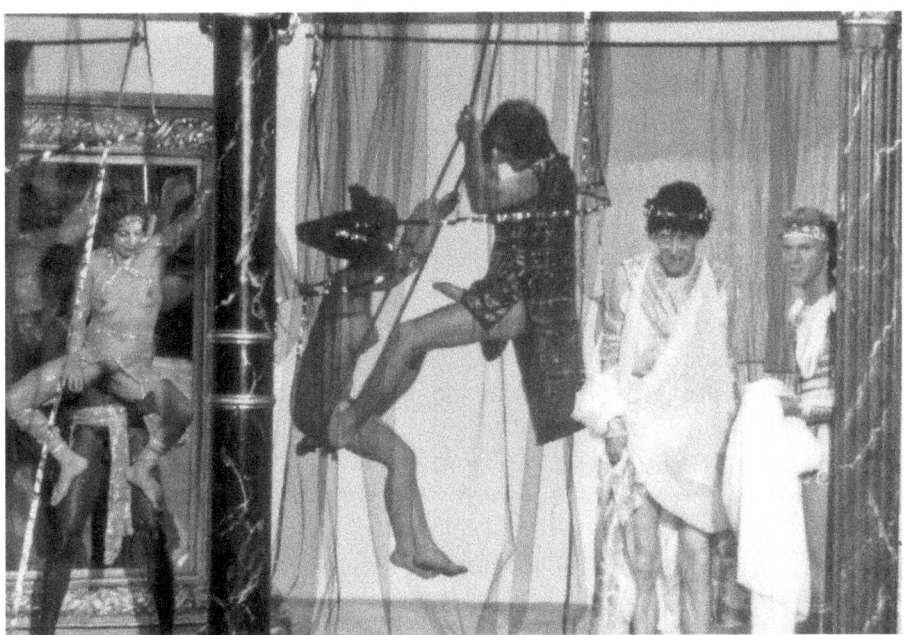

Top: In Scene 6a, Tiberius (O'Toole, second from right), and Caligula (McDowell, right) pass demonstrations of sex acts, while talking about the benefits of nymphs and satyrs. Courtesy Photofest. *Bottom:* In Scene 6b, Tiberius and Gemellus make a zigzag climb to the top level where sex acts are performed. Courtesy Photofest.

the provinces. Tiberius credits himself with years of service to the state and recommends it to Caligula, even though he believes he has not been given sufficient recognition for his loyalty to Rome. He said he prefers private life, but importantly, he thinks he would have been killed if he were not emperor. Live in the seat of power or do not live at all seems to be the message. An environment of hatred, treachery, and terror has always surrounded him, he confides in the eighteen-year-old.

They return to the helpless soldier. Filled with wine, Tiberius stabs him in the abdomen, and blood and wine gush from the wound. This routine job has to be done to maintain strict discipline, and Tiberius is a disciplinarian. He must convince everyone that he has the mental will and strength to maintain his supremacy. Viewers may be aghast at the violent acts, but Tiberius zips through these tasks impassionately. Macro cuts off the man's genitalia, which are shown in close-up before being thrown to hungry dogs. Tiberius speaks rapidly, saying that the Romans only want power and pleasure; they are swine and he is a swine herder. He excludes ordinary citizens in his ref-

In Scene 6c, Tiberius (Peter O'Toole, center) offers Caligula (Malcolm McDowell, second from right) poisoned wine that Caligula gives first to Gemellus (Bruno Brive, second from left). They are flanked by an unidentified attendant and slave girl. Courtesy Photofest.

erences; he concentrates on the outrageously eccentric, arrogant, wealthy class. Later, we see the impact of his thoughts on Caligula, who studies the Roman hierarchy in all its self-indulgence, gluttony, and sexual obsessions. There is pervasive disgust with the wealthy and powerful as they gorge themselves. This reflects the immorality of power, a major theme being developed by Tinto Brass.

Young Tiberius Gemellus arrives, Tiberius's grandson, and the emperor offers a drink to test Caligula, who cleverly offers it first to Gemellus. The emperor seems amused, but prevents Gemellus from sipping the wine. From consulting seers, Tiberius knows Caligula will not die by his hand. He predicts that Caligula will kill Gemellus, and that someone will kill Caligula. A slave immediately drinks the poisoned wine and dies, illustrating how trivial her life is considered to be by the wealthy class. This is another example of the class struggle in Roman times. If Caligula had drunk the wine, he would not have been worthy of the position of emperor. Tiberius and Gemellus leave. Alone, Caligula excitedly stamps orders as if he were emperor; later he will illustrate the dullness of some of the emperor's official routine. By Scene 34 such activity is a boring reality for the head of state.

Tiberius lived until he was seventy-seven.[16] His story is more complicated than Caligula's. Obsessed by fear, Tiberius ruled by means of it. He did not return to Rome during the last eleven years of his reign (A.D. 26–37). He was able to rule in absentia because he had absolute power over life and death and kept a relentless network of spies and military operatives. He built a tall lighthouse near the palace so that he could see all of the naval traffic for miles around, and he could flash messages to the mainland. With a sense of miserly necessity, he accumulated a substantial fortune so that he did not have to depend on the senate to approve and finance his activities.[17] Arguably, he deserved to live as he chose, for he had served Rome well. With little gratitude from the people and realizing the ravages of old age, he may have lived in decadence as a voyeur, draining what little enjoyment was left in his declining years, regardless of gossips and critics; however, the viewer is unaware of this backstory. While Tiberius lived, the empire was stable, despite some economic fluctuations and potential wars.[18] His agenda was minimal, and the public grew increasingly discontented.

SCENE 7 • This scene takes place in Caligula's bedroom. Although Caligula is sleeping with Drusilla, apparently in Tiberius's palace, this is of no consequence; he awakens from a dream recalling Tiberius's prediction of being killed. Drusilla calms him, only to be frightened by a bird caught in mesh netting covering the bed. (In literature a blackbird is a pervasive omen of misfortune. The blackbird may indicate it is caught in its own destiny and no longer has free will.) Drusilla reviews his positive prospects for succession and that eases his mind. He wants to make Drusilla his queen, but she ignores him. He is committed to marry Macro's wife, Ennia Naevia, whom he raped after his first wife died.

Elsewhere in his bedroom, Caligula is ready for his first shave.[19] Until now he has worn a light beard, commonly referred to as peach fuzz. The first shave often symbolizes a transition to manhood, a time when a young man receives the *toga virilis.* No such ceremony is held, however. Caligula is pleased with himself. Ennia enters and invites him to take charge of his future and hers. He grabs her breasts and she screams, as if she were unexpectedly hurt. Their relationship is political and neither seems to be enthusiastic about a future together.

SCENE 8 • In a bath close to Caligula's bedroom, Nerva has slit his own wrists, a common way to commit suicide. Tiberius is unable to save him. The importance of suicide in Roman society is substantial, and considered an acceptable way to die if a person finds continuing life is futile. Disfavor with the emperor or criminal offense resulting in long imprisonment are other reasons for suicide. A sword to the abdomen, starvation, and poisoning were common methods. The concept of personally terminating one's life because

In Scene 8, Tiberius is unable to save Nerva (Sir John Gielgud) from suicide. Courtesy Photofest.

of impairment or being of no further productive use is important to the understanding of pagan life. This scene may be particularly disturbing because it suggests that old Nerva will endure no retribution; he is merely slipping away peacefully at a time of his own choosing. The setting for a tub, raised on black marble steps, is unusually large, and is another interior built against a cyclorama without walls. This adds concentration to Caligula's curiosity about death and the afterlife.

SCENE 9 • Caligula hears the commotion and rushes to Nerva.

SCENE 10 • Nerva, who plays the abstract role of Tiberius's conscience, remains true to righteous principles, and Tiberius appreciates his dedication without compromise. Nerva complains about the reprehensible behavior of Tiberius, who was once a good man; and he refers to Caligula as a "reptile." Viewers do not know why Nerva has such low regard for him; inasmuch as Caligula had no real power. As Tiberius leaves, Caligula uses Nerva's impending demise for pointers about the afterlife. Throughout the film Caligula seeks assurances that there is life after death and that the gods are immortal. Tiberius exits saying that is nonsense, but he recognizes such myths are some-

In Scene 10, left to right: Macro (Guido Mannari), Nerva (Gielgud), Ennia (Adriana Asti), Tiberius (O'Toole), and Caligula (McDowell) at the scene of Nerva's suicide. Courtesy Photofest.

times useful. The scene depicts this method of suicide as a reasonable solution. Nerva says he is in no pain and is just becoming sleepy; in other words, this method of committing suicide looks easy and comfortable. Disappointed that Nerva experiences only sleep and darkness and does not see Isis, Caligula calls him a liar and pushes him under the water.

SCENE 11 • The next morning, after what seems to be a night of unexplained debauchery, shows the results of hell on earth. The viewer sees displays of several people, including the speaking statues, who have been raped, tortured, and murdered by stakes and swords. This is a theatrical showcase of horrors that parallels the showcase of sexual proclivities shown earlier, only those people were alive and these are dead. Caligula witnesses the cruelty, which may be a minimal representation of what he probably saw on Capri during his teen years, but viewers would not know this.[20] Charicles reports that Tiberius is in poor health, but could live another year. Apparently impatient, Caligula seeks the allegiance of Macro by kissing him on the mouth, supposedly a tighter bond of unity than a handshake. Moody Macro, flabbergasted, responds by putting his arm over an open flame. These are the acts of ultimate commitment.

SCENE 12 • This scene takes place in Tiberius's bedroom. Viewers become aware that two or three scenes may be played in these large bedrooms. In a brief cutaway, which is not explained or developed, Claudius rolls dice while Gemellus watches. This shot is a good reminder of the potential contenders for emperor. Viewers do not learn what fate holds for either of them. They do have a sense that fortunes turn on luck. Life is capricious.

SCENE 13 • The shot widens to reveal Tiberius on his death bed. Relatives and servants are assembled, but no guards are present to protect his interests because Macro is their commander. Calig-

In Scene 12, Claudius (Giancarlo Badessi) rolls dice as a reminder that fortunes change in an instant. He will become emperor. Courtesy Photofest.

In Scene 13, Macro (Guido Mannari) strangles Tiberius (Peter O'Toole) after Caligula fails to do it. Courtesy Photofest.

ula has Macro usher everyone from the room. Up to this point Caligula had been dressed in elegant tunics, cloaks, and modified breastplates; however, now he wears an odd gold costume of stiff net, resembling a ballet dancer's tutu that barely covers his derriere. While Caligula vigorously attempts to remove the imperial ring from Tiberius's finger, Tiberius awakens and discovers his intentions. Caligula is a strong young man, but no match for Tiberius. So Macro strangles Tiberius with a black mesh scarf. This is a subtle reference to the blackbirds being caught in the netting over beds shown in previous scenes. Repeating the blackbird motif through the drama is a purposeful construction carrying perhaps a message from the gods: Caligula must fulfill his destiny. Dramatically, the mesh is useful because viewers can see the agony on Tiberius's face. If the deed is to be done, better it be done quickly. This action could be prolonged, but it is not. It is well planned. It sets the course for further disposition of characters; namely, Macro and Gemellus. The true circumstances of Tiberius's death were probably natural causes, but this choice is made on dramatic grounds. Gemellus has seen the murder; therefore, at the scene's end Caligula completely reverses course when he greets him with his "we must love each other" ruse.

After collapsing seven years in ten scenes Caligula has lost his youthful innocence, and the scenes of exposition are concluded. He looks tired and the lines are deeper in his face. The depth of his crimes are beginning to register. He has no closet like Dorian Gray in which to hide his miseries. At this point dark shadows and harsh lighting contribute to his descent. A superficially conceited attitude penetrates the character. He has lost the charm of a lover and sweetness of a youth; in other words he is no longer a character whom viewers want to succeed. Unlike in *A Clockwork Orange*, wherein the viewer always wants Alex to be acquitted of his bad boy ways, Caligula is entangled in lewd or violent acts that are difficult to forgive. When that happens to the leading character in a film, viewer interest may wane. Delicate decisions are called for. The danger is that becoming emperor may appear more compelling than being emperor. Caligula's problem is to retain his throne and his life. The logic of utopia, if applied, would show Caligula catering to the public will, as the action rises.

SCENE 14 • Tiberius, his face covered by a mask, lies in state. The viewer is not sure where he is, presumably on display before the senate in Rome. Caligula, Drusilla says, is lord of the world, as the senate names him emperor

In Scene 14, Caligula, with Drusilla (Teresa Ann Savoy) at his side, becomes emperor after Tiberius's funeral. Ennia (Adriana Asti) stands between McDowell and Savoy. Courtesy Photofest.

with Claudius as fellow counsel and Gemellus as Caligula's heir by adoption. Exercising his powers from the start, Caligula insists that Drusilla and his sisters be given equal allegiance. He knows the senators are weak and self-serving; therefore, he leads with strength.[21] The theme Tiberius previously expressed — that the emperor and the senate are natural enemies — is joined. This notion does not hold up very well, inasmuch as Caligula has not been denied anything.

In fact, the people of Rome hated Tiberius and were ready to throw his body into the Tiber River. They were delighted that "Little Boots" was emperor. They had great expectations, and Caligula began his reign with popular gestures of granting amnesty and giving money to the soldiers from the huge treasury his frugal predecessor had saved. If viewers had been given relief from incessant wickedness, the case for Caligula's popularity could have revealed a complex personality of highly likable traits offset by cruel periods perhaps prompted by recollections of the deaths of his family and by personal loneliness and neglect during his upbringing.[22] If Tiberius had spent more time impressing Caligula with the role of benefactor to the people, Caligula might have had a more positive focus for his reign. None of this is on the screen.

SCENE 15 • Caligula's bedroom. By Scene 15, in Caligula's bedroom, the claustrophobic effect of filming in a studio becomes a factor. As Caligula and Drusilla make love again, they believe they are being spied upon through the mouth of a large wall medallion. A dominant feeling viewers get is that palace life is without privacy.

SCENE 16 • Caligula investigates the intrusion by looking behind the wall where he finds two men preoccupied with fellatio, and he chases them away. If this act is not related to the narrative, and it is not, then it should not be in the film. The only plot point addressed in this scene is that Drusilla wants Caligula to get rid of Macro rather than Gemellus.[23] This is the worst possible advice she could give him, and he has no clear reason to take it. Heretofore, she has had an undue influence over him, but within the constraints of reasonable cause and effect.

SCENE 17 • In an open corridor leading to a multipurpose arena, in front of the imperial guard, Caligula tells Gemellus to name the one who murdered Tiberius. The encounter is a surprise. Among the members of Caligula's entourage, Macro seems to be trustworthy, but Drusilla's advice has prevailed. Gemellus identifies Macro, and he is arrested by Chaerea, who is in line to become commander of the guards after Macro's execution.[24] Getting rid of Macro is essential, for distrust in the head Praetorian is intrinsic to the job. Caligula must remember Tiberius's problems in eliminating Sejanus, but viewers do not know this. It is not on the screen.

SCENE 18 • Again in Caligula's bedroom, two men argue over land rights, and Caligula makes a meaningless, capricious judgment. Caligula seems to do almost everything in some part of his large bedrooms. Various bedroom settings tend to look alike. The bed is surrounded, not so much by walls, but rather by set pieces, such as columns and drapes. The impression is that everybody uses these rooms, with minor adjustments in placement of the set pieces and lighting. Centrality in Caligula's surroundings would have added strength and definition to his character; insubstantial circumstances weaken a perception of who he is and what he stands for, which is not unexpected in a twenty-year-old.

SCENE 19 • In another room that looks like a bedroom, presumably Ennia's, men are ejaculating into a cup to provide a beauty lotion for Ennia. Such a treatment is within reason due to Roman faith in the regenerative power of sperm. Caligula urinates at the edge of the room perhaps to show his contempt for her or Macro, whose death the senate has authorized. When Ennia learns of his sentence, Ennia spits in Caligula's face in protest and is exiled to Gaul. Viewers cannot empathize with the self-centered, promiscuous Ennia until they realize she cares for Macro. In seconds, this scene contrasts regeneration with renunciation in a few shots and lines of dialogue. Unfortunately, Caligula cannot distinguish between his friends and his enemies.[24] Caligula has a stuffed likeness of Incitatus in the room; this is another pervasive reminder of an important symbol.

SCENE 20 • In another huge space where Caligula and Drusilla carry on an intimate conversation, the large theatrical stage dimensions are once again preserved. In fact, living space for the palace residents was rather small, except in the palace of Augustus. Drusilla tells Caligula he must marry a respectable lady of the senatorial class. He must have an heir. His responsibility is absolutely clear to her, and even though he would rather play sex games within his comfort zone, she insists he meet his obligations, as she grabs his covered genitals.

SCENE 21 • In the atrium in Drusilla's house, the priestesses of Isis are meeting. This lovely setting consists of a shallow pool surrounded by columns and gauze drapes, which float when people pass by them. There is no architectural context for the setting, except that the pool is surrounded by columns, with eunuchs sitting on ledges between them. It does not seem to be indoors, where it would be surrounded by the rest of the house; instead, it is a singular entity, which illustrates the theatrical nature of the staging in the overhead shot pictured. This approach to scenic art direction prohibits the production from being realistic. Clearly the settings waver between being realistic (Tiberius's palace, the arena, the wedding villa, Caligula's courtyard bedroom, and some exteriors) and being theatrical, isolated from the con-

Top: In Scene 21a, the priestesses of Isis (played by uncredited Penthouse Pets) are gracefully exhibited in lesbian encounters. Courtesy Photofest. *Bottom:* In Scene 21b, Caligula, dressed as a woman, visits the priestesses of Isis at his sister's request. Courtesy Photofest.

text of other scenes (numerous bedroom scenes, Nerva's bath, the temple, government interiors, and Drusilla's house).

Ordinarily, men are not allowed at the gathering. Caligula is disguised as a woman, which he liked to do occasionally. The Vestal Virgins ignore him while he looks for a wife. This was a fine occasion for the beautiful Penthouse Pets to perform lesbian acts, while the story remains centered on the task at hand. Although one woman masturbates, the potential for lesbian sex is restrained. The women relate gracefully to each other. The positions of the women to the pool and the circle of columns allows for many lovely pictorial compositions like those in *Penthouse* magazine.

This scene is appropriate to the narrative and is much superior to the later unnecessary sexual encounters in Scene 27. Caligula sees two women he likes. One is the virgin Livia, who is about to be married to a young officer named Proculus, and her opposite, a sexually experienced divorcee, Caesonia.[25] Despite Drusilla's advice, Caligula selects Caesonia.

SCENE 22 • Beyond a few gauze curtains and adjacent to the pool is the altar of Isis. The limits of the area are undefined. Here Caligula isolates Caesonia and has anal sex with her. This is another example of pagan openness. Maybe he is testing her willingness and skills as a sex partner. Neither char-

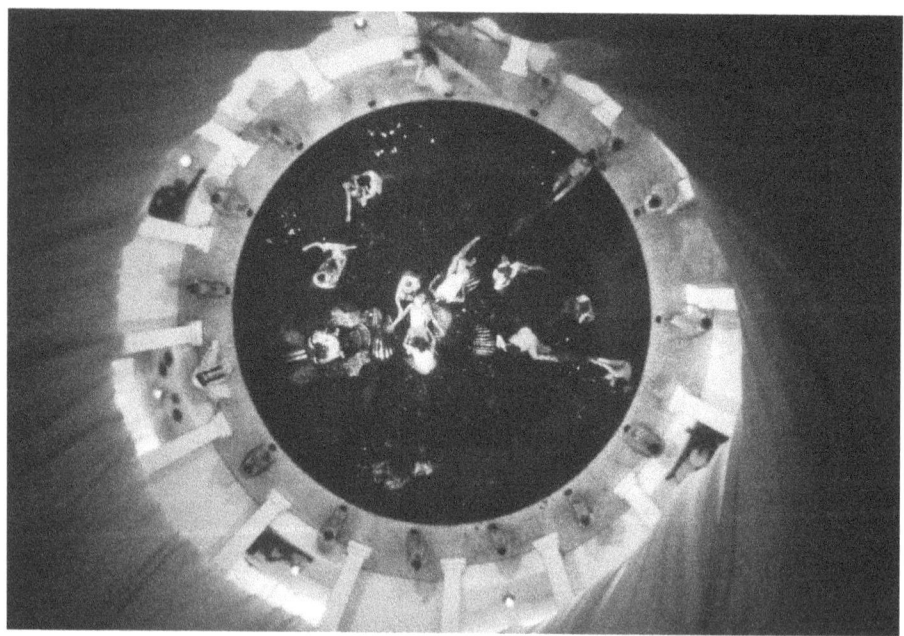

An overhead view of Drusilla's circular pool with the Vestal Virgins is shown only in the *Io, Caligola* edition. Courtesy Photofest.

acter seems passionate about the opportunity. There is little emotion — no heat, no affection. Caligula approaches most women as conquests. He is doing his duty but this is in contrast to his amorous approach to Drusilla in earlier scenes. Technically, the anal intercourse is arranged as a two-shot in profile, with plenty of clothing to cover the act itself.

This scene aptly illustrates the difference between most adult films and traditional mainstream films. Adult films sell explicit visual sex acts sweetened by an appropriate audio track, usually with few words, grunts, and groans. The movement is quick and mainly devoid of showing caring between partners. The mental concentration for adult models is often forced: Is she enticing enough? Is he going to be able to ejaculate? Viewers may assume that adult performers are having a good time, but in truth, their genuine emotions may be internalized or ignored, so that complete concentration can be applied to the physical outcome viewers want to see. Adult models often play themselves, and they do not try to become believable characters or pretend to be someone else. Mainstream actors depend upon becoming the character; that is, being credible as someone else. If the viewer believes in the actor's character, the actor creates a vicarious experience for the viewer.

In scene 22, Caligula and Caesonia do not show mutual attraction, but they do hint at compatibility. Viewers should be able to see what the actors' characters are thinking. Caesonia tries to gracefully submit to Caligula and to show him why she is well qualified for the title of empress at least from a sexual perspective. No torrid activity occurs, nor could a viewer expect it. They just met. Yet, this is a scene where adult and traditional action could merge. The actors, in this instance, do not interact sufficiently. They are not seductive; and consequently, viewers have difficulty empathizing with them. In fact, Caesonia was Caligula's fourth wife. It is reasonable to believe that she would have known how to please him, and it would have been interesting to see how her methods of enticement would have compared with Drusilla's. She had the responsibility for stimulating the emperor. She should have rivaled Drusilla.[26] Instead, a viewer may ask, why her?

The importance of this scene is that it was the critical moment at which adult techniques should have blended with traditional character acting. Viewers do not expect the leads to perform adult sex acts unless they are adult stars, but viewers do expect their characters to believe in what they are doing, and in this instance, to be seductive. Often viewers are not sure the actors are experiencing anything. Certainly these actors do not demonstrate the excitement of a joyful encounter. Perhaps the commonality of pagan sexual experiences have reduced this pleasure to a mechanical process. Here the pages of *Penthouse* should have guided the romantic high standards of human ecstasy — beautiful characters engaged in an intensely absorbing and erotic sex act. This is one of the few scenes that should have illustrated how reasonable it is for explicit sex to become part of traditional films by adding a few more frames of love-making. Technically of course, adult models could have been substituted for the actual sex moments. Later Brass said that he did not shoot explicit sex, and even if he did, he might not include it in the final assemblage of the film. This was another opportunity for Guccione and Brass, however, to affirm one of the main objectives of producing the movie.

SCENE 23 • A crowded Roman arena is the backdrop for demonstrating some of Caligula's eccentric preferences. For example, Caesonia is on a leash so that she will remain faithful to him, at least until she produces his child. The occasion for this festive event is the beheading of Macro. He is buried in the sand floor of the arena with only his head visible. An enormous and elaborate machine with circulating blades at ground level separates Macro's head from his body, as seen only in the unrated version. The action in the arena is not as compelling as watching skillful gladiators challenge each

In Scene 23a, at the arena, Caligula (Malcolm McDowell) discusses the marriage of Proculus and Livia with Longinus (John Steiner, in black cloak). Drusilla (Teresa Ann Savoy) is seated on Caligula's right. Photograph courtesy General Media Communications, Inc., and Robert C. Guccione. Used by permission.

In Scene 23b, Caligula responds with satisfaction to the arena crowd. Courtesy Photofest.

other or various animals, something popular with audiences for decades. In some films, by the time gladiators get into the arena a viewer has an emotional investment in one or more of them. The gladiators in *Spartacus* (1960) and *Gladiator* (2000) have the same empathic effect. Death is the result of a contest. But there is no contest between a machine and a helpless human being already buried. This novel construction, which has no known historical basis, was expensive and arguably not worth the money.

Caligula notices the couple Livia and Proculus, who are betrothed, and he manages to get an invitation to their wedding. This prompts outrageous acts that do not strengthen the plot, except to reinforce his cruelty.

SCENE 24 • Caligula arrives late for the wedding of Proculus and Livia. Prominently placed in the setting are large penises. Caligula says he wants to bestow his blessing on the bride and groom. The wedding guests are a raucous, lusty bunch wildly enjoying themselves, while the shy bride and groom are just hoping they will get through the revelry so that they can enjoy each other alone. Caligula has established by now that he is a volatile person, and no one wants to upset him. Everyone is supportive of the couple on this important day, so the tensions are set. Livia and Proculus perform admirably in what must have been a difficult sequence, which clearly illustrates Brass's logic of power, forcing people to do immoral and inhuman acts.

SCENE 25 • In the kitchen behind the banquet hall Caligula forces Livia to lie on a hard table so that he can rape her, and check to see whether she is a virgin by producing a blood spot as proof. The young woman is devastated, but Caligula, with wicked nonchalance, immediately turns to Proculus to fist him while still wearing his imperial ring. Naturally, their pleas go unheeded. The deeds are sufficiently heinous in themselves that they are not graphically shot, as a director would do for an adult film. The understated acting of the Italian couple intensifies their compassion and provides pathetic counterpoint to Caligula's outrageous use of power. Caligula is aloof, sneering, and seems to be interfering with this ceremony only because he can. Up to this time, Caligula has been reasonably likeable, and he could be forgiven for most of what he has done by applying some rationale such as his own fears, possible conspiracies, bad education, and his youth. Now, however, whatever ambivalence viewers may have had has disappeared, and interest in the rest of the film, if there is any, rests with curious sidebars to the main narrative.

In Scene 25a, with the wedding feast in progress, Caligula bestows his blessing on Livia (Mirella Dangelo) and Proculus (Donato Placido) in the kitchen. Courtesy Photofest.

For a film to succeed in mixing adult and traditional values viewers must like — or love to hate — the main characters. There is also a serious aesthetic inconsistency to be considered; namely, if the principal story and mise-en-scène of *Caligula* have become unrealistic, then why would the sex scenes need to be realistic?

SCENE 26 • This scene takes place in Caligula's bedroom and courtyard. It is a stormy night with thunder and lightning. Caligula, sleeping nude, is awakened by the weather and sees the fleeting figure of Gemellus across a large adjacent courtyard. Caligula seems to go after Gemellus, but then regresses to his childhood, repeats his boots dance as if he were experiencing a nightmare, and wanders around the courtyard. This could be another opportunity for providing exposition, a chance to incorporate flashbacks of the horrors Caligula experienced in his early life — the death of his heroic father, the exile of his mother, cruel punishments for relatives, and the mental torment of constant debauchery on Capri. A useful comparison may be the experience of Aulus Vitellius, two years younger than Gaius. He lived his adolescence on Capri as one of the homosexual prostitutes referred to as *spintriae*. Suetonius wrote that Vitellius used his body to help his father gain position and status. In early life he was hurt, resulting in a limp. Vitellius was also known to role-play, rather like Caligula, and to seek favors from the emperors. The psychological impact of his years on Capri may explain in parallel his brief sadistic reign in A.D. 70. This exposition is not included, however.[27]

In Scene 25b, Caligula rapes Livia and checks to see whether she is a virgin. Photograph courtesy General Media Communications, Inc., and Robert C. Guccione. Used by permission.

Caligula slips and falls in the courtyard. Caesonia and Drusilla rush to presumably comfort him, but they find equal comfort in consoling each other, although this seems to be an unexpected attraction.

SCENE 27 • In a bedroom behind the medallion in Scene 16, where two men were briefly shown previously, two Penthouse Pets appear in the roles of Messalina and Agrippina Minor, who actually became Claudius's wives. Shooting this scene was an afterthought and so their integration into the main narrative was impossible to add belatedly. The scene could be interpreted also as a fantasy projection of Drusilla and Caesonia from the previous scene, and the characters could have blended in if they had been identified earlier in the story. Their lesbian interlude is the kind of scene Guccione apparently thought his *Penthouse* readers would expect, and he wanted the women featured in some way. Later they would appear in a lovely pictorial gallery for the magazine. It seems that he had found himself with a conundrum: how could he have the women in the movie without having them in it? He simply put them in unexpectedly without being able to integrate them into the narrative; a hot lesbian encounter that did not blend in with the rest of the drama. The women are credited on-screen but he allowed the scene to be edited out of all variations except the unrated edition. They are suitable as an adult insert within that context.

In a plush bedroom the very attractive women engage in what is typical lesbian activity shown in adult movies. This and the orgy scene are the only prolonged hardcore scenes in the picture. The women may be recognized from earlier in the narrative, especially as priestesses at Drusilla's meeting. They engage in kissing, cunnilingus, and vaginal and anal finger penetration, and a trembling movement suggests orgasm. This post-production scene was shot by Giancarlo Lui and Bob Guccione, mentioned elsewhere.

SCENE 28 • Caligula arrives at a palace banquet hall on his white horse, Incitatus. Claudius rolls his dice and seems to see an omen that is not made part of the story. Caligula announces he will be a god when he is dead. While deity status was a persistent concern for him, the title of "god" is not uncommon for truly distinguished heads of state. Caligula, unlike Alexander the Great or Augustus Caesar, has done nothing outstanding to earn the respect the title represents. If a leader received this title, temples were established and maintained in his name. A cult was developed so that believers could worship him. Tiberius fought many wars and faithfully served in government during his lifetime, but he made no claim that he was or should be recognized as a god. Even so, Caligula becomes obsessed with attaining the status of a god.[28]

At the dinner, Caligula learns that Gemellus is taking an antidote probably to prevent possible food poisoning. He claims the antidote is to ward off a fever that is taking many lives in the city. Caligula declares this incident an act of treason and sentences Gemellus to death.[29] Drusilla is angry and calls Caligula an "amateur"; her reference is unclear. Possibly embarrassed,

Caligula slaps her and she exits. In an attempt to change the mood of the party, Caligula eats the allegedly poisoned food, laughs, pretends to be poisoned and recovers. The scene is amusing because it shows that Caligula never misses a chance to perform. Caesonia is supportive, but Caligula is uncertain about what he has done. He orders Caesonia to dance. Caesonia, dressed in jewels, dances for Caligula and the guests. The choreography is not particularly unique or erotic. How would a lady, who seems to be several months along, express herself? If Caesonia's character had been better defined, then the dance might have been more expressive and relevant. Wouldn't such a previously promiscuous woman be skilled in dancing?[30]

SCENE 29 • Caligula had a marble stall built for Incitatus, apparently the one living being he could trust. The pair are alone when viewers learn that Caligula has caught the fever.

In Scene 27, two Penthouse Pets as Messalina (Anneka Di Lorenzo, left) and Agrippina (Lori Wagner) enthusiastically engage in a lesbian encounter. Photograph courtesy General Media Communications, Inc., and Robert C. Guccione. Used by permission.

SCENE 30 • On dark streets, numerous bodies, evidently dead from an unidentified disease, are being piled up for cremation. This scene, though seemingly unrelated to Caligula, sets the murky tone for much that is to follow.

SCENE 31 • In Caligula's bedroom, Caligula and Incitatus are in bed. Caligula tells Drusilla he is seriously ill. She has no concerns for herself, as she tries to comfort him. Caesonia is sent to get their lawyer, Longinus.

In Scene 28a, Caesonia (Helen Mirren), known for her beautiful body, dances for Caligula and guests. Courtesy Photofest

SCENE 32 • In a room nearby, Caesonia is with Longinus, the family adviser. Perhaps Chaerea is out of hearing range when he notes that it would not be a good time to kill Caligula because a civil war might break out. This implies that Caligula remains popular with the people, even though he has lost the respect of many of those closest to him, especially Chaerea. The question is still puzzling—why would Chaerea lead an assassination plot from which there does not appear to be any benefit for him? This question has been asked for centuries. To complicate matters at this point,

In Scene 28b, Caesonia, though pregnant, dances for Caligula and banquet guests. Courtesy Photofest.

In Scene 31, Caligula, with his horse Incitatus in bed, seems to be out of his mind and incurable to his doctor, Charicles (Leopoldo Trieste). Photograph courtesy General Media Communications, Inc., and Robert C. Guccione. Used by permission.

viewers do not know whether Gemellus is dead, Drusilla has any power, or whether Caesonia's child might become heir, with Caesonia as regent.

SCENE 33 • This scene takes place again in Caligula's bedroom. Longinus has come to Caligula's bedside to change his will in favor of Drusilla. Whether it is completed is unclear. Drusilla gets in bed with Caligula and he recovers quickly. In fact, Caligula's fever or severe illness lasted about one month. Much speculation has claimed his mental penchant toward cruelty began after he was restored to health. This trait was demonstrated long before this scene.[31] Today trauma experienced by youths is treated extensively.

SCENE 34 • Caligula tolerates the routine bureaucratic life at the palace by stamping his approval on documents.

SCENE 35 • A torture chamber displays a collection from the mundane to the weird; none is more bizarre than Proculus held in a sling. Some historians claim that Caligula held a latent jealousy of him; others say this was because Proculus had hair and Caligula was losing his. More profound is the notion that Proculus represents good, like Scipio in Camus' *Caligula*. In any case Proculus's body is being cut so that blood seeps out of it slowly, giving

In Scene 33, Longinus (John Steiner) goes to Caligula's bedside to name Drusilla his heir. Courtesy Photofest.

Caligula time to ask the same questions he asked Nerva: "Does he see Isis?" In an unexpected act, a fellow soldier mercifully wields a fatal blow and Caligula is angry. This scene, coming after Caligula's illness, demonstrates the extreme cruelty he now seems to crave. According to Brass's theory, the logic of utopia may be overwhelmed by the logic of power, contaminating him and making Caligula abusive and cruel.

The body of the dead Proculus is caressed by Pets, who then urinate on it. The acts in this scene are explicit and revolting. Caligula tells Longinus to send his genitals to his wife Livia, but his penis is cut off and fed to a dog. Perhaps this violent repetition illustrates Caligula's mental state or it may be a test of the public's tolerance for violence, including sadomasochism, then and now. These acts and Caligula's fundamental enmity toward Proculus are speculation. Additionally, what this scene does show is that simulated body parts and adult film models can substitute for well known legitimate actors in explicit actions and scenes.

SCENE 36 • A bird appears again, mostly to remind viewers how important omens were in the lives of Caligula and those around him. This insert could have had more meaning. Scenes 35 and 36 accelerate the rising action, as Caligula nears his mental breaking point. The bird is the omen of destiny that Caligula cannot control. While Scene 35 shows Caligula on a downward trend as the logic of power becomes devoid of human traits, Scene 36 has him consumed by malicious behavior. He is evil. The blackbird reminds him that his end is near. Scenes 37 and 38 reveal that Caligula lacks control over his destiny. The goddess Fortuna has abandoned him, his desire for a male heir is thwarted, and his sister dies.

SCENE 37 · On an elevated stage, presumably in the palace, a small crowd awaits the birth of Caesonia's baby. Caesonia, her face behind a mask, gives birth — explicitly pictured — to a girl that Caligula prematurely calls a boy. Caligula celebrates by calling Caesonia empress of Rome. Afterward, Drusilla faints; she is ill with the fever and everyone flees. This scene combines the lifecycle's beginning — bloody, violent, miraculous — with Drusilla's approaching death.

SCENE 38 · In Drusilla's bedroom, she is dying. Caligula prays to Isis and smashes her statue when she fails him. In torment, Caligula licks Drusilla's nude body, while remembering earlier times in a montage of happy

In Scene 37, Caesonia, shielded by a mask, gives birth to their daughter, Julia Drusilla. Courtesy Photofest.

occasions. His motivation is a primitive response rather like an animal licking its dead mate. There is no sense that the Romans had faith in their gods any more than the multitudes believe in their gods today. They prayed to them for public display and to be on the "safe side" if they turned out to be real. Grief can be dispelled in different ways and this short scene shows some of them. It was not as simple to shoot convincingly as a routine burial in most movies. In the end Caligula's despair explodes in a scream.

SCENE 39 • The scene opens on a street in Rome. During a month-long mourning period Caligula wanders the streets. On an outdoor stage he sees a satire about his administration and society. At the bottom of a living triangle are slaves, in the row above are the people, next is the army, and on higher levels are the tribunes and senators. At the apex is the emperor, played by Mnester, who was in fact Caligula's occasional lover. An actor playing the role of Drusilla cries out, "Let's make love." Furious, Caligula knocks down the rows of actors forming the triangle. He and several street people are thrown in jail.

SCENE 40 • In a room in the palace, Caesonia and Longinus contemplate where Caligula might be. This brief scene also helps establish that Caesonia is probably not involved with any conspiracy.

SCENE 41 • The street ruffians are rounded up and thrown down a chute into a holding cell. The prisoners are mostly a mixture of low life. One woman is engaged in cunnilingus. The main figure in the rabble is an unidentified entertainer, Giant. He is providing amusement as a magician by taking valuable items from a woman's vagina. As he is about to take Caligula's imperial ring, he recognizes a resemblance.

SCENE 42 • Caligula returns to the throne with Giant at his side. Dressed in drab clothing, he demands that the senate declare him a god.[32] There is no clear cause and effect here. He simply repeats the lines said at the beginning of the film: "I have existed from the morning of the world ... I am no man, and therefore I am [a] god." The line still does not make sense. Longinus says Caligula is mad, but the senate is politically evasive and will not stand up to him, and by its acquiescence allows a madman to dictate. The senate confirms him as a god. Caligula shows his contempt for the senators. He tests them by forcing them to imitate sheep. After the death of Drusilla, Caligula goads the senators to do outlandish, irrational things. Favored senators who lived well do not want to jeopardize their status by aiding the others he destroys. This becomes a speculative basis for senatorial participation in his death, but no reference is made to possible collusion between the Praetorian Guard and senators. The logic of utopia has been consumed by power and Caligula at the height of his reign is also near the end of it.

SCENE 43 • Back in the bedroom, Caesonia baits Caligula with a scepter.

A shot of the dungeon into which Caligula and Giant are thrown in Scene 41. Courtesy Photofest.

Whether they care for each other and whether he is truly crazy are arguable. He checks with Longinus about the depleted treasury. To remedy the current financial crisis, Caligula proposes that the state run a brothel as an income source. This is another scene which defies logic. Caligula's logic is that the richest men in Rome are the pimps, which is not true, and he knows he cannot recover sufficient funds from a one-time sex event to cover the state's debts. Caligula's peculiar grasp of logic begins in Scene 4. Due to the infrequency of reference, it is not easy for viewers to follow it. The notion that Caligula is going to do something "good" for the country is absurd, but having ships maintained as floating brothels is not completely far-fetched.

SCENE 44 • The skeleton of a galley that Caligula uses as a brothel looks like

In Scene 42, Caligula returns to the senate with new demands. Courtesy Photofest.

In Scene 44a, the orgy separates the principal actors from those having sex. Photograph courtesy General Media Communications, Inc., and Robert C. Guccione. Used by permission.

it cost more to build than he would ever receive in return. Caligula really did have a bawdy house at the palace for a while.[33] The ship is used as a device to further the notion that Caligula is mad, but it could also be said that he was just desperate for money. In actuality, Caligula had difficulty raising money for the central government, but this is not mentioned. From this point on, the script moves further and further from reality. Coincidently, on two levels this is the moment of crisis in the picture. *Caligula* has to have a brothel to satisfy the storyline and to consummate once and for all the traditional and adult film experience. Viewers have been waiting for the moment when couples copulate to the satisfaction of adult and traditional movie audiences. This is a difficult collaboration.

Caligula and Caesonia preside over a busy orgy of partially clothed bodies. Unfortunately, the activity consists mainly of unrelated body parts engaged in fellatio, touching genitalia, breast licking, cunnilingus, anal fingering, whipping, and a few seconds of vaginal intercourse resulting in ejaculation. No leading actors are involved; and therefore, without an investment in the characters, there is not a great deal of interest in watching miscellaneous body parts engaged in sex. The Penthouse Pets and unidentifiable good-looking extras provide what action there is. Chaerea's soldiers in gold body armor perform a variation of Caligula's boots dance and a painted white hermaphrodite-like clown, reminiscent of *Fellini Satyricon* and *Sebastiane,* smacks his brilliant red lips in approval.

At the orgy's conclusion Caligula, commands the static ship to sail to Britain.[34]

SCENE 45 • On a river bank near Rome, Caligula, with Giant, engages in a fanciful invasion of Britain. Naked foot soldiers and clothed horsemen charge across a stream. Some collect papyrus as a token that they have engaged in the campaign. This so-called madness is an odd way to bring

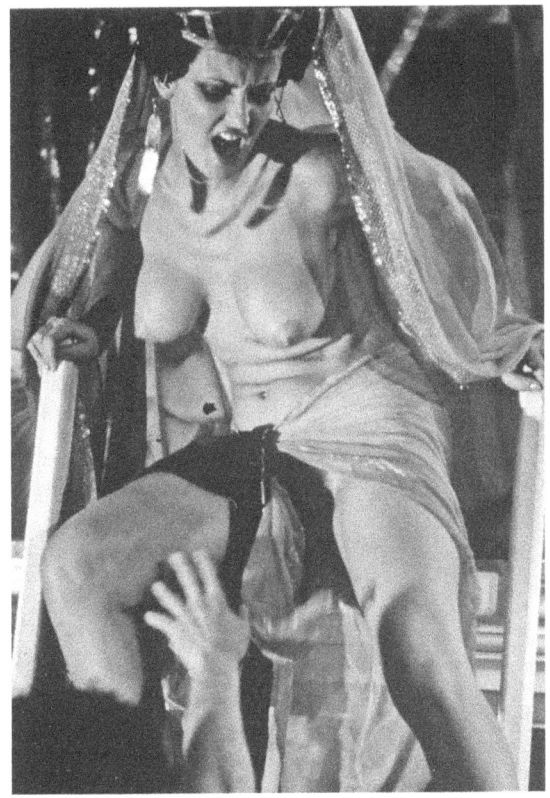

In Scene 44b, the moments of climax are the high point of the orgy scene. Courtesy Photofest.

the narrative to crisis. In reality, Caligula's résumé has him continue a rather tranquil, domestic reign. He was not called upon to wage wars against rebellious territories as Tiberius did, but he did make thoughtful judgments in settling disputes in northern Germany and in northern Africa. He took a contingent, believed to be as large as 250,000 troops, across Gaul, arriving on the northwest shores to determine whether he should invade Britain. The date is uncertain, and crossing the English Channel may have been treacherous. He may have met a dissident British warlord at sea, but little came of the meeting.[35] He had a lighthouse built and on the shore soldiers gathered seashells (not papyrus) as souvenirs. None of this adventure is in the movie. So he decided to return to Rome, raising money along the way. Presumably he had plenty of time to take on the British tribes later.[36] (Claudius does precisely that during his reign.) Is this the logic of a madman?

SCENE 46 • Caligula rides Incitatus into the banquet hall again. Naked

Above: In Scene 44c, Caligula (McDowell, top) commands that the static ship sail to Britain. Caesonia (Helen Mirren) is in front of Caligula, echoing his pose. Courtesy Photofest. *Opposite, top:* In Scene 45a, with Giant (Osiride Pevarello) at this side, Caligula commands soldiers in a faux battle outside of Rome. Courtesy Photofest. *Opposite, bottom:* In Scene 45b, Caligula has his troops gather papyrus rather than sea shells, and listens to a sea shell, presumably because he is mad. Osiride Pevarello as Giant is to his right. Photograph courtesy General Media Communications, Inc., and Robert C. Guccione. Used by permission.

slaves are serving food and the papyrus canes are paraded before the guests. Thinking of one of the ways he could raise money, he terrorizes wealthy Romans with confiscation of their lands and threatens their lives. Caesonia warns him to watch out for Chaerea. Caligula is aware of Chaerea's enmity, but unlike his action against Macro and Gemellus, he ignores it. Why? While all questions are seldom answered in a movie, key questions should be answered to bring satisfactory closure to the story.

SCENE 47 • Chaerea and others plot to kill Caligula. The true nature of this conspiracy is interesting in itself, but the film does not develop Chaerea's character.[37] Building to the assassination might have been a more compelling conclusion. One view asks what were Chaerea's mounting concerns about Caligula's behavior that brought him to the point of assassination. Chaerea does not seem to want more power for himself. Nor is there any explanation what would happen to him or whether there was any forethought as to who would rule in Caligula's place. Would assassination make the empire a better place for the Roman people without a designated successor? With no heir apparent and the empire without leadership, wouldn't it be worse off? Would

In Scene 46, revelers celebrate Caligula's return from Britain and Gaul. Courtesy Photofest.

Rome be in a position similar to Tiberius's indecision about an heir at the beginning of the film?

SCENE 48 • An exhausted Caligula climbs a stairway leading to his bed chamber. Caesonia tries to comfort him when a bird appears again. This transitional scene is used to set up a dissolve to Chaerea's breastplate, which has a bird engraved on it, and to foreshadow the grand stairway that is the site for Caligula's demise.

SCENE 49 • A stage at the end of the arena shows Caligula and his family rehearsing a play about the Egyptian gods Osiris and Isis. Caligula has the role of Osiris. Caesonia and their daughter are casually rehearsing. Faux blood that was to be used in the play is spilled accidentally. This is a bad omen, but he is not upset—"This is only a play." He seems to have matured a great deal since the start of his reign. Nearby, Chaerea and Longinus plot the murders. Some writers, including Gore Vidal, speculate that, despite his youth, Caligula sought death. This interesting concept is difficult to understand and is not developed in this story. Supposedly Caligula is happily married and loved his little girl. There is a sense of finality in this rehearsal, however, for it may be a veiled attempt to reconcile with Isis, suggesting that Caligula has done as

In Scene 51a, Chaerea stabs Caligula in a moment reminiscent of his ancestor Julius Caesar's death. Photograph courtesy General Media Communications, Inc., and Robert C. Guccione. Used by permission.

In Scene 51b, Caesonia is lying dead on the steps after trying to help Caligula. Photograph courtesy General Media Communications, Inc., and Robert C. Guccione. Used by permission.

much as he could during his short life, and perhaps some sympathy is returned to him.[38]

SCENE 50 • In the arena, Caligula, in a flowing white toga, walks toward a grand marble staircase, apparently opposite the stage.

SCENE 51 • The white marble staircase and Caligula's white costume are a visual setup for a bloodbath. Caligula runs on ahead of his family and up the staircase, alone. He is intercepted by Chaerea, who stabs him in the abdomen, and other soldiers follow his lead. The killing is premeditated and brutal, with lots of red blood on the white clothing and stairs. Caesonia rushes to his aid, only to be slaughtered also. Their daughter's head is smashed by a soldier who was actually assigned to the murders. Their corpses roll to the bottom of the stairway for the final shots of Caligula's bloody body.

Quickly Caligula's gold crown and imperial ring are passed along to Claudius, and attention focuses on him.[39] As the blood is being washed off the stairs, Incitatus gallops into the arena. Is there symbolism here? Has the spirit of Caligula been freed to live on in immortality? Is he to be remembered throughout time? Has he achieved the impossible? Is he a god after all? The final shot, a faint reminder of the blood-streaked gold coin at the beginning of the movie, now shows blood streaming down Caligula's upside-down face.

As credits roll, the controversies over *Caligula* have just begun.

In Pursuit of Profit

After the completion of the masterwork, it became obvious that an edited edition or editions would be essential if Caligula were to be accepted in theaters worldwide. Restrictions in countries, even those known to be supportive of artistic endeavors, were wide-ranging. The first indications of how severe they might be were the result of Italian censorship. These edits accrued to the *Io, Caligola* edition and are noted in the scene descriptions that follow, with the unrated edition described first, the rated version second, and the *Io, Caligola* version third. The rated edition, edited for cable television, obviously took the biggest loss; excising these scenes completely omitted Caligula's major illness early in his reign and most of its consequences. Because timing is so important to censorship — a few frames may make all the difference — some scenes contain only a few shots of a sexually explicit moment and may be merged with similar moments.

Plot Structures

Typically, a film with linear or chronological structure has an initial situation or exposition describing the protagonist(s) in action sequences. Sec-

In Scene 51c, Caligula's family is murdered and the bodies roll down the steps. Courtesy Photofest.

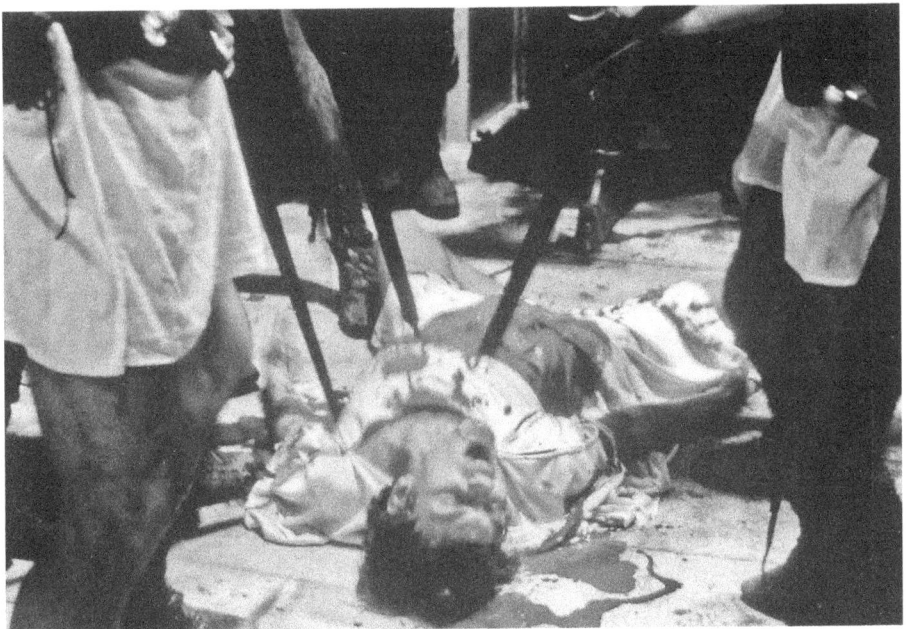

In Scene 51d, the final shot is a close-up of Caligula's upside down bloodied face. Courtesy Photofest.

ond, the protagonist runs into a problem with the antagonist(s). This problem gets bigger in a continuum of complications known as "rising action." Third, the protagonist eventually reaches a point at which he or she (or they) seem unable to resolve the problem. This is the crisis. Fourth, usually following quickly, the protagonist's problem will be resolved favorably or unfavorably. This is the climax. Fifth, with the resolution revealed, the protagonist may be shown as he or she lives happily or dies—the falling action.

In *Caligula,* Caligula is introduced in Scenes 1–13 (exposition), he becomes emperor in a series of actions and is overwhelmed in Scenes 14–32 (rising action), he cannot resolve the main problems he faces because of a growing conspiracy in Scenes 33–46 (crisis), he is assassinated in Scenes 47–50 (climax), and Claudius becomes emperor in Scene 51 (falling action).

Layered over this plot structure are the demands of adult filmmaking that require scenes resulting in physical orgasms. In other words, a dual climax is necessary: one to satisfy adult fulfillment (in Scene 44) and a second climax to meet traditional narrative requirements (in Scene 50). It might be said that a third layer is imposed on this structure, also. It involves the director's theory, applying the logic of utopia in Scenes 1–13 (the murder of Tiberius), the logic of power in Scenes 14–35 (the murder of Proculus), and the logic of folly in Scenes 36–51 (the assassination of Caligula). The unrated edition of *Caligula* provides these necessities.

A minimal synopsis of the scenes as they appear on the screen for the unrated, rated, and *Io, Caligola* versions follow, illustrating the extensive attempt to marry traditional story and sexually explicit scenes. Note the fleeting multitude of shots and scenes. Parentheses are used to indicate lapsed time within the scene; for example, (01) indicates one minute into the scene. My comments are in brackets. Screen credits follow.

Caligula. Unedited, Unrated. Letterbox, Scenario and Credits. Twentieth Anniversary Edition. 1979/1991. Color/156 minutes.

Titles. 01:00	PAGAN ROME 37 AD–41 AD
	Music: Drumbeats with faint chorus humming.
	WHAT SHALL IT PROFIT A MAN IF HE SHOULD GAIN THE WHOLE WORLD AND LOSE HIS OWN SOUL. MARK 8:36 [Printed on full screen]
Scene 1. 02:30	Forest. Shepherds tend sheep. Two white horses graze. Caligula and his sister Drusilla, semi-nude (one breast shows), wear white tunics. They run; he kisses her breast and swings her over his lower torso to Khachaturian's *Spartacus*.
Titles. 00:20	Caligula gold coin with blood streaks on the face. Caligula voice-over: "I have existed from the morning of the world ... I am no man and so I am a god."
Credits. 01:45	Bob Guccione and Penthouse Films International present
	Malcolm McDowell
	Teresa Ann Savoy
	Helen Mirren
	and Peter O'Toole in
	CALIGULA
	[Prokofiev's *Romeo and Juliet* begins.]
	with John Steiner, Guido Mannari, Paolo Bonacelli, Leopoldo Trieste, Giancarlo Badessi, Mirella Dangelo
	introducing Anneka Di Lorenzo and Lori Wagner
	featuring Adriana Asti
	with John Gielgud as Nerva
	Art Director Danilo Donati
	Director of Photography Silvano Ippoliti

4. Editions of Caligula

Film Editor Nino Baragli
Production Manager Mario Di Blase
Original Music by Paul Clemente
Musical excepts from works by
Aram Khachaturian and Sergei Prokofiev
Adapted from an original screenplay by
Gore Vidal
A Bob Guccione Franco Rossellini production
Principal Photography by Tinto Brass
Editing by the Production
Additional scenes directed and photographed by
Giancarlo Liu and Bob Guccione

Caligula. Edited, R-Rated, Letterbox, Scenario, and Credits. Twentieth Anniversary Edition. 1979/1991. Color/102 minutes.

Titles. 01:00	Same as unrated edition.
Scene 1. 02:00	Same narrative content, although some shots may vary slightly.
Titles. 00:20	Same.
Credits. 01:45	Same.

Io, Caligola: In Italian, Letterbox, Scenario, and Credits. Felix Cinematografica. 1984, Color/124 minutes.

Titles. 00:10	Minerva Video Gruppo Curti Comunicazione
Scene 1.	Omitted.
Title & Credits. 02:10	A great hall. Mask of Tiberius lying in state [Scene 14]. Narrator voice-over. Full names on full screen. Music begins. McDowell, Savoy, Mirren, O'Toole IO, CALIGOLA with Steiner, Mannari, Bonacelli, Trieste, Badessi, D'Angelo with the participation of Asti, with Gielgud in the role of Nerva Adapted from an original screenplay by Gore Vidal Dialogue for the second edition by Franco Rossellini

Director of Photography Ippoliti
Edited by Enzo Micarelli
Scenery Costumes Designer Donati
Musical excerpts by Kathcaturian, Prokofiev, Renzo Rossellini
Produced by Franco Rossellini, Bob Guccione for Felix Cinematografica s.r.l., Penthouse Films International
Principal Photography by Tinto Brass
Edited by the Production
Director of Production Sergio Galiano
Post Production Coordinator Enzo Natale
A Production by Franco Rossellini[40]

Scene 2. Unrated 02:15	Dissolve to Caligula's bedroom. Caligula, with the light beard of a teenager, is dressed in a blue [or white] tunic; Drusilla wears a white tunic with perhaps a thong. They are in bed discussing her sex life (her relations with her husband). Guard commander Macro interrupts them; Drusilla hides. Macro tells Caligula that Emperor Tiberius has summoned him. Caligula inquires about his wife, whom Caligula has promised to marry after their divorce. Macro leaves. Drusilla says she will follow Caligula.	
Rated 01:45	Same. Omitted are some shots of Caligula and Drusilla in bed.	
Io, Caligola 00:30	Scenes are substituted. Caligula, dreaming, and Drusilla are in bed. A bird is caught in a mesh drape. Caligula is horrified. Caligula's somersault is omitted.	
Scene 3. Unrated 00:45	Exterior, road. Caligula in a sedan chair passes mostly naked men working. Soldiers are in tunics and breastplates. Macro warns Caligula about Senator Nerva, Tiberius's tutor.	
Rated 00:30	Same with less nakedness.	
Io, Caligola 00:45	Insert of an unidentified rock island and sounds of waves. Scene follows as above.	
Scene 4. 01:25	Dissolve to hallway to the bath. Caligula is greeted by Nerva, who hates him. Nerva complains about the deaths of his colleagues in Rome. Whipping and screams are heard faintly in the background.	

Rated 01:20	Same.
Io, Caligola 01:25	Same.
Scene 5. Unrated 06:45	Interior bath. Caligula descends to a large pool. Women breast-feeding babies, nude young men and women called "fishies," guards, and slaves of the empire surround the pool. Tiberius arises from the water and asks Caligula to perform a dance from childhood when soldiers nicknamed him "Little Boots." The fishies, with close-up shots of genitalia, join Tiberius in the pool, while a reluctant Caligula dances. (02) An unidentified Claudius enjoys the activities. Tiberius and the fishies get out of the pool. (02:30) Then he dresses behind a drape held by servants. Tiberius tells Caligula he has let him live and asks Nerva to help mold Caligula into an emperor. Nerve says Tiberius is the third emperor after Julius and Augustus Caesar. Tiberius needs a successor. (04) Gemellus, a blood grandson, is a teenager; Caligula is a grandson by adoption, and Claudius is mentally challenged. (05) Claudius is present when Tiberius says he is "nursing a viper in Rome's bosom." Caligula dumps Claudius in the pool, as they leave.
Rated 5:30	Same with less nudity.
Io, Caligola 06:45	Same as unrated.
Scene 6. Unrated 10:00	Upper chamber with three levels in the background. Tiberius ascends to a large chamber where a soldier is being punished for drinking. Macro ties his penis with the soldier's bootlaces and a bladder of wine is poured into his mouth. (01) Accompanied by a black female slave, Tiberius and Caligula pass "speaking statues," slaves of the empire, (02) engaged in suggested and actual sex acts—masturbation, snake fetish, intercourse, and anal finger penetration. (03) Some freaks have multiple body parts such as eyes or hands. Caligula claims the people love Tiberius, but he says, "No. They fear me, and that is much better." (04) They return to the helpless soldier, whom Tiberius stabs in the abdomen with a sword; wine gushes from the wound. Macro cuts off his genitals to feed the dogs. (05–06) These visuals of sex and violence tend to overwhelm

Tiberius' references to his years of service to the state. The people are "wicked beasts," he insists, but recommends that Caligula continue to serve them. Tiberius stamps documents. (07) The senate is the natural enemy of any Caesar, he says, and he knows everything that is going on. (08)

Gemellus arrives. Tiberius offers a poisoned drink to Caligula, but Caligula offers it first to Gemellus. Tiberius's slave drinks it and dies. (09) As he leaves with Gemellus, Tiberius predicts that Caligula will kill Gemellus and someone will kill Caligula. Alone, Caligula stamps documents as though he were emperor.

Rated 07:20	Omitted are the soldier's punishment and most of the "speaking statues" performing sex.
Io, Caligola 05:45	Omitted are most of the soldier's punishment and over one-half of the "speaking statues" sequence, including normal and abnormal female genitalia, Macro tying a bootlace on a soldier's penis, medium close-ups of breasts, a penis, and a female using a dildo, a female handling a penis, a pan shot of a woman's vulva, a woman around an erect penis, a group orgy, and male penetration. Tiberius's voice-over dialogue concerns nymphs and satyrs.
Scene 7. Unrated 04:00	Caligula's bedroom. Caligula awakens from a dream. He recalls Tiberius's threat to perhaps kill him, just as he may have killed his family. He is with Drusilla, whom he wants to make queen. (01) He is frightened by a bird caught in the drapes. Drusilla eases his mind by saying that Gemellus is too young, Claudius is regarded as incompetent, and Tiberius is too old. (3) Later, Ennia, Macro's wife, comes in while Caligula finishes his first shave. Now that Caligula is a man, Ennia urges him to be the master of his destiny. He grabs her breasts and she screams. (04)
Rated 01:05	Omitted is the first part of the scene; the shaving scene with Ennia is retained.
Io, Caligola 02:00	Scene is similar to above.
Scene 8. Unrated 01:00	Nerva's bath. Nerva has slit his wrists and is bleeding to death. He hates what his life has become. Tiberius tries to save him, but he is too late.

4. Editions of Caligula   173

Rated 00:20	Same.
Io, Caligola 00:20	Same.
Scene 9. Unrated 00:30	Caligula's bedroom. Caligula hears the commotion and goes to Nerva's bath.
Rated 00:30	Same.
Io, Caligola 00:30	A wide transition shot of the bath includes Macro and Ennia.
Scene 10. Unrated 03:00	Nerva's bath. Nerva refers to Caligula as a "reptile." Nerva says he watched Tiberius murder his family. Tiberius says he has always been surrounded by enemies, then he exits. Caligula asks Nerva about death and whether he sees Isis. Nerva says nothing is happening. Caligula calls him a liar and drowns him.
Rated 02:50	Same.
Io, Caligola 03:00	Same.
Scene 11. Unrated 04:00	Upper chamber of the bath. Morning. Some men and women from the sex slave displays have been raped, tortured, hanged, or murdered with stakes or swords, crucified, or killed while suspended in a sling. (01) Chores begin to clean up this violent, brutal scene. Caligula sees the cruelty; Charicles, a physician, tells him that Tiberius is near death. (02) To gain his loyalty Caligula kisses Macro on the mouth, and Macro swears his allegiance to Caligula by putting his fist over an open flame.
Rated 00:50	The first part of the scene is shortened; the second half is omitted.
Io, Caligola 03:00	The first-half horrors in the unrated edition last thirty seconds. Omitted are a shot of a bloody vulva; a long shot of a hermaphrodite's genitals; a close-up of a nude dead female being carried by a clothed man; a man's head in a cage; a long shot of chained nude females; a medium shot of a multi-eyed, multi-mouthed figure next to a penis sculpture; a male dwarf; a medium shot of a penis;

shots of a dwarf and four other men wearing
gold belts and genital pouches; a long shot of three
nude women; a medium close-up of a female
posterior; women cleaning stairs and a walk;
chained animals; a medium shot of women with
large breasts that bounce as they trot; a long shot
of a nude male tied to an upright post; a man leading
a horse; a long shot of nude women cleaning a walk
while men are clothed; women carrying amphorae;
four men bathing in blood; a close-up of Caligula's
reaction; blood spatters on a wall; a close-up of a
wedge penetrating an unseen body; a medium shot
of a spiked pole; a close-up of a bloody penis; a
medium shot of a vulva on a rope spiked with spurs;
a long shot of women whipped in a suspended swing.
Total running time is about two minutes. The second
part of the scene is retained.

Scene 12. Unrated 00:10	Nearby room. Claudius rolls dice while Gemellus watches.
Rated 00:10	Same.
Io, Caligola 00:10	Same.
Scene 13. Unrated 06:00	Tiberius's bedroom. Tiberius seems near death and so relatives, a doctor, and servants are present. Caligula motions to Macro to make them leave. Caligula tries to pull Tiberius's imperial ring off his finger. Tiberius awakes, demands the ring back; Caligula refuses and is about to kill Tiberius. Instead, Macro strangles Tiberius by putting a black mesh scarf over his head, so his final agony is seen. Caligula knows Gemellus has seen the killing. Afterward, Caligula tells Gemellus they must love each other.
Rated 06:00	Same.
Io, Caligola 06:00	Same.
Scene 14. Unrated 04:30	A great hall. A mask of Tiberius lies in state. Caligula is lord of the world, Drusilla says. Everyone is dressed in black with gold designs on cloaks and robes. Caligula accepts the emperor's title from the senators. He learns

4. Editions of Caligula

	that Tiberius was not popular. To enhance his own popularity, he declares general amnesty and gives a bonus to the soldiers. The senate names Claudius a fellow counsel and Caligula accepts Gemellus as his son and heir by adoption. Caligula forces a reluctant senate to swear allegiance to him and Drusilla. Macro warns Caligula about Gemellus.
Rated 05:00	Same.
Io, Caligula 05:00	Same.
Scene 15. Unrated 01:30	Dissolve to Caligula's palace bedroom. Viewed through a scrim, Caligula and Drusilla make love while being spied upon through the open mouth of a large, wall-mounted, sculptured medallion.
Rated 01:30	Same.
Io, Caligola 01:30	Same.
Scene 16. Unrated 00:50	Room behind the medallion. Two men are engaged in fellatio lasting fifteen seconds. Caligula chases them out, while Drusilla suggests through the hole in the wall that Caligula should get rid of Macro rather than Gemellus.
Rated 00:30	The fellatio is unrecognizable.
Io, Caligola 00:30	About five seconds of male-on-male fellatio is in progress, then a penis shot, and a cutaway to Drusilla at the medallion before Caligula chases them out.
Scene 17. Unrated 03:10	Exterior, arena corridor. The medallion motif appears on the walls. In front of the imperial guard, Caligula, dressed in red robes trimmed in gold, tells Gemellus to name the killer of Tiberius. Gemellus names Macro. Macro is arrested by Chaerea, whom Caligula promotes to commander of the guards.
Rated 03:10	Same.
Io, Caligola 03:10	Same.
Scene 18. Unrated 01:50	Caligula's bedroom. Caligula and Drusilla are present when two men present cases over land rights. Caligula makes a capricious judgment.

Rated	Omitted.
Io, Caligola	Omitted.
Scene 19. Unrated 03:20	Elsewhere in the palace. Men ejaculate into a cup to provide a beauty treatment for Ennia; Caligula urinates at the edge of the room. Ennia is told that the senate has authorized Macro's death, and Caligula confirms Chaerea as commander of the guards. Ennia spits in his face and he banishes her to Gaul.
Rated	Omitted.
Io, Caligola 02:45	The real ejaculations and Caligula's urinating are omitted
Scene 20. Unrated 01:50	Palace room. Drusilla tells Caligula that he must marry a respectable lady of the senatorial class; he wants to marry her. She insists as she grabs his covered genitals.
Rated 01:50	Same.
Io, Caligola 01:35	Same.
Scene 21. Unrated 03:30	The atrium in Drusilla's house. The priestesses of Isis are meeting. Disguised as a woman, Caligula looks for a wife. Caesonia scatters rose petals. Livia, a virgin engaged to Proculus, (01) a soldier, appeals to Caligula, but he picks the divorced Caesonia, whom Drusilla calls the most promiscuous woman in Rome. (2) The three minutes of lesbian sex acts, including masturbation, are mostly suggested rather than explicit.
Rated 01:45	Omitted is some nudity and all sexual activity.
Io, Caligola 02:00	Omitted are a medium shot of women half-lying in a shallow pool and shots of caressing, massaging breasts, vulvas, and kissing; close-ups of two women kissing, of breasts, of masturbation, a medium shot of kissing, close-ups of a woman, a vulva, a long shot of the group; and Caligula standing with Drusilla. Total running time is about fifty seconds. An overhead shot of the pool shows eunuchs sitting between the columns.
Scene 22. Unrated 02:30	Altar of Isis. The horned Egyptian idol is in an adjacent area. Caligula has anal sex with Caesonia, which is limited to a side view of her buttocks. (02) Clothing covers the action.

Rated	Omitted.
Io, Caligola 02:00	The sexual activity is covered by clothing or omitted.
Scene 23. Unrated 02:25	Roman arena. From his emperor's box, wearing a purple satin tunic and gold cloak, Caligula throws eggs at victims. His entourage also throws eggs. Caesonia is led around on a leash to assure her faithfulness. Macro is decapitated by a whirling blade under a wall-like machine that cuts off heads protruding from the ground. (02) Proculus and Livia are seen. Longinus arranges for Caligula to attend their wedding party.
Rated 02:20	Same, except the decapitation of Macro is omitted.
Io, Caligola 03:20	Macro's decapitation is omitted. Added is a challenge in the arena that Proculus survives.
Scene 24. 03:00	Wedding banquet hall. Large phallic symbols are present. Dressed in red-orange, Caligula and his retinue are greeted by Proculus and family. (01) Caligula says he wants to bestow his blessing. (03)
Rated 03:00	Same.
Io, Caligola 03:00	Same.
Scene 25. Unrated 04:30	Kitchen. In a room behind the banquet hall Caligula rapes Livia and checks to see if she bleeds like a virgin. She does. (02:30) He greases his hand, the one wearing the imperial ring, to fist the naked Proculus. There are no penetration shots of either action.
Rated 00:30	Caligula's intentions are established and concluded, but the actual rapes are omitted.
Io, Caligola 02:30	Livia is raped but only the intent and outcome with Proculus are established. The rape is shot as a close-up of Caligula's face. Livia cries, Caligula makes a blood check, there is a transition to Proculus and preparation for fisting with imperial ring, Proculus mounts a table, and Proculus's rape is depicted via a close-up on his face. Caligula, as an afterthought, inserts a flower in the grease covering Proculus's posterior.
Scene 26. Unrated 03:30	Caligula's bedroom with the medallion. A stormy night. Caligula is in bed with the nude Caesonia. Gemellus, seen in an adjacent courtyard, is threatening

	to Caligula. Caligula runs into the courtyard, falls, gets up, and does his "boots dance" in the nude. Caesonia and Drusilla comfort him. He kisses Drusilla's breasts; Drusilla and Caesonia kiss.
Rated 01:50	Same narrative. Some of the courtyard action and final embrace are omitted.
Io, Caligola 03:00	The scene is like the unrated version with minimum edits.
Scene 27. Unrated 03:00	Scene 26 dissolves to 27. This is noteworthy because Drusilla and Caesonia's caressing is followed by two women, Messalina and Agrippina, engaged in explicit sexual activity in the room behind the medallion. Furnished with a bed, two Penthouse Pets engage in explicit sex consisting of rimming, kissing, cunnilingus, vaginal and anal finger penetration (1:30) that results in erotic tremors. The last shot is an upside-down face shot of a Pet, which somewhat resembles Caligula's final upside-down shot. This similarity is aesthetically undesirable. Edited outtakes show the scene with an audio track of humming and thunder as heard in the opening credits. The print of this Guccione-Lui scene is too dark.
Rated	Omitted.
Io, Caligola	Omitted.
Scene 28. Unrated 06:45	Banquet hall. Caligula rides in on his white horse. Claudius rolls dice and seems to see an omen. Caligula says he will be a god when he is dead. He offers Gemellus some food but is offended when he discovers Gemellus is taking an antidote for poison. Gemellus says it is for fever that is rampant in the city. Gemellus is arrested and will die for treason. Furious, Drusilla calls Caligula an "amateur." He slaps her and she leaves. To enliven the party, Caligula pretends to eat the poisoned food and orders the pregnant Caesonia to dance.
Rated 06:30	Same.
Io, Caligola 06:30	Same.
Scene 29. Unrated 01:00.	Quarters for Incitatus. Caligula, alone with his horse, vomits from fever

4. Editions of *Caligula*

Rated	Omitted.
Io, Caligola	Same as unrated version.
Scene 30. Unrated 00:15	Exterior street. Many people have fever and bodies are being cremated in open fires.
Rated 00:15	Same.
Io, Caligola 00:15	Same.
Scene 31. Unrated 02:45	Caligula's bedroom. A sedated horse and Caligula are in bed together. The doctor and Caesonia are beside the bed. Later, Drusilla arrives. Caligula says he is dying; Drusilla contradicts him. (02) Caligula wants Longinus to write his will.
Rated	Omitted. Caligula's much-debated illness (that may have caused his "madness" resulting in a penchant for cruelty) begins here. All references to this are omitted here and in later scenes.
Io, Caligola 02:00	Caligula's desire to have his will written is omitted.
Scene 32. Unrated 00:30	Courtyard. Caesonia goes to get Longinus, and may have overheard Chaerea say that it is not a good time to kill Caligula, that the people love him and civil chaos might break out.
Rated	Omitted.
Io, Caligola	Omitted.
Scene 33. Unrated 03:00	Caligula's bedroom. Longinus arrives to rewrite Caligula's will. Caligula is about to give the empire to Drusilla; he regrets their quarreling. She gets into bed and Caligula recovers. A man offers his life if he recovers and Caligula accepts it.
Rated	Omitted.
Io, Caligola	Omitted.
Scene 34. Unrated 01:30	Business chamber. Caligula stamps documents. Life is dull.
Rated	Omitted.
Io, Caligola 01:30	Same as unrated edition.

Scene 35. Unrated 04:20	Torture chamber. Proculus is in a sling. Caligula, in a black tunic, stabs him and repeats the questions about death he asked of Nerva. Does Proculus see Isis? (02) Proculus's bleeding body is caressed by women, who then urinate on it. Caligula tells Longinus to give Proculus's genitals to Livia. (03:30) Proculus's penis is cut off and a dog eats it. These acts are explicit and repetitious.
Rated	Omitted.
Io, Caligola 02:30	Reduced torture; no urination or genitalia are shown. Caligula's line about sending Proculus's genitalia to Livia is omitted.
Scene 36. Unrated 00:15	Caligula's bedroom. The bird reappears.
Rated	Omitted.
Io, Caligola 00:15	Same as unrated.
Scene 37. Unrated 03:10	Dissolve to a stage in the palace. Before a crowd Caesonia gives birth to a girl that Caligula prematurely calls a boy. Dressed in white, Caligula plans to celebrate by marrying her and declaring her empress of Rome. But Drusilla is ill with fever and faints. Everyone flees.
Rated 03:10	Same.
Io, Caligola 03:10	Same.
Scene 38. Unrated 05:30	Drusilla's bedroom. Drusilla is dying. Caligula prays to a statue of Isis. Seeing his grief, Caesonia enters and quickly leaves. Drusilla dies. Caligula smashes the idol. (03) Caligula licks Drusilla's nude body, remembering earlier times of happiness in three flashbacks, then carries her to what seems to be a temple and screams. In court Brass said that the original intention was to express the depth of Caligula's pain, not necrophilia. He said that the flashbacks may have prompted the misreading of the scene.
Rated 06:00	Omitted is Caligula licking Drusilla's nude body; other scenes are substituted.
Io, Caligola 06:00	Same as above.

4. Editions of Caligula 181

Scene 39. Unrated 06:20	A street in Rome. Caligula, wearing a blue, hooded cloak, wanders aimlessly; mourning is in effect for a month. He sees a pageant — a living triangle represents society with slaves at the bottom, on higher levels the people, the army, tribunes of the people, and senators, and the emperor at the apex. Playing Drusilla, an actor says, "Let's make love." Caligula knocks over the triangle. He and many street people are put in jail.
Rated 05:30	Basically the same.
Io, Caligola 05:30	Same as above.
Scene 40. Unrated 01:00	Palace chamber. Neither Caesonia nor Longinus know where Caligula is.
Rated	Omitted.
Io, Caligola	Omitted.
Scene 41. Unrated 02:50	A jail holding cell. Caligula joins prisoners. A woman is given cunnilingus. A poor magician named Giant takes valuable items from the woman's genitals. (01:30) He is about to take Caligula's imperial ring, but then he recognizes the ring.
Rated 02:00	Same narrative. The ring-finding trick is omitted.
Io, Caligola 02:00	Same.
Scene 42. Unrated 02:10	Throne room. Caligula, dressed in a green satin cloak and gold breastplate (and accompanied by Giant), returns and forces the senators to declare him a god: "I have existed from the morning of the world ... I am no man, and therefore I am a god." Longinus says Caligula is mad, but the senate confirms him as a god. Caligula's brazen attitude goads the senators into imitating sheep. Despite outrageous acts, the senators tolerate him. Black drapes fall from the ceiling, as mourning for Drusilla ends
Rated 02:10	Same.
Io, Caligola 02:00	Same.

Scene 43. Unrated 01:25	Caligula's bedroom. Caligula has absolute power. Caesonia gives him a scepter. He asks Longinus about the state of the treasury. To improve it, Caligula proposes a brothel.
Rated 01:25	Same.
Io, Caligola 01:25	Same.
Scene 44. Unrated 10:50	A galley built as a brothel. In general, Caligula, in gold lamé, and Caesonia, in red, preside over a busy orgy of partially naked bodies. Caligula sells sex for five gold pieces. Explicit sex acts include brief shots of fellatio, (03) touching genitalia, breast licking, cunnilingus, anal fingering, (05) masturbation and more fellatio (07). Longinus wears a gold metallic toga, and Chaerea is in a silver guard uniform. The two plot Caligula's demise while Caligula chides them about liking boys. (09) Soldiers enter to do a variation of Caligula's boots dance. In the final twenty seconds, a Pet brings one man to climax, as Caligula gives the command for the static ship to sail to Britain.

The sex in this scene is justified as part of the "logic of power" theme. Power exercised here is violent and not pleasureful. This is the scene that requires the most attention if it is to be satisfying to everyone, filmmakers and viewers. Every person needs to know precisely what is expected. Movies are shot in brief segments. For some directors ninety seconds of final screen time is a full day's work. Viewers needed to understand the layout of the galley, and they would have benefited from a few minor cast introductions, as partiers arrived. The shots driving the main continuity involve Caligula, Caesonia, Chaerea, and Longinus; they have the dialogue.

The sex partners, soldiers, dancers, and atmosphere people needed a continuity of their own that blends with the main action. The principal performers energizing the sexual activity are Agrippina and Messalina, but they are not established sufficiently as characters and tend to look alike, making them virtually unidentifiable as leaders of the sex action. When group sex is not blocked specifically, it looks like strangers lost in a miscellany of unrelated body parts. The censor has the job of trying to preserve the narrative, while extracting legally obscene frames.

In addition to the continuity mentioned in Scene 44, the fleeting sex activity on the screen in the unrated

	edition is approximately as follows: close-up of a penis; intercourse in profile (no faces); nude body parts (no faces); medium shots of fellatio; an unknown face; a female's face during anal sex; close-ups of groups of Pets; finger sucking; breasts; penis; kissing women; fellatio by a Pet; faces of two women and a man in cunnilingus; a man and woman having intercourse; a woman giving fellatio; shots of kissing, footlicking; close-ups of anal fingering by a man; and male and female genitalia. The scene moves toward its end with a medium shot of intercourse with a Pet, fellatio by Pets, the entry of soldiers doing Caligula's boots dance, Caligula and Caesonia with arms waving, a close-up of a faceless male ejaculating as cries, laughter, bell ringing, and music intensify in volume and accelerate in pace to a weak visual sex climax and transition to the next scene.
Rated 05:45	Nudity is minimized and explicit sex acts are omitted.
Io, Caligola 04:50	Some women perform fellatio, rimming, anal finger insertion, and fondle a dwarf. Everyone seems to be having fun and participants are often smiling. Two women kiss, Caligula and Caesonia appear with outstretched arms and soldiers enter to dance.
Scene 45. Unrated 02:50	Exterior, river shore. Caligula with Giant continues more strange behavior, a fantasy invasion of Britain located across the river. Papyrus serves as the enemy, for Caligula "must have some proof he conquered Britain." The foot soldiers are naked; the horsemen are not. They charge forth to carry out the emperor's whim.
Rated 01:40	Same except some nakedness is omitted.
Io, Caligola 02:40	No naked soldiers appear at first. Seashells are gathered near a river and forest. Naked soldiers attack papyrus. In his tent of mesh netting, Caligula laughs. Giant is nearby.
Scene 46. Unrated 05:20	Banquet hall. Caligula, dressed in black sequins and gold trim, rides Incitatus into a dining hall where naked slaves serve food and papyrus canes are exhibited. Caesonia warns him of mounting hatred. He repeats Tiberius's line: "Let them hate me, so long as they fear me." To balance the budget, Caligula announces that the property of some senators who failed Rome will be confiscated. They are

	arrested. Caesonia says to watch out for Chaerea. "I think he intends to kill me," he replies.
Rated 03:30	Same.
Io, Caligola 05:00	Same.
Scene 47. Unrated 00:25	Street. Chaerea and others plot to kill Caligula.
Rated 00:25	Same.
Io, Caligola 00:30	Same with some shot variations. Closes on the moon.
Scene 48. Unrated 02:25	Main hall and stairs to the bed chamber. Caligula climbs it; he is exhausted. Caesonia tries to comfort him and a bird appears, frightening her, but Caligula is no longer afraid of the bird.
Rated 02:15	Same.
Io, Caligola 02:25	Same.
Scene 49. Unrated 01:30	Stage, part of the arena. A bird emblem is on Chaerea's tunic. Dressed in white, a happy Caligula and family rehearse a play. Caligula is the Egyptian god Osiris and Caesonia is Isis, who restores Osiris after he has been cut to pieces. Their child is with them. Fake blood for the play is accidentally spilled. Nearby, Chaerea and Longinus plot the demise of Caligula and his family.
Rated 01:30	Same.
Io, Caligola 01:30	Same.
Scene 50. Unrated 00:45	Arena walkway. Caligula and party walk to the grand marble staircase opposite the stage.
Rated 00:45	Same.
Io, Caligola 00:45	Same.

Scene 51. Unrated 04:00	A marble stairway. As he runs up the staircase, Caligula is encountered by Chaerea. Chaerea stabs Caligula in the abdomen with his sword and other soldiers follow his lead. Caesonia comes to his defense. She is killed and the child's head is smashed. Giant is beheaded. Their bodies roll to the bottom of the stairway. Caligula's gold crown and imperial ring are passed on to Claudius, and attention then turns to him. As the stairs are being washed, Caligula's white stallion is released into the arena. The final close-up shot is of blood streaming down Caligula's upside-down face.
Rated 04:00	Same.
Io, Caligola 04:00	Similar to above. The final shot is of Incitatus with Caligula and family in the background.
Credits. Unrated 01:45	Cast (in order of appearance)

Caligula	Malcolm McDowell
Drusilla	Teresa Ann Savoy
Macro	Guido Mannari
Nerva	John Gielgud
Tiberius	Peter O'Toole
Claudius	Giancarlo Badessi
Gemellus	Bruno Brive
Ennia	Adriana Asti
Charicles	Leopoldo Trieste
Chaerea	Paolo Bonacelli
Longinus	John Steiner
Livia	Mirella Dangelo
Caesonia	Helen Mirren
Mnester	Richard Parets
Sudura Singer	Paula Mitchell
Giant	Osiride Pevarello
Proculus	Donato Placido
Director of Post Production	Giancarlo Lui
Unit Manager	Sergio Galiano
Sound Engineer	Claudio Maielli
Dialogue Director	Louise Vincent
Script Continuity	Carla Cipriani
Make-Up	Guiseppe Banchelli
Hair Stylist	Jole Cecchini
First Assistant Director	Piernico Solinas
Casting Directors	Paolo Heusch Robert Tatti
Choreographers	Tito Le Duc Pino Pennesi

Special Effects	Franco Celli
	Marcello Coccia
Architects	Giovanni Natalucci
	Franco Velchi
Set Dresser	Luigi Urbani
Wardrobe Mistress	Gloria Picone Mussetta
Wardrobe Master	Gregorio Simili
Master of Properties	Gianpiero Grassi
Supervising Sound Editor	Winston Ryder
Dialogue Editor	Archie Ludski
Sound Editor	Roger Van Engel
Assistant Editor	Peter Krook
Dubbing Mixers	Gerry Humphreys
	Robin O'Donoghue
Technical Equipment	Cinenoleggio
Costume Rental	Ferani Veste
Shoes	L.C.P. Di Pompei
Wigs	Rocchetti-Carboni
Props	Rancate of Sormani
Accounting	SOC. G.E.S.C.A. SPA
Unit Photographer	Mario Tursi
Special Photographers	Eddie Adams
	Jerry Bauer
	Stan Malinowski
	Claudio Patriarca
Unit Publicists	Walter Alford
	Maria Ruhle
Assistant to the Producers	Leslie Jay

A Penthouse Films International
and Felix Cinematografica S.R.L. Production
Re-recorded at Twickenham Studios, London, England.
Filmed at Dear Studios, Rome, Italy
Copyright Penthouse Films International, LTD
MCMLXXIX
All Rights Reserved

Rated 01:45	Same.	
Io, Caligola 01:00	Same background. Several different credits.	
	Malcolm McDowell	Caligula
	Teresa Ann Savoy	Drusilla
	Helen Mirren	Caesonia
	Peter O'Toole	Tiberius
	John Steiner	Longinus
	Guido Mannari	Macro
	Paolo Bonacelli	Chaerea

Leopoldo Trieste	Charicles
Giancarlo Badessi	Claudius
Mirella D'Angelo	Livia
Adriana Asti	Ennia
John Gielgud	Nerva
Supervisor of Production	Alessandro Mattei
	Augusto Marabelli
Camera Operator	Pino Di Biase
	Enrico Sasso
Wardrobe Mistress	Gloria Picone Mussetta
Sound Engineer	Claudio Maiella
Boom Operator	Giuliano Maibelli
Production Secretary	Carla Cipiani
Makeup	Giuseppe Branchelli
Hair Stylist	Jole Cecchini
Assistant Director	Piernico Solinas
Casting Director	Paolo Heusch
Assistant Casting Director	Roberto Tatti
Assistant Choreographer	Peno Pennesi
Special Effects	Franco Celli
	Marcella Coccia
Architects	Giovanni Natalucci
	Franco Velchi
Set Dresser	Luigi Urbani
Technical Equipment	Cinenoleggio
Costumes	Farani Veste
Footwear	L.C.P. di Pompei
Wigs	Rocchetti-Carbone
Properties	Rancate of Sormani
Accounting	ATA Soc. GESCA S.p.A.
Unit Photographer	Mario Tursi
Unit Publicist	Walter Alford
	Maria Rhule
Dubbing	C.D.
Dubbing Director	Ferruccio Amendola
girato negli studi	Dear International S.p.A.
Titles	V.G. s.r.l.
Editing	Stefano Morandi
Film Inserts	Franco Rossellini
Editing for Current Edition	Idea Cinematografica
IO, CALIGOLA	
scene tagliato[44]	

Cinema Censorship in the Seventies

    The release of *Caligula* signaled the reevaluation of violence, sex, nudity, and language in the movies. What some believe was the second "golden era" of American cinema in the 1970s had come to an end, a time in which great movies addressed great themes—*M*A*S*H* (surviving battlefield and medical bureaucracy in wartime), *Chinatown* (enduring political corruption and incest), *All the President's Men* (forcing a president to uphold the Constitution), *One Flew Over the Cuckoo's Nest* (struggling against inadequate mental health care), *Saturday Night Fever* (fighting intrinsic neighborhood prejudice), *Apocalypse Now* (killing without cause), *Star Wars* (seeking meaning in the universe). The effort to expand artistic freedom with *Caligula*, by combining sexually explicit and violent scenes, was about to be tested on the world stage, not only by censors but by audiences. For *Caligula* to be a success, it had to survive at the box office. As illustrated in the previous analysis, the main story was reduced to getting rid of a leader through assassination. As world censors removed shots and scenes of sexual content, they left most scenes of violence and many of substantial nudity. Foul language was not at question.

The shocking values preserved in *Caligula* were intensified and summarized in its world release, as many critics, distributors, and government censors tried to reshape the inevitable future it signaled. But they could do little. Violence dominated sex on the surface until sex became violence, and then they were shown to be inseparable. The semen in the adult-bordello scene of climax was mirrored by the spilling of blood in the scene of assassination; that is, penis for sword, semen for blood. The parameters for future films would be stretched to more outrageous limits, with additional latitude for language in other kinds of films. The box-office results would soon show the public's preference for the unrated edition of *Caligula*, but, to pacify governments and businesses, edited versions were made available almost immediately. What the public did not know, it would not know. *Caligula* preserved the long-held belief that motion pictures are a business first and an art second.

Ars Longa, Vita Brevis

The outstanding documentary *The Battle Over Citizen Kane* (1996) declares that *Citizen Kane* is as much about the life of Orson Welles as it is about the life of William Randolph Hearst. A similar perspective has been advanced regarding *Caligula:* that it is as much about Bob Guccione as it is about Caligula. Certain comparisons could be made, but not about Guccione and Caligula. Caligula had two father figures who were mentors: Germanicus from whom he learned that being a winner and an entertainer had important public appeal, and Tiberius from whom he learned that distrust and fear were central to survival in a world where conspiracies abound. Caligula lived too short a life to define what he would have become as a leader and he may have suffered from what many refer to today as post–traumatic stress disorder, which in some people is disabling.

If a comparison were to be made, Guccione's life would be closer to that of Tiberius. Not in the alleged pederasty, of course. The comparison lies with building his own empire, merging two New York mansions into his palace, maintaining traditional macho strengths, collecting significant works of art, having and using his own money for independent projects, and maintaining a harem of beautiful women around him. These similarities have some substance, but do not stand up very well because Tiberius and Caligula were politicians and Guccione is an artist, who happened to run a publishing and media empire. As an artist, Guccione would have had more impact if he had spent more time on *Caligula*, but he chose not to. He did not realize that one of his principal claims to lasting fame would be *Caligula* and its impact.

5

RELEASE, HISTORY AND IMPACT

With a smile of acknowledgment, the drumbeats promoting *Caligula* first appeared in *Playboy*, not *Penthouse*, when critic Arthur Knight wrote his annual review "Sex in Cinema" in 1977. An explicit color photograph shows Caligula and Tiberius talking in front of his "Speaking Statues." This placed *Caligula* among such traditional films as *Apocalypse Now*, *The Spy Who Loved Me*, *Equus*, *The Deep*, and Tinto Brass's *Salon Kitty*, in which Teresa Ann Savoy services a Nazi SS officer (Helmut Berger). The adult industry provided an ample collection of hardcore (*Honeypie*), softcore (*Goodbye Emmanuelle*), and parodied current or classical stories (*Shampoo/Blowdry*, *Cinderella*).[1] It could be said that *Caligula*, being placed in such illustrious company, was already accepted as a mainstream motion picture.

During the 1970s and 1980s, big stars and major producers and directors of traditional, theatrical films went on promotional tours. Although the tours were somewhat costly, they did generate excitement for pictures the public may have known little or nothing about. The tours visited heavily populated areas. After Clint Eastwood directed his first film, *Play Misty for Me* (1971), Ronald Neame directed *The Poseidon Adventure* (1972), and Joan Rivers starred in *Rabbit Test* (1978), and a decade later after Charlton Heston directed and acted in *Mother Lode* (1982), Terry Gilliam directed *Brazil* (1985), and actors Matthew Modine, Nicholas Cage, and director Alan Parker wanted recognition for *Birdy* (1985), they personally visited with newspaper critics, radio reporters, television hosts, and sometimes college students.[2]

Alan Pakula's *All the President's Men* (1976) supplied media outlets with one of the best press kits ever assembled. It included several pages of biographies, production notes, black and white 8 × 10-inch glossy photographs, a 35mm film strip showing how the *Washington Post* city room was constructed in Hollywood, a poster, and audiotape interviews with producer

Walter Coblenz, actors Robert Redford and Dustin Hoffman, director Alan Pakula, and designers George Jenkins and Gordon Willis. The objective was to anticipate how the media might be willing to promote the picture if the information were easily available in print, pictures, and sound. The Watergate story was one of the best promoted movies of the period.[3]

Except for Guccione, only a few Pets promoted *Caligula*. Instead, nontraditional methods were used; that is, anything that would create free publicity. The idea was that *Caligula* had enough attention-getting aspects that the media would report them as news, and in the seventies celebrity visits to cities were often news. Concentrating on newsworthy aspects of the film would provide greater public anticipation for its release than paid promotion. Favorable word of mouth comments from the public or "buzz" was always preferred to prepared press releases.

Besides, those who ordinarily would promote the film wanted to distance themselves from it. For the most part they scattered. A disgruntled press denied access during the shooting and some of the actors made few comments. Malcolm McDowell is alleged to have said: "I'd like to think I gave a pretty creditable performance with material that was pretty difficult to get through." In 1979 Helen Mirren's one-line summary was: "It's an irresistible mix of art and genitals." "I've never opened my mouth to denigrate 'Caligula,'" Mirren told the *New York Times*. "I was pretty young when I made that — not physically so much as inexperienced in film. And you know what? It was a great experience. It was like being sent down to Dante's *Inferno* in many ways."[4] By 1979 most of the principals were supposed to be unhappy about the film, their scenes, or some personal details; these comments seem contradictory today. Guccione wanted free publicity and he knew how to get it. With a fiery attitude toward the press, he required reviewers and everyone else to pay the premium ticket price to see it. Members of the press, who often got complimentary passes to review movies, could consider this a news story or an insult and write spiteful comments. The situation was potentially a public relations nightmare. It was another gamble for Guccione.

The Rating Dilemma

Naturally promotion and advertising are supposed to encourage the public to see the picture for reasons that motivate its production — enjoyment, information, and vicarious experience. Previous to the time *Caligula* entered the market, the newspapers became skittish about running advertisements for X-rated or unrated adult films. The *New York Times* said that beginning 1 July 1977, guidelines for pornographic films would be limited to single-column displays up to one inch long. They could include name of the film, cinema location, screening times, and an "adults only" label. Offensive titles or references would be prohibited.

Broadcast media tended to be even more cautious about referring to these films even though the Supreme Court had established its position on obscenity. No amount of promotion could get *Caligula* on television because the networks believed the American public was puritanical. So the battle over broadcast television programs scrubbed them in production. The FCC reported 32,438 complaints about sex on television in 1973 and 11,716 in 1975, with the rate continuing to drop. The public condoned violence, however. "The networks learned their lesson. ABC had retreated so far that it refused to touch R-rated films unless they were first reedited by the producers and rerated by the Motion Picture Association to bring them down to PG or G-rating. In 1974, when ABC aired *Midnight Cowboy*," *American Film* reported, "it cut twenty-three minutes from the original film. Gone were all references to homosexuality, prostitution, and drugs, as well as all profane or even irreverent phrases. A number of scenes crucial to the viewer's understanding of the film's plot were eliminated."[5]

Guccione decided that he did not want *Caligula* labeled "X" by the Motion Picture Association of America so he did not submit it for a rating. An "X" would have prohibited advertising in most newspapers. It might not have been reviewed. Shopping malls would not have allowed its exhibition, and large retail stores would probably not have sold it. "X" meant pornography in 1979, and Guccione thought his picture deserved a rating that described it as suitable for mature adults.

In anticipation of what was to come, he arbitrarily designated *Caligula* "MA," for mature audiences. Today MA is in common use, especially for cablecasting. This was another risk, for the decision could have endangered its place among mainstream feature competitors. Guccione anticipated the new designation that the MPAA agonized over for a decade. As late as 1990, adamantly against adding a new designation, MPAA president Jack Valenti said that over 450 films were rated on an average year. Only two or three films have this problem. "We have to be fair," he insisted, according to reporter Glen Collins. In addition, Valenti said that it would be difficult to distinguish between serious and exploitative films, Collins wrote. "Sometimes the distinctions, say, between 'erotic' and 'porn' are not that easy to judge."[6]

The MPAA concluded that "X" was an inappropriate rating for any serious picture designated for the mainstream theatrical marketplace, but it took little leadership in making this distinction during the eighties. As sales increased profits for the adult and European films that showed greater flexibility in content, the MPAA came up with a new designation for motion pictures containing themes, nudity, sexuality, violence, and situations intended for adults exclusively and not children seventeen and under. "NC-17" was given for the first time to Philip Kaufman's *Henry & June* (1990). The story is based on a diary kept by Anaïs Nin, who has sex with author Henry Miller (whose *Tropic of Cancer* and *Tropic of Capricorn* were published in the United States in 1961, after an obscenity ban of thirty years) and his wife June; however, as Jeff Miller wrote in the *Houston Chronicle*: "Great stretches of this film, sex scenes included (sex scenes especially), are boring enough to make wallpaper come loose from the paste."[7] Whatever sex takes place, if any, happens in the dark. The MPAA motive, in part, in giving the movie an NC-17 was to establish its copyright. Other purposes of ratings are to indicate whether a film is suitable for children, to tempt adults to see it, and to stimulate business. Adults should make their own decisions, which was precisely what Bob Guccione wanted them to do.

Caligula was unique. To be successful it had to get favorable attention from a conservative public that preferred to attend films that did not invade its comfort zone. At the time the public held a mixed view as to whether adults should be allowed to screen and view sexually explicit films; and even if they did, the experience was presented in a shameful context. This was a continuation of the same fight that Hugh Hefner and Guccione had entered by initiating their magazines in previous decades. The objective, beyond the movie's content itself, was to give courage and opportunity for adults to see and enjoy an adult biographical story that contained graphic scenes. *Caligula* purported to expand attendance to sophisticated adults who would find violence and sex realistic and acceptable within the right narrative. *Caligula* emerged from the progress made by pornographic filmmakers to produce sexually explicit pictures that would penetrate the social stigma that kept most adults from seeing such explicit films.

Unquestionably, adult films with interesting and universal themes were improving throughout the 1970s, notably, *Deep Throat* (1972), which has a humorous story claiming everyone has the right to sexual satisfaction; *The Devil in Miss Jones* (1972), which contends that a woman cannot be punished after death for a sex life she did not have while living; *Behind the Green Door* (1973), which shows that a woman can enjoy sex with whomever she chooses and even the voyeurs of the world will get off on her experience; and *The Opening of Misty Beethoven* (1975), which returns to a favorite male theme that a woman needs a master teacher to perfect the art of love. But none of these films came close to having the breakthrough potential of the well-financed *Caligula*.

The so-called "golden age" of pornographic films was six years long. During this period, roughly 1969 to 1975, the industry went from teasing moviegoers to showing them explicit sex in detail. It went from little legal guidance to the Supreme Court's decision on determining obscenity through jury trails. It originated with amateurs from all over the nation, many of whom were refugees from the drug scene on the coasts. Most of the performers were referred to as models, since they had no acting training or perhaps ability. A few models developed reputations for attracting movie fans and could become celebrities by appearing on stage. The changes taking place in the adult movie business seemed slow, but from a larger viewpoint a great deal happened. Directors with artistic sensitivity were emerging and so were a few studios that were able to invest in them. The changes were rough, but they were present. Yet, neither men nor women were welcomed into mainstream theatrical entertainment. Male models were no better off than female stars. While this may seem unusual, it is not, particularly if the duration of a model's career is put into perspective. Whether the actor or model is in adult or traditional films, if he or she has four years of fame and fortune, that means good fortune. From inception to conclusion the model may have a decade or so in the spotlight. This will give the person enough time to use celebrity status to develop another line of work. By the late 1970s few adult models had converted their work into successful business entities. They may have received several hundred dollars per scene, but most of their work had no residual benefits. Seka was one of the earliest adult stars to find a way to be properly compensated for her on-screen work.[8]

The era was one of human discovery, and toward that some believed that abandonment of one's present state of mind in exchange for new perceptions induced by drugs was desirable. Adult stars and many traditional actors were very young, and the effects of narcotics—reinforced by the introduction of increasingly obvious sexual displays in music and dance—established a climate for "letting it all hang out." Hedonistic enjoyment was a good thing. In cinema, adult filmmakers said they wanted respect and freedom of expression most of all.

As the seventies became the eighties, many adult films began with the American flag flying briskly and a voice representing the Free Speech Legal Defense Fund saying: "All Americans are now being faced with a continuing campaign of censorship and harassment by the government at all levels. We are all going through a difficult [time] concerning our personal rights— rights guaranteed to us by the First Amendment...."[9] *Caligula* symbolized the transition from the 1970s to the 1980s. If *Caligula* proved to be the crossover film everyone hoped for, the more the adult and traditional picture companies could broaden their parameters. Naturally, a lot of hope for greater freedom of expression was riding on *Caligula*. If *Caligula* took in a lot of money, it was widely believed that an amalgam of adult/traditional movies might follow. "The public would have lost the First Amendment if it hadn't been for adult producers fighting for it from 1970 to 1985. Mainstream films benefited, but none of the big studio guys wanted to be associated with pornography," according to Bob Augustus, an editor for *Caligula*. The Adult Film Association of America had a membership of 285 and had already been an active voice for thirteen years, fighting off the censorship threats of Citizens for Decency through Law (CDL). More than 135 higher quality X-rated films were released in 1982 to 894 adult theaters. The adult theaters held up well despite television, cable, and video distribution. The AFAA promotion said, "Videocassettes have replaced the stereo as the instrument of seduction in the 1980s."[11]

Caligula was not just another film; it was poised to become a seminal feature picture in the history of cinema.

Caligula's Premieres

Caligula made its first appearance in a private screening in May 1979, in a 210-minute, nonjudged preview at the Cannes Film Festival in France, referred to in *Variety*.[12] Having settled his legal disputes with Tinto Brass and Gore Vidal during the previous two years, Bob Guccione debuted the public viewing of *Caligula* in Italy on 14 August 1979. After a week authorities thought it was too explicit and it was withdrawn from the theater for reediting.[13] For its debut in the United States, *Caligula* opened on 21 October in Hollywood. *Variety* said: "With the biggest investment ever in porn to play with, Tinto Brass in a creative fit of paranoiac obsession, sifts through the pages of first century Rome under syphilitic Tiberius and epileptic Caligula to demonstrate the unlimited baseness of the human condition [from a story by Gore Vidal]." The highly respected *Les Cahiers du Cinéma* said that *Caligula* had been "amputated of 20 minutes by censorship" prior to screening. Then it went into a scathing review: "What could be a very good show at 'L'Elysée-Montmartre' [a cabaret where the Can-Can was first created] becomes an absolutely infect [sic] product on the big screen. The audio is incredibly hard-pressed, as if audience members were all deaf. For two hours, *Caligula* distills a profound boredom: no progression, some zoom outs in order to show off the scenery and processions of erratically edited close-ups." The review concludes, "Caligula reenacts pagan cinematic ritual: The one where bodies are sacrificed and offered to the scenery."[14]

Ronald Reagan had just taken office as president of the United States, and a more conservative attitude was sweeping the country. As a protective measure, Guccione asked the U.S. attorney general's office to view the film; it assured him *Caligula* would not be prosecuted at the federal level, but local governments could file suit against it and that could hurt national distribution. Even though Guccione said he would support them, most local exhibitors did not want to deal with public disapproval or the expense of a possible trial.[15]

Displeased, but undaunted after the four years of investing time and money in it, Guccione rented the Trans Lux East Theatre, changed the name to the Penthouse East, and premiered *Caligula* on 1 February 1980 in New York City. I attended on opening night or soon thereafter. The 516-seat theater seemed intimate, and the line ran down the block, impressively four abreast. Tickets were at a premiere price of $7.50, which hinted at the inflationary prices they would rise to in years ahead. No one was supposed to attend free. I was excited to see an adult film produced in the mainstream Hollywood tradition and exhibited in a respectable cinema. On screen *Caligula* is a flood of incredible activity that appeared to be more violent than sexual, and I thought the audience was trying to absorb it. The graphic scenes flowed from the screen in such rapid succession that the story tended to be overwhelmed between explicit moments, which the color film seemed to capture in garish saturation, but without precise definition. There is a lot to absorb and to fill in if the viewer is not familiar with the story. Afterward, I did not hear much discussion about the movie. Perhaps viewers were mulling it over privately. What had we seen?

Of course, this was not the first time a premium price was charged for a sensational film. That honor goes to David Wark Griffith. He charged $2.00 for viewing his blockbuster, the most controversial film in cinema history, *The Birth of a Nation* (1915). It caused riots and gave Griffith international fame. Films have been picketed and I have attended one or two movies that were interrupted because of a bomb threat (including *The Last Temptation of Christ* in 1988). Crowds have been commonplace at theaters where promotion has been effective and the word has been that stars might appear. *Caligula* did not create riots, nor were there bomb threats. Public protests were organized. Neither the adult nor the traditional film industry came forward to support Guccione's attempts to bring motion pictures in line with the cultural tsunami forming on the horizon.

Critics in Los Angeles and New York struggled to write a fair assessment of the film. It was difficult to tell whether they did not like the movie, pornography, or Guccione (sometimes described as "a tough man," "difficult to like"), or were just trying to be witty at the picture's expense. No question the critics generally panned *Caligula*. It was credited as a massive undertaking, a generally accurate story, a fine performance by Malcolm McDowell, and having lavish settings and costumes by Danilo Donati. Mixed complaints put an unflattering spin on just about everything. Most of the dissatisfaction was

The Caligula poster (one-sheet). Photograph courtesy General Media Communications, Inc., and Robert C. Guccione. Used by permission.

with the degrees of sex and violence, much of the editing, some performances, sound quality, and accoutrements that were somehow confused with Guccione's personal disco nightlife in New York. Critics have no responsibility for evaluating a movie based on the producer's expressed objectives. Instead, they tend to assess it on whether *they like it* based on their memory in seeing hundreds of films, knowledge of the industry, background in journalism, research in film history, and insight regarding the cultural values of the nation.

Even so, at the end of the first eighteen days the Penthouse East Theatre had taken in over two hundred twenty-two thousand dollars; in other words, about thirty thousand people had seen it. This was a respectable start.[16]

World Distribution

Between 1980 and 1984 the unrated edition of *Caligula* was released in most of Europe, Australia, Canada, South America, and Southeast Asia. Viewing was linked to the age of consent in each country. In Sweden that was fifteen, in other Scandanavian countries and France that was sixteen; elsewhere it was eighteen. It was not released in Russia until 1993.

Doggedly, Guccione kept *Caligula* in the marketplace throughout the 1980s by running it continuously in New York and a few theaters he owned or leased. Much of the highly touted cost of *Caligula* would be written off through tax credits and overseas production. This strategy enabled him to regain his original costs by mid-decade, said one distributor. No matter what the critics wrote about the movie, Guccione had a world press of his own. He had the advantage of promoting *Caligula* through *Penthouse,* having estimated worldwide monthly sales at 5,350,000. Franco Rossellini had joined the company as associate international publisher for the magazine. In May 1980 *Penthouse* ran a special *Caligula* issue. It featured a pictorial on its production, a long interview with Guccione, some tie-ins to men's fashions, and many humorous cartoons on ancient Rome. In June a photo layout featured Anneka Di Lorenzo and Lori Wagner in their love-making scene that Giancarlo Lui and Guccione shot separately.[17]

The magazine layout illustrated aesthetic differences between watching the women in motion and viewing them in still pictures. The women, wearing elaborate mid–first century Roman wigs, tended to lose their individuality and their personal identity; nevertheless, they appeared to have a spontaneous and delightful sexual encounter. One of them assured the media that the sex was real. The still photo display allows the reader to take in the ambiance in which their escapade occurs; it looks posh. By contrast, the context for the moving picture sequence is clandestine, the bedroom setting is not as lush, the women do not seem to be as relaxed as they are in the still poses. The stills concentrate on only smiling and happy faces; the movie's sex action feels strained. The frozen moments are romantic glimpses of their encounter, the moving reactions include grimaces and perhaps painful expressions. In order for the climax to be visually expressive, the women engage in a shaking movement, to graphically demonstrate the orgasm supposedly surging through them. The *Penthouse* photo spread is prettier, more romantic and inviting than the two-day cinematic experience, partly because it goes by so quickly, and the viewer cannot retrieve an act, a glance, or a touch in motion that is reserved for the pages of *Penthouse*. The still photographs could be retouched, framed, and adjusted with meticulous care, especially when lighting is critical. These are noteworthy differences in the nature of media.

The Metamorphosis of Movie Men

In 1980 three different types of male movie stars appeared on the screen. John Travolta in *Urban Cowboy* represented the past, a macho man. Richard Gere in *American Gigolo* signified the future, the emergence of the metro man. Malcolm McDowell in *Caligula* served as the transition.

Urban Cowboy tells the story of a young fellow who moves from central Texas to Pasadena, Texas, to find a better life in the oil business. Other than his new job, his principal place of interest is the honky tonk — Gilley's. Country star Mickey Gilley owned the Pasadena hangout that attracted a few thousand true believers in the Texas way of life on weekends. They were good old boys, rednecks maybe looking for a little exercise, a fight, and loads of beautiful young girls who liked to dance the Texas two-step and play stupid. The drunken guys, who *were* stupid, tried to hold on to the reins of a rodeo-styled mechanical bull designed to throw their ass into a bale of hay. Around two in the morning the drunken boys and girls paired off, and each pair got into a truck with a shotgun in the back parked in the rut-filled dirt lot outside. This was the traditional life.

An American gigolo, who makes his money as an escort to very wealthy older women, has to keep himself in excellent condition so that he looks handsome and can maintain his sexual stamina. Julian Lay is a very nice guy who may get thrown out of bed, not off a mechanical bull. He is a metro man, a narcissist, who spends his money on an enormous wardrobe, not because he needs it, but because he wants to look perfect. He does not get involved with the women he goes out with. He knows that intimacy leads to responsibilities and he does not want any. He insists on being a beautiful, unobtainable free spirit who is paid a lot of money for a short ride. In one scene, Julian, nude, having met a client's expectations, gazes out a venetian blind that stripes his genitalia with shadows, suggesting that he is in an illegal profession; but to the mainstream movie business this picture shows that it is just a few frames away from being an explicit, adult sex film.

What is basic to these characters is that they make bad choices, behave badly, and fail to use their male assets effectively. The cowboy gets his girl in the end, but the escort is framed for rough sex ending in a murder and it looks like he will lose his freedom to a wealthy, older woman who is willing to save him from prison. What is perceived of the future is the descent of the macho American male, who did well enough in previous decades helping women get equality and control. In the 1980s, the male was yielding his essence — that which made him who he was — to the female. "Today's sensitive heroes cook, clean, and take care of junior while the women are out of the picture," wrote Dave Kehr in *American Film*.[18] Ten years after the Vietnam war a reevaluation of what makes a real man began in print media, according to Samuel Osherman in his 1985 book *Finding Our Fathers*.[19]

A macho man does not need a woman to succeed. And at first Caligula does not need a woman. He just uses her for political or sexual reasons. Then he finds someone who addresses his political responsibilities and gives him a child before they are married to prove she is up to the task. Along the way to fatherhood, he realizes that she is nurturing to him and to the child. The emperor and the gigolo illustrate the transition in contrast from a young man who managed an empire to the dependent fellow who could not manage his own life. Of course, the traditional cowboy gets his girl and rides into the sunset, albeit in a pick-up truck. The cultural change that was taking place in 1980 was huge, and *Caligula* — in its story, its production, and its future — would have complex ramifications for the movie industries and in showing what it means to be male in the decades that follow. A 2007 study shows that fathers do 67 percent more housework and 50 percent more childrearing than they did in 1982, according to *Details*.[20] Is this a good thing, the manly thing to do?

Fortuna

In 1981 the goddess Fortuna must have smiled on Guccione. Business was never better. "Ten years ago, the approach was to stick a picture of a pretty girl in the ad and hope for the best, budgets are increasing. There's more adult product out there."[21] Penthouse announced plans for cable television. This strategy enabled Guccione to feature plays on the Penthouse Entertainment Network/Pet Network, along with advertising and promoting Telemine, an adult-oriented movie channel. Later, Playboy and two other adult channels — Eros (softcore films) and Private Screenings (all movies) — were competition.[22] Fortunately for Guccione the perfect technological achievement — the videotape recorder and playback — made it possible to buy or rent *Caligula* for private viewing. Adults no longer had to go to adult theaters across the country to see it. As quickly as possible the adult industry switched from film to videotape production; adult theaters were in decline and their existence was often being challenged by local city governments and self-appointed moralists who could claim they had a constituency but never were forced to prove it.

As *Caligula* went into national theatrical distribution, resistance to the film was apparent. In Houston, for example, the Texas Center for Media Awareness (formerly Morality in Media in Texas) became sufficiently active to help write and get two anti-obscenity laws passed in the Texas Legislature. The Texas Center for Media Awareness encouraged the formation of chapters to stop "pornography" and "offensive media" that were threatening "to our family, to our community, to our nation, and to our civilization." As the screening debut date of 16 October 1981 neared, it urged people to contact the prosecuting attorney and the Houston Police Department's vice division. Conferences on obscenity, pornography, and violence were held, and *Caligula* was "temporarily halted in the state of Texas." An unsigned pamphlet was circulated claiming: "Caligula — This movie, if unopposed, can legally establish the standards for the City of Houston."[23]

This was not really true. Jury trials of adult films throughout the seventies and eighties were shaping the community standards. *Caligula* premiered at the River Oaks Theatre, a specialty art house run by the Samuel Goldwyn Company, later a Landmark Theatre. Houston artist Rika Waldrop, attending opening night, had this impression: "I thought of blood. It was like a Caravaggio, lush." Her reference was to painter Michelangelo Amerighi Caravaggio (1565?–1610) who art historian Helen Gardner said selected his subjects from the lowest classes, painting figures in scenes with a realism that at times approaches the photographic. "This chiaroscuro of strong concentrated lighting and sinking all else in shadows," Gardner wrote, was "violent."[24] Then there were the sculptures of Lorenzo Bernini (1598–1680), a consummate portraitist who captured emotional intensity. His *Portrait of Constanza Buonarelli* "caught a transient expression which we are sure must have been most characteristic of his sitter," and for his altar piece *The Vision of St. Theresa* he "cast aside all restraint" to reveal "the saint swooning in ecstasy" when an angel pierced her heart, or some say a bit lower down, with a flaming arrow. "If we compare the face of his swooning saint with any work done in previous centuries, we find that he achieved an intensity of facial expression which until then was never attempted in art," according to E. H. Gombrich in *The Story of Art*.[25] Bernini and Caravaggio's masterpieces must have influenced Guccione, Vidal, and Brass, artists themselves, before the film-production process adulterated their efforts.

Homosexual Influences on *Caligula*

Caligula does not appear to have been a homosexual; he was married four times between ages eighteen and twenty-seven because he was desperate to produce an heir. After he came to power, he drove out the homosexuals living on Capri, but he did have shameless homosexual experiences within the context of pagan life.

In an article on venereal disease that appeared in a 1977 issue of *Hustler*, a reference was made to a mysterious disease noticed in San Francisco's gay community. The discussion that this new disease received in the press was linked to easy sex and the homosexual community. The early reports suggested that it was an exclusively gay infection, probably having to do with the promiscuous lifestyle attributed to homosexual men. This was a rush to judgment that proved to be extremely harmful to both heterosexuals and homosexuals. Being labeled a gay disease that had no cure, the number of illnesses mounted rapidly; in addition, homosexuals were further ostracized.

The only full-length feature to immediately follow *Caligula*'s lead was *Centurians of Rome* (1981), produced by Hand in Hand for the gay market.

After a credit crawl influenced by *Star Wars*, the story begins in the Roman countryside, where Demetrius (George Payne), who looks like a latter-day Steve Reeves of 1960s Hercules fame, and his lover, Octavius (Scorpio), are at the mercy of soldiers who insist on collecting overdue taxes. Having no money, Demetrius, sold as a slave, is purchased by Caligula.

Octavius, meanwhile, is lusted after by the guard commander (Eric Ryan), who insists on sex with him and then offers to help him free Demetrius. Many night scenes showing the soldiers priming Demetrius sexually for the emperor are too slow and dark, having been shot in torch light. Demetrius is taken to Caligula's tent. Caligula (Michael Flent) is an affable, pretty twentysomething who likes risky, romantic experiences with men, and allows Demetrius a limited opportunity to fist him. Flent's amusing portrayal of Caligula, unafraid and in control, is the opposite of Robinson's and McDowell's characterizations, and suggests the reasons the Roman citizenry may have been more accepting of and entertained by Caligula. In other words, these traits offer a unique perspective on what it might have been like to be a spoiled youth in search of himself while he ran an empire. Typically the sex action is observed in long shots around set pieces. The men are hairy seventies guys, quite good looking and believable as human beings; nothing like the hotly lit, hard-driving, rather impersonal competitors of late eighties gay films. In the end Demetrius and Octavius escape and the guard commander becomes Caligula's favorite partner.

Centurians of Rome, according to Bijou Video, cost one hundred thousand dollars and benefited in part from a train robbery in England, making it one of the most expensive gay films of all time.[26]

The Reagan administration failed to mention Human Immunodeficiency Virus/Acquired Immunodeficiency Syndrome (HIV/AIDS) in public, while the principal focus was on the gay community. In the first half of the 1980s, numerous men in the arts communities began to come down with the disease, which had many manifestations. In 1985, Rock Hudson, the personification of maleness in mainstream movies, admitted that he had AIDS, and had done everything possible to cure it. Doris Day, Hudson's leading lady in *Pillow Talk* (1959) and other delightful movies, stood by his side as he wasted away before television cameras. With two hundred fifty thousand dollars from the estate, Elizabeth Taylor, who starred opposite Hudson in George Steven's *Giant* (1956), founded the American Foundation for AIDS Research with Dr. Matilda Krim. By mid-decade, the public began to realize that the virus was non-preferential, and being spread at a rapid rate in heterosexual populations. In 1987, Althea Flynt, Larry Flynt's wife, died of the virus that she may have contracted from a blood transfusion she had before blood donors were screened for the disease. By the end of the decade it seemed like everyone knew someone who had the virus. The personification of maleness in the adult sex industry was John Holmes, aka Johnny Wadd. He made *The Rise and Fall of the Roman Empress*, starring Ilona "Ciccolina" Staller, a future member of the Italian Parliament, knowing he had AIDS. Holmes died in 1988.

The initial AIDS cycle claimed thousands of lives, and dramatic events were staged, such as displaying in Washington, D.C., a patchwork quilt honoring each death. Candlelight vigils were held in San Francisco to pressure the government to find a cure. Intense competition between scientists in the United States and France isolated the virus. Meanwhile, the principal preventive measure was for men to wear condoms, which gay filmmakers began to allow about 1990, thus giving reluctant men permission to save their own and others' lives. Adult heterosexual production companies were less inclined to require condoms. Dominating and ravishing helpless women is a common theme among adult video's best sellers, and male models had to demonstrate they could deliver a great deal of semen after coitus interruptus. (Male viewers do not want to see condoms being used on-screen because they do not like using them in real life.) Currently, condom use has become a ritual in most adult and mainstream pictures. Inadvertently, AIDS and same-sex relations began to appear frequently in 1980s mainstream, as well as adult, films: Edouard Molinaro's *La Cage aux folles* (1978), Arthur Hiller's *Making Love* (1980), and Paul Bogart's *Torch Song Trilogy* (1988). Various AIDS oriented films followed, that enabled the public to get acquainted with gay and lesbian lifestyles, paving the way for such breakthroughs as Showtime's series *Queer as Folk*, (2000–2005) and Ang Lee's *Brokeback Mountain* (2005).

Whether the AIDS virus existed during first century Rome is unknown, but as slavery and means of transportation increased, it is possible. Certainly a number of diseases such as syphilis were common, and there was no way of stopping their devastating consequences.

The Conservative Cycle

The ripple effect of censorial protests continued throughout the eighties. In 1983, the Texas Center for Media Awareness reported: "Commercial pornography is a national industry, conservatively estimated to reach a traffic of at least two to three billion dollars a year." Such adverse publicity resulted in adult magazines being wrapped in brown paper or being available only on request by consumers at major outlets like convenience stores. Pier Paolo Pasolini's *Salò: 120 Days of Sodom*, originally released in 1975, had just opened at the River Oaks Theatre when the Houston Police Department confiscated it. The film involves teenagers who are kidnapped and taken to a villa in Salò, the headquarters of Benito Mussolini's Fascist government during its last days (1944–1945). The leaders—a duke, a magistrate, a banker, and a bishop—represent the power groups that have sent the youths to war and, in this case, to be sacrificed to the sexual appetites of their elders. Intentionally brutal, the leaders parade the boys and girls around nude and forced them into a series of gross activities that include defecation, urination, and unwanted sexual engagements, so degrading that one or two of them commit suicide. Loosely based on the writings of the Marquis de Sade, the film shows the depravity of a leadership group, acts of sadomasochism wherein bloody violence is perpetrated on the youngsters. The film concludes with the theme that evil will continue to persist in a world of unredeemed humanity.

In 1983 Landmark took the case to court and I was one of several who testified as to Pasolini's intentions in making the film and to his brilliant record as a great Italian cinematic artist (*The Gospel According to St. Matthew*, 1964), novelist (*A Violent Life*), and poet. Some films such as *The Decameron* (1971), and *The Canterbury Tales* (1972), based on classic works by Boccaccio and Chaucer, were declared obscene by the courts and were delayed in having a public viewing, making Pasolini a fascinating and controversial figure. Landmark won the case (*Harris County vs. Landmark River Oaks Theatre*, 1983), but it had a disquieting effect on exhibiting controversial pictures for years thereafter. It was well known that Pasolini was a homosexual, who was killed in Ostia the year after the release of *Salò*, supposedly because he made an offensive remark to a young man or perhaps for political reasons.

Pasolini, it will be remembered, had hired Franco Rossellini early in his career. Homosexual influence was notable in the making of *Caligula* because some of the key contributors were gay.

As early as 1981, General Media issued an R-rated edition of *Caligula*, but it failed to find its niche. In 1984, General Media reissued an R-rated edition of *Caligula*, but it became quickly obvious that the dramatic power and intention of the original film had been fundamentally destroyed. The narrative, which depends on Caligula's madness to sustain its rationale, is entirely deleted from the R-version. The development of Caligula's character as to his vices, his priorities, and paranoia concerning conspiracies threatening his life are not sufficiently established. Bob Guccione's personal touches — with the Penthouse Pets in scenes of lesbianism and a few minutes of homosexual fellatio — are deleted and the principal orgy scene on the galley is cut in half so that the explicit sexual frames are omitted. The unrated original film is outrageously gutted. As noted in the previous chapter in scene-by-scene detail we see what can happen to a picture if it is "edited" to meet commercial requirements in distribution or for reasons of censorship.

So the R-rated edition was withdrawn from the market, but this did not mean that it was stripped completely of its commercial value. Running 102 minutes, and claiming to be "The Most Controversial Film of the 20th Century," it was reissued in letterbox format in 1991 and later on DVD. The public in the 1980s did not have the perspective to realize that the reason *Caligula* was a success rested on the unrated version; therefore, there was a relative void of about ten years when the R-rated editions distributed to disappointed viewers had lackluster sales. Nowadays the public has rediscovered the 1980s and the unrated *Caligula,* not the rated one, which has had fifty-four minutes cut. The outrageous scenes of violence and sex are omitted, as defined in the previous chapter: men ejaculating for a beauty preparation, anal sex with Caesonia and Livia, mutilation of Proculus, the aftermath of Caligula's illness, and the sexual climax in the brothel sequence. With these omissions, the reasons for outrage against the R-rated *Caligula* are substantially moot. The rated edition was sufficiently sanitized for family video distributors and was suitable for cablecasting in the United Kingdom and in the United States at the turn of the 21st century.

Nineteen eighty-four was also the year Franco Rossellini managed to get the rights to produce another version of *Caligula* through his company, Felix Film, and Penthouse International. This is the Italian-language version, *Io, Caligola,* discussed earlier. Significantly, no universal criteria exist for censorship, in the United States or elsewhere. Censorship is common, however. The tastes of the individual countries are paramount; therefore, tolerance is based on what the populations of each country are presumed to find acceptable. The general notion prevails that Asian and American films tolerate greater violence and less nudity and sexuality than European films. Several countries have specific restrictions related to religious beliefs. Homosexuality and lesbianism are tolerated to some degree in most countries, but gay male sex is less acceptable or is discreetly managed.

About the time *Caligula* was being shot, French cinema had eliminated most of its concerns regarding sex, and this brought greater pressure on the American filmmakers to do the same thing. Many American films of the sixties and seventies that were rated "X" have been re-rated as "R" today. Nevertheless, the Italian censor's judgments relevant to *Io, Caligola* were a matter of degree—how much was shown, how long was it on the screen, and how detailed was it. Male genitalia was often eliminated but female genitalia was not; both tended to be eliminated if they were placed in a violent context. The running time of *Io, Caligola* is thirty-two minutes less than the unrated edition: seventeen minutes are devoted to sex and the remainder are rearrangements and inserts selected by Franco Rossellini.

The reason *Caligula* is a seminal Omega-to-Alpha benchmark is that it is positioned as the transitional summary of the sex and violence of the 1970s to the more extreme sex and violence of the 1980s. Rossellini's 1984 *Io, Caligola* is much more liberal than the R-rated edition considered suitable for VHS and cable distribution to American and English audiences. Cultures are constantly changing and the levels of censorship change with them.

The Mafia and the Meese Commission

Generally it was said that Mafia bosses detested pornography and prostitution, but that greed drove them into these highly profitable businesses because the Mafia was well suited to handle distribution and exhibition, areas where the money was. The Mafia became involved in *Deep Throat* because the original financing came from a Mafia family. *Deep Throat* was financed by a loan that Anthony Peraino, a member of the Joseph Colombo crime family, gave to his son Louis "Butchie" Peraino. With the unprecedented success of *Deep Throat*, the five New York Mafia families quickly infiltrated every aspect of the pornography businesses, coming to own theaters, motion pictures, and people who made them.

While the pornography businesses were seeking greater freedom and respect during the seventies, they were increasingly vulnerable to gangland's top bosses. Two of the most ruthless figures were Michael Zaffarano, of the Bonanno family, who opened the Pussycat movie houses and was a major Mafia money collector, and Robert Di Bernardo of the Gambino family, who was into labor racketeering as well as pornography. Di Bernardo chose to remain inconspicuous. These men, along with others, played their roles cautiously and well. The public was barely aware of their existence. Law enforcement authorities, however, tracked them constantly. When small-town theater owners began to take in huge sums of money, city officials called in the Federal Bureau of Investigation. In some communities pornography had spread to stage sex, paraphernalia, and prostitution ranging beyond their jurisdictions. When they realized that mob influence in the adult movie business was nationwide, they sought help from the FBI.

In 1977 a major federal operation was established in Miami, using the acronym MIPORN. The men and women from the FBI were less known than the mob figures; nevertheless, a lead officer was special agent William P. "Bill" Kelly, who with others carefully tracked the criminals. After two years of intensive investigation, in 1979 MIPORN carried out a big operation, arresting fifty-eight alleged criminals in thirteen cities. Forty-nine were convicted, including some of the Perainos. Michael Zaffarano had a fatal heart attack when he was fleeing FBI arrest. Robert Di Bernardo disappeared. An account of what happened to him is told in *The Other Hollywood*, a collection of interviews, assembled by Legs McNeil and Jennifer Osborne.[27] Between 1969 and 1981, about fifty underworld characters, including pornographers, may have been killed by the mob, according to the Meese report.[28]

The biggest problem for adult films in seeking respect was their limited content, consisting of weak scripts and a too-substantial dedication to explicit sex scenes. In the early eighties there was an effort to imitate the mainstream industry by satirizing its films and by originating fresh material. For instance, to impress upon critics that adult cinema had arrived, Platinum Pictures circulated a press kit, including biographies, photographs, and a 45rpm music disc, to promote Chuck Vincent's *Roommates* (1981), a sort of early *Sex in the City*. Vincent coauthored the story of three women trying to survive in New York. Veronica Hart is the victim of a married man (Phil Smith) who has sex and leaves her, but she finds happiness with another handsome boyfriend (Jerry Butler). "It could be Brook Shields in *Blue Lagoon* brought to its ultimate conclusion," the press kit claimed.[29] Samantha Fox tries to overcome her past as a hooker, and Kelly Nichols meets a guy (Ron Hudd) at a disco. They get stoned and have sex in a surreal fantasy that converges pleasures of the bygone seventies era. The trio are "scintillating," according to *Swank*, and Al Goldstein wrote, "Porn grown up; style and substance poetically provocative."[30] This was the *Caligula* experiment replicated within the adult film industry. To this day serious attempts continue to be made, but they are relatively few compared with the cheaply produced adult movies. In 2006, two of the few Italian films with subtitles referencing the ancient genre were *Empire of Caesar* and *Marc Antony*, a two-part gay series retailing at over one hundred dollars on DVD. They have a vague continuing storyline referring to a conspiracy against Caesar and show some effort has been made with the settings.

For the second time in about twenty-five years, a U.S. president authorized a commission to study pornography in America. In 1985, President Reagan asked his attorney general, Edwin Meese III, to make recommendations on how to control the spread of pornography. The attorney general established the Attorney General's Commission on Pornography. It consisted of seven men and four women of various backgrounds and political persuasions. More witnesses testified against pornography than for it, and after several months the Meese commission produced a remarkably long and detailed document that concluded:

> First, the Commission expressed an unmistakable condemnation of sexually explicit material that is violent in nature. There is no place in this culture for material deemed legally obscene by the courts which depicts the dismemberment, burning, whipping, hanging, torturing or raping of women. Secondly, we were also unanimous in our condemnation of sexually explicit materials which depict women in situations that are humiliating, demeaning and subjugating. Thirdly, our Commission was unanimously opposed to child pornography in any form.[31]

By 1986, the Meese Commission reported on every aspect of adult sex businesses, including movies, videos, peep shows, book stores, cable television, satellites, print, and paraphernalia. The Commission issued ninety-two recommendations, particularly targeting phone sex services that had become prevalent since the break-up of the American Telephone and Telegraph Company, cable and satellite television companies that transmit potentially obscene programs, and adult stores that allowed live sexual contact in booths and/or contributed to health risks. In addition, it agreed no one under eighteen years of age should be admitted to adult establishments.

What was evident at its conclusion was that public demand for sex products was very high. The Commission reported that over the period of study, about one hundred adult sex movies were distributed to seven hundred cinemas, bringing in approximately five hundred million dollars at the box office. The average production cost of a 35mm or 16mm adult film was around seventy-five thousand dollars. Within five years two million households subscribed to sexually explicit programming, with the Playboy channel providing the main service to seven hundred thousand subscribers. Despite frequent deplorable conditions, the adult bookstore businesses, with booths that accommodated anonymous live sex, brought in more than two billion dollars per year in profits. In 1985 over seventy-five million adult videos were rented from nineteen thousand outlets. Of these, *Adult Video News* (AVN) estimated seventeen hundred were new; they cost four to six thousand dollars apiece to produce a sixty-minute video and perhaps ten to twenty thousand dollars to videotape a ninety-minute feature. The retail price was sixty to eighty dollars each. The Meese Commission estimated that there were over fifty thousand different titles. Most of the estimated twelve to twenty-four production companies were located in California.

The Meese Commission was criticized by major media for flawed data and biased reporting in a crusade against the adult industry, which might result in censorship being imposed on media in general. Even so, the Commission did put into perspective the relationship of 1970s crime syndicates and the adult movie businesses since pornographic films became profitable. Although Guccione said he never was involved with the Mafia, he continued to take risks. One was an Atlantic City casino that failed. By the mid–1980s, with *Penthouse* profits at a peak and with *Caligula* at the break-even point, the Meese Commission began to put pressure on media distributors of adult magazines. "Since 1986," according to the American Family Association, "more than 20,000 stores nationwide have dropped the sale of sexually explicit magazines. Significantly, "7-Eleven, Rite Aid, Kmart, CVS yanked *Penthouse* from their shelves, costing Guccione tens of thousands of sales off the newsstand, a huge blow to his bottom line."[32] *Penthouse Forum* covered the Meese report in detail, and it waged a public relations battle against the Commission, bringing much more attention to the Commission's work than it otherwise might have had.[33] In turn, the Meese Commission pressured the 7-Eleven convenience store chain to stop selling sex magazines. Without widespread distribution, *Playboy*, *Penthouse*, and *Hustler* sales began to suffer huge losses. Within less than ten years Guccione's substantial fortune, estimated at two hundred million, was severely curtailed by an inability to deliver products to the public. Without the delivery of these popular magazines, the fight for adult freedom and perspective in the marketplace diminished.

Progress in the Freedom Fight

Of the three adult magazine publishers—Hefner, Guccione, and Flynt—it was Larry Flynt who stuck his neck out the farthest and was shot down. *Hustler* can be revolting in ways—it takes the term "sexually explicit" to the extreme, but it is very funny at times and taps into what a lot of people are really thinking but do not want to admit. Flynt says, "I'd rather have ten truck drivers than one college professor reading HUSTLER."[34] In 1978, while on trial for obscenity charges, Flynt and an attorney were shot after they left a diner near the county courthouse in Lawrenceville, Georgia. The bullets ripped into his torso and lodged in a nerve center near his spine. He lost the use of his legs. Years later he learned that the crime was perpetrated by a racist, Joseph Paul Franklin, who was upset over photographs of a black man with a white woman.[35] Painkilling drugs and depression might have taken his life if it were not for his wife Althea Leasure Flynt and conscientious medical care.

Instead, Flynt's story is one of amazing recovery and resumption of publishing the raunchiest of the major sex magazines. The struggle was part of continuous challenges to his life and fortune. Flynt's magazine was a major purveyor of satirical cartoons and stories commenting on the celebrities, political figures, and issues of the late twentieth century. It was only a matter of time before *Hustler* would offend a prominent religious leader; and when he published an ad that lampooned television evangelist Jerry Falwell (1933–2007) Falwell alleged that it was beyond the limits of parody, and brought a forty-five million dollar lawsuit. The case went to the Supreme Court. If Flynt were less wealthy or less dedicated or less battered by the "slings and arrows of outrageous fortune," the case might not have gone so far; but Flynt was preserving the fundamental right of press freedom (that also included the movies) stated in the First Amendment. "Free speech is not freedom for the thought you love, but freedom for the thought you hate the most," he said.[36]

On 24 February 1988, the Supreme Court ruled in favor of Flynt. Chief Justice William Rehnquist wrote the opinion for the court. It "upheld the right of the press to print cruel satires on anybody in public life. The vote was 8–0," Christopher Hitchens reported in *Vanity Fair*. The victory was sweet for Flynt, but once again showed that rights granted in the Constitution had to be preserved through vigilance and struggle. Despite the myriad arguments litigated against pornography in the United States, the adult print and film industries have made major contributions to clarifying the basic rights of all Americans.

Only eight years had gone by since *Caligula*. Porn magazines, undermined by the Meese Commission, had survived, and the four-year presidency of George H. W. Bush had begun with a noticeable change in the air; the networks began to relax censorship rules. Contraception methods were discussed on ABC's *thirtysomething*, a bisexual man spread AIDS on NBC's *Midnight Caller*, and graphic pictures showed the internal workings of sex organs on CBS's *Inside the Sexes*, Elizabeth Jensen observed in the *New York Daily News*.[37] Language was loosening up, with previously forbidden words used in news and entertainment. Even commercials suggesting that condoms might prevent AIDS, previously prohibited, began to appear, as the FCC relaxed its grip during the latter years of the Reagan administration.

Larry Flynt's trial drew the interest of producer-director Oliver Stone, who made *The People vs. Larry Flynt* (1996). The film was R-rated for language, nudity, and sexual content, and it soft-pedals *Hustler* as a blue-collar *Playboy* by calling it more honest — "something the film needs to be," said one reviewer.[38] Woody Harrelson played the irrepressible Flynt.

Two years earlier Oliver Stone had directed Harrelson in *Natural Born Killers* (1994), an endless river of blood and sex stretching across the desert, which he and his lover (Juliet Lewis) litter with almost as many corpses as there are cacti. Their devastating killing spree is mirrored in a media display that a news reporter (Robert Downey, Jr.) presents to the public as a master showman. *Variety* said: "*Natural Born Killers* is a heavy-duty acid trip, quite possibly the most hallucinatory and anarchic picture made at a Hollywood studio in at least 20 years. A scabrous look at a society that promotes murderers as pop culture icons, as well as a scathing indictment of a mass media establishment that caters to and profits from such star-making, this is Oliver Stone's most exciting work to date strictly from a filmmaking point of view."[39] The screenplay was based on a story by Quentin Tarantino, whose penchant for killers, bloody and cruel, would offer a unique imprint over the next several years.

Collectively, Guccione, Flynt, and Hefner had fought the battle for press and film freedom for four decades, investing their lives and fortunes in the cause. *Caligula* is a particularly important example of protecting cinema freedom in that struggle. All three had become involved in film ventures as producers or as subjects. Part of Flynt's story had been told in a major motion picture and the Hefner and Guccione biographies were yet to be written. Guccione's role to this point was far-sighted. He was an independent producer without a studio, he had little experience in filmmaking, but he had considerable understanding of the media businesses, especially the print business, and he was a gambler. He was lucky, too, because *Caligula* appeared just as the public was searching for a more suitable venue in which to satisfy its private fantasies — the home theater. Furthermore, having substantial success with marketing *Caligula*, Guccione decided to celebrate that success in 1989 by offering the "special tenth anniversary edition" of *Caligula* that he boasted "may well be the most controversial film in history." An "epic story of Rome's mad emperor," the box cover said, featuring "his unholy sexual passion for his sister, his marriage to Rome's most infamous prostitute, his fiendishly inventive means of disposing of those who would oppose him." Epic? Mad? Unholy? Most infamous prostitute? In addition, he offered "cinematic giants," for his cast had become increasingly famous and the Penthouse Pets, as a group, were even better known than before the movie.

With the Hollywood preoccupation of selling major studios to giant conglomerates that owned newspapers, cable and phone companies, movies, and even toys, this structure enabled a corporation to move its products around its communication outlets until it found a place for them. The rapid changes in the mainstream movie industry resulted in little interest in ancient-genre films. Guccione's effort to reenergize interest in *Caligula*, one of the few ancient genre films of the 1980s, helped to keep alive the notion that the ancient cycle would become prominent again.

Bad Boys Live Longer

Made and released in the lingering moments of the decade, Steven Soderbergh's *sex, lies and videotape* (1989) is a drama about an affair that a man (Peter Gallagher) has with his wife's sister (Laura San Giacomo), casually told by James Spader to the wife (Andie MacDowell) as he videotapes her. It won the Palm d'Or at the Cannes Film Festival. The R-rated film mixes simulated sex, profanity, and some violence. It was a restating of the basic *Caligula* formula: produce your own movie, include sex and violence, and feature good-looking young actors. The film *sex, lies and videotape* was a remarkable achievement because the story was written in eight days, shot in one month, edited in four weeks, and made for $1.2 million. Its success gave new hope to the traditional and adult film industries that there was undiscovered fresh talent, and the potential for a high profit-to-cost ratio. As was well known, the aspect of the motion picture business that best illustrated this formula was the growing adult-feature–video industry, increasingly resilient though hit hard by HIV/AIDS and the Meese report.

Invited to the 1988 Democratic National Convention was actor Rob Lowe. He stayed at a nearby hotel where he had sex with an underage girl and videotaped it. Criminal charges were not pursued, and a civil case was settled in time for him to portray a sociopath whose depravity is uncovered on videotape in Curtis Hanson's *Bad Influence* (1990). The live bedroom incident, believed lost at first, surfaced as a high-priced illicit item in the adult video market. Although it could have ruined Lowe's career, the video proved to be ahead of its time.[40] For a few celebrities who only wanted or needed attention, exposure was a good thing. Television's *Baywatch* actress Pamela Anderson and her "bad boy" rock musician husband Tommy Lee revealed their intimate love-making on a home video that is far more graphic than anything in *Caligula* and sold it like any other sexually explicit adult film (1997). The notice this video received temporarily preserved and extended their celebrity status, and thereby improved their marketability for work in entertainment.[41] Likewise, heiress Paris Hilton, not yet twenty, who costarred in a television comedy, exhibited herself in a sexually explicit videotape with a boyfriend. Distributed as *1 Night in Paris*, it suggests that nudity and intimate acts the couple were engaged in had wide acceptance in the nineties generation.[42] Whether these videos were originally intended for world distribution does not matter. Once they are in existence, just as history has shown with Hedy Lamarr's nude swim in *Ecstasy* (1933), they can never be withdrawn from the marketplace.

Live stage shows offered some new excitement, as the Playboy and Penthouse franchises invested in upscale cabarets. Along with a multitude of other nude, topless, or similar men's clubs, women were featured as pole dancers and showgirls. The "gleefully vulgar, and more stupid and steamy" Paul Verhoeven's *Showgirls* (1995), produced for a staggering $40 million, was widely panned — and widely viewed, not so much in cinemas but on cable television before it was sold in stores in NC-17 and R-rated versions.[43] The story concerns an incredibly selfish woman, Nomi Malone (Elizabeth Berkley), who will stop at nothing to accomplish her dream of being the head dancer in the revue at the Stardust Hotel, Las Vegas. The comedy is crass and funny, the action is immoral and corrupt; and though it is fiction, unstoppable ambition is what much of the public believed motivated success anyway, and not only in show business. *Showgirls* was a take-off of *All About Eve*. It has a savage rape scene and gratuitous showgirl-on-showgirl action. Critics and audiences claimed they did not like it, but its tenacious promotion kept it in the news and on cable and DVD. Dutch director Verhoeven (*Basic Instinct*, 1992), making *Black Book* in 2006, claimed he was saying bye-bye to big budgets and salaries so that nobody could say he had too much nudity in his pictures. "As for sexuality, it comes from my belief in sex, my pleasure in sex, and my strong conviction that it's a wonderful communication system," a view that Tinto Brass articulated while making *Caligula*.[44] *Showgirls* contributed to a banner year of nearly $5.5 billion at the box office. Tape sales were at a record $6.7 billion, with video outpacing theater revenue three to one.

Meanwhile, the female interest in men's clubs had increased since 1993. This resulted in cleaner, more attractive venues, attended by women and men. A few clubs, such as La Bare, had specialized in men stripping for women since the late seventies. The egalitarian clubs became an important enough part of the culture to be shown on such television series as *The Sopranos*.

Showgirls was followed by a bigger critical casualty, adapter-director Andrew Bergman's *Striptease* (1996). Erin (Demi Moore) takes up pole dancing at a men's club because she needs the money to provide a good home for her seven-year-old daughter. Empathy for Erin in this slow, dark, and boring narrative is nothing like that for Nomi in the upbeat *Showgirls*. Though panned, these films were played repeatedly on cable television. Demi Moore survived nicely, too, by being paid $12.5 million, making her the highest-paid actress for a single film.

Replaying a movie repeatedly, no matter what is said about it, is another reminder of a distribution technique Guccione popularized so that he could keep *Caligula* in the public conscience. Networks had become subsidiaries of multimedia conglomerates, and they were to repeat these movies until they found an audience for them, usually on cable or DVD.

Seventies and eighties nostalgia was another factor. In a New York lounge best known for good-looking bartenders, two veterans juggled wine bottles, throwing them at each other and catching them like circus jugglers do. This skill was delightfully demonstrated in Roger Donaldson's *Cocktail* (1988). The tale stars Tom Cruise as a former Army man who is trained by his older buddy (Bryan Brown) in the hottest techniques for attracting young ladies. *Cocktail* was rated R for brief nudity, language, and a suicide (by the older vet after mounting debts and a failed marriage). In 1997, the flashback film *Boogie Nights* featured the disco days as viewed from the perspective of the 1970s sex film business. Supposedly patterned after the life of John Holmes, it was a well received story about an aspiring young guy (Mark Wahlberg), who has what it takes to be a video stud, verified by a brief shot of his large instrument (that Wahlberg denied was his). As he becomes successful, he also realizes that the industry can be a special place where some of the frequent social outcasts can find solace and even a home with each other. Burt Reynolds, as the fatherly porn-company producer, won an Academy Award for Best Supporting Actor. These films, in part, were heirs to *Caligula*'s legacy of greater sexual freedom on screen, except that the lead actor in *Caligula* was unashamedly nude and unidentified body parts were not substituted for those of lead actors, and *Caligula*'s scenes were never sensationalized with the use of foul language, unnecessary in a script attributed mainly to writer Gore Vidal.

During the Clinton administration, enforcement of the nation's obscenity laws was a low priority, and pornography became widely available, mainstream entertainment. One key crime figure whom many believed was the king of porn, Ruben Sturman, previously referred to as being a pioneer of the business when he began selling adult films out of the trunk of his car, had been indicted for selling what was now being distributed by some of America's largest cable, satellite, and hotel corporations. They were earning, but not always reporting, several hundred million dollars a year from adult entertainment. On 27 October 1997, Sturman died in a prison hospital in Lexington, Kentucky. The *Chattanooga Free Press* wrote: "The smut lord is dead.... But the evil he and his court-coddled colleagues have done — the degradation of our nation's culture and the corruption of our youth — lives on."[45] By mid-decade, total adult video sales had become three times the revenues of traditional cinemas.

The big indiscretion of the 1990s, as it turned out, was not an actor's youthful antics, but rather those of President Bill Clinton. His 1998 affair with intern Monica Lewinsky cued an international media frenzy that was exaggerated beyond its importance from the outset. Was it caused by pussy power or penis power? The public, the press, and certain politicians spent millions of taxpayer dollars to penetrate the depths of their after-hours predilections. The president's judgment ignited a Republican effort to impeach him. In his videotaped interrogation, he looked like a lad caught with his hand in the cookie jar. The president had lied and then tried to cover it up, in part by redefining sex, as any good lawyer might do. Interestingly, many young people of the nineties defined sex as having intercourse; they said humans beings did not really have sex unless "they went all the way." Fellatio, therefore, may not really be sex, although it meets our 1970s definition of "penetration and wet." An investigation conducted by Kenneth Starr and the media's unstoppable repetition of the story prevented Clinton from conducting a great deal of public business. This became another topic for culture analysts to research, as Maria St. John has shown in her article, "How to Do Things with the Starr Report: Pornography, Performance, and the President's Penis."[46]

Another scandalous event took place on 1 February 2004 during the halftime musical interlude at the National Football League's Superbowl game. During a five-second moment, singer Justin Timberlake appeared to tear a part of Janet Jackson's costume to reveal a shielded nipple on a nude breast. The occasion, allegedly seen by ninety million viewers, some of whom were children, brought embarrassment to the CBS producers, an unprecedented FCC threat of a fine of over half a million dollars, and increased fame to the vocalists. By the twenty-first century the concept of "transparency" in government, which previously referred to flawless integrity in handling public business, had extended to the sex life of the president, to lives of celebrities, and to lives of regular citizens eager to exhibit themselves on the Internet.

During the last years of President Clinton's second term there was a media attempt to synthesize the notion that some urban men were better in touch with their sensitive feminine side; to wit, the metrosexual man had fully evolved as being more dependent on women and sensitive to female needs, but young males remained reluctant to surrender themselves to marriage when they could have a "relationship" instead.

Remember Augustus's scolding of the young men of Rome for not meeting their responsibilities to have a home and families? The young Roman was more like the American gigolo than Caligula. This perception was quickly shattered when George W. Bush swaggered forth to take the office of president of the United States. The macho man of the 1970s— remember *Urban*

Cowboy—was in control, and the metrosexual guy was hard to find. The conservative values President Bush brought with him from Texas permeated his administrative style and decisions. A domestic agenda quickly turned into a wartime commitment. Had the macho man returned?

The DVD Difference

The shadow of uneasiness in the motion picture business was pervasive throughout the 1990s. Teens to fortysomething crowds were not buying tickets at the mainstream cinemas like they once did. Some feared that regular moviegoers were viewing films on home computers, or renting movies at low cost, or seeing adult films on pay-per-view. By 1996, in order to compete, the major film companies began selling their libraries one film at a time on DVD, a lightweight, shiny, seven-inch disk, rather than one ticket at a time at the box office: $19.99 vs. $7.00. Producers promised the re-released old movies on DVD would have enhanced picture and sound quality. Some classic films were cleaned and reprinted from the original negative. Sometimes original footage the director wanted, called the "director's cut," was added, along with commentary from those involved in creating the film. Occasionally a documentary, such as *The Making of Caligula*, and perhaps printed information and pictures were included. No one asked whether viewers wanted to collect movies. How many times does a person want to see the same movie? It was assumed that the public wanted to collect movies.

From the producer's viewpoint, a DVD release had sufficient additional information that the DVD should be reviewed again as though it were a new motion picture. Reviewers got more work. This was perfect for producers. Movies with subject and production details that were not initially looked upon favorably had a new chance to be better understood and reevaluated by younger audiences. New editions of *Caligula* definitely benefited in the process. At the very least, it was reconsidered a "cult" film that special audiences would want to rent or buy. Moviegoers divided into groups. Large audiences attended a blockbuster, if the stars and story were appealing and millions of dollars went into its production. Teenagers went if their friends were excited about the performers and the subject. Young adults and those with families opted for low-budget rentals shown at home or in second-run neighborhood cinemas. Groups of older adults, minorities, and special interests went to see those pictures that appealed to ethnic, racial, or lifestyle backgrounds at smaller, independent cinemas; foreign films found small audiences in art houses.

With the enormous financial returns from Steven Spielberg's prehistoric *Jurassic Park* (1993) and James Cameron's romantic *Titanic* (1997), the decade ended with yet another flashback to the previous one. Granted, the average cost of making a traditional Hollywood feature in 1990 was forty million dollars and that cost had increased to over two hundred million. Still, *The Blair Witch Project* (1999) was made by student actors for thirty thousand dollars and took in one hundred million dollars after its stellar opening at the Sundance Film Festival. With this huge cost-to-profit ratio, the writer-directors Eduardo Sánchez and Daniel Myrick had dramatically underlined a film's marketing potential, not only on DVD, but also on the Internet. New product demands were coming from various audiences due to increased dissemination over more broadcast and cable television channels.

Particularly appealing to younger audiences were live-action and animated stories loosely based on the tales of Hercules and biblical stories— Kevin Sorbo in the television series *Hercules, the Legendary Journeys* (1990s), Ryan Gosling as *Young Hercules* (1998), Disney's *Hercules* (1998), and the DreamWorks adaptation of the Ten Commandments story, *The Prince of Egypt* (1998). Mature audiences, although they could get laundered movies, so-called family-friendly versions of theatrical mainstream pictures at chain distributors, preferred uncensored movies that included sex, nudity, violence, and the language of the original production. *Caligula*'s long-fought battle with censors, that damaged many films from *Apocalypse Now* in 1979 to *Queer as Folk* in 2005, was still being fought, but at least adults had shopping options thanks to multiple formats and various distributors. By 2003, television programs and motion pictures were available on DVD, which had become 60 percent of Hollywood's business, mainly a male-oriented world in movies and a female-oriented world on television.[47]

Return to Paganism

Beside the live shows and the virtual experiences provided on multimedia as the Internet became more significant, moral values were changing throughout the world. Exposure through media to other cultures forced changes just about everywhere. By the mid–1990s the ancient genre began to return, as media competition forced networks to broaden their appeal to a diverse marketplace. Besides cartoons, the live-action dramatic programs were mainly Christian stories about Jesus, his relatives, and well-known biblical figures in familiar stories.

In the early twenty-first century — two thousand years after Caligula — the human problems facing society were remarkably similar to those in ancient Rome: hunger, immigration, insufficient mercenaries to fight on distant battlefields, and polarization of wealth. Women were still hunting for good men, ones who would love them, share caring for the kids, have employment, and remain faithful. Television capitalized on these concerns and capably illustrated them to a growing female audience in the HBO comedy series *Sex in the City*, which is the occasionally amusing tale of four liberated, attractive, professional women who have difficulty finding love. Well into their thirties with biological concerns mounting, the comedy plays out in numerous sexual encounters, as the women living in Manhattan sleep with several men without finding satisfaction. Despite the fact that most of these women did not have a happy love life or get a husband who lives up to their expectations, the series spawned another media success, as ABC TV's *Desperate Housewives* (2004). This satire concerns the plight of thirtysomething wealthy women seeking or trying to hold on to husbands or boyfriends, and/or a happy family life. At times the women are portrayed as stewing in futility, with their only escape to engage in acts like burning down a house. Some of these women are also sleeping around while they are looking for a mate. The comedy is narrated by a woman who has committed suicide already. Each woman is a well-known character type — a zany divorcee (Teri Hatcher), an adulterer (Eva Longoria), frazzled mom (Felicity Huffman) and control freak (Marcia Cross). The bewildered men in this comedy try to maintain their distance but the women are constantly plotting ways to get their attention. Some of the men are no bargain and are hesitant to get involved in the mess at Wisteria Lane, but of course they do.

The quest-for-a-man theme mutated into a live-on-film reality television series, ABC-TV's *Hooking Up* (2005). Here were glimpses of about a dozen women emailing résumés and retouched pictures to men who responded by doing the same thing. Finding a husband or even a suitable boyfriend proved to be no easy task, even with a worldwide database. The men used the term "hooking up" as a euphemism for having intercourse; the women seemed to be looking for a "meal ticket." Various efforts to get men and women together on camera so that they could assess their dates and experience meeting each other did not work out — the encounters were dull and disappointing for participants and viewers alike.[48] As David Brooks wrote in the *New York Times*: "Now young people face a social frontier of their own. They hit puberty around 13 and many don't get married until they're past 30. That's two decades of coupling, uncoupling, hooking up, relationships and shopping around. This period is not a transition anymore. It's a sprawling life stage, and nobody knows the rules."[49] By 2007, women were making up 56 percent of the television audience. The mating show idea persisted, as desperate programmers, trying to attract men, offered twenty-to-one odds in *The Bachelor* (2007). The show was premised on the notion that an overachieving, handsome male would bond with one of twenty women, who were screened to be well above average in qualifications, especially pulchritude.

The matchmaking even filtered into the lives of college students. MTV's *The Real World* (2003) showed about a dozen undergraduates who were supposedly attending a major university, but were actually more concerned about living in an off-campus communal apartment. The young men were interested in only two things: getting drunk and getting laid, evidently in that order. The women, slightly less sedate about the task of finding a husband, were cast into a nurturing role of trying to understand and support the self-absorbed young men. Cameras were rolling all the time; occasional brief nudity, mostly when someone was taking a shower, was lightly blurred out. Individual backgrounds were woven into the multiple storylines. Coping with unfortunate experiences that happened to them occasionally, the students did not seem to study, work or need money. Certainly none had the terrifying challenges attributed to Caligula and his family. Even if Caligula had been crazy, he was better prepared to handle his life and successfully rule an empire than these privileged undergraduates. Showing the life of a twentysomething of the first century and the lives of several twentysomethings, supposedly sane, in the twenty-first century, is revealing. These telecasts targeted to general audiences reveal most of these young adults as confused, helpless, poorly educated, arrogant, and depressed, sometimes engaged in destructive behavior. A similar view of young adults is portrayed in media advertising; young people seem to want everything and to work for little or nothing.

Thanks to new media, people can now limit their communications to electronic fantasies. Men and women can turn on their DVD players and masturbate to the extent that their imaginations allow, without ever getting involved. The adult video industry has been only too glad to assist them by providing every experience possible from a world cast of capable actors. Narcissism, especially as demonstrated by celebrities, is rampant. Everything and everyone, the message appears to be, can be bought or sold on a credit card.

Bloated corporations, overtaxing government bureaucracies with bottomless appetites, arrogant military power, lazy politicians rendered powerless by lobbyists, and religious organizations weighted down by pomp and bad behavior have forged the yoke imposed on poor citizens. Outside North America, large populations cultivate fields of poppies and gather coca leaves. The luxurious lives of Americans and international celebrities are displayed on billboards, flaunting wealth. American youths, especially those of privilege, tend to conclude that instant gratification is their right. A drug that seems to addict many is the drug of instant celebrity — by winning the lottery, by surviving extreme contests, or perhaps by displaying performances of human degradation. As the mother of porn star Belladonna told ABC news anchor Diane Sawyer, in a discussion about media corporations that profit from pornography: "I hate them. I hate that their kids get to go to college, live in a beautiful home, go on wonderful vacations, and my daughter has to, and will, suffer for that."[50] By 2004, pornography was a $10 billion industry that became increasingly closer to fusing adult entertainment with theatrical motion pictures. Adult entertainment has become mainstream, outgrossing all other entertainment businesses.

Vivid Video's president Bill Asher, a suave Dartmouth graduate, said: "We have good sets, good plots, attractive people who can hopefully speak and act. Everything you can expect to see in a mainstream movie."[51] Bob Guccione's premise for producing *Caligula* has come true and is being repeated. He wanted to make a traditional movie with sexually explicit scenes. Asher wants to make sex films with the same traditional values, including good acting and writing.

Admittedly, Guccione's *Caligula* may have gone to some extremes not yet reached in traditional Hollywood films, but much of the mainstream motion picture industry is subtly infusing adult content while continuing to wear the mask of old Hollywood. Meanwhile, the adult moviemakers become more traditional in style. The difference between mainstream and adult films continues to narrow. Several adult studios are even located in the San Fernando Valley, within a few minutes drive from Disney, Warner Bros., and Universal Pictures.

Resurrection of the Classical Genre

Various movies of the twenty-first century show the convergence of violence, sex, and nudity, and an increase in crude language in adult and traditional films. Frequently, these pictures are about the relatively small percentage of people who are wealthy leaders. The motion pictures produced about the Roman Empire in earlier decades usually focused on this same small group. Besides a half-dozen biographies of biblical leaders, NBC's *The Odyssey* (1997) and ABC's *Cleopatra* (1999) hinted at a renewed interest in the ancient (classical) genre. *Cleopatra* is a merger of the narratives well known in Shakespeare's plays *Julius Caesar* and *Antony and Cleopatra*, the former being a history of a famous murder and the latter a romantic tragedy. In the first half of *Cleopatra*, Cleopatra (Leonor Varela) entices the weary Caesar (Timothy Dalton), who uses her for political and playful purposes; but in the second half, the macho Caesar is replaced by the metro Marc Antony (Billy Zane), who is no match for the enchantments of Cleopatra. The television drama runs an unmerciful four hours. Exteriors of ships battling at sea and interiors decorated with the riches of Egypt make the film marginally watchable despite copious interruptions with commercials.

To announce the return of the genre, using the wonderful advancements in computer technology, Ridley Scott's *Gladiator* (2000) presented Rome in its unbelievable second century glory. Maximus (Russell Crowe), an officer of the Roman army, is deceived by his own government, sees his own family murdered, is sold into slavery, and fights his way back to Roman leadership by killing Emperor Lucius Aelius Aurelius Commodus (Joaquin Phoenix), who ruled from A.D. 180 to 192. The movie includes scenes of bloody combat, some deviant sex, and breathtaking views of Rome in its days of splendor. This film has strong male appeal. Winning Academy Awards for Best Picture and Best Actor in 2001 the ancient narrative was off to a solid start.

Less than three years later, Peter O'Toole starred in *Augustus,* which repeats the same story as *Cleopatra,* but from a different perspective. The elderly Augustus, in narrative exposition and flashbacks (when he is played by a younger actor), tells about the sacrifices he and his family made for the preservation of Rome. The focus for this film is Augustus's relationship with his daughter Julia (Charlotte Rampling). The principal events, showing how Augustus gained control of the empire, are relatively accurate. This version has forceful but less disagreeable women, beautiful vistas, and crowded battle scenes shot at Hammanet Studios, Tunisia. The significant line passed along from *Caligula,* which was borrowed from the gospel of Mark, has Augustus asking, "What if a man conquered the world but lost his soul?" In this film that seems to mean a man's essence as a caring human being. To make sure that this does not happen, Augustus on his deathbed retrieves Julia from banishment so that she can forgive him for forcing her to give up the man she loved to marry Tiberius. The movie adds another *Caligula* touch in that its makers sought a world market — it was released with Spanish and French subtitles.

This was the second time that the Augustan period had appeared on the screen. Oddly, *Empire* would repeat this period two years later, and *Rome* would do the same thing one year after that. Within six years, ABC, Columbia/Sony, and HBO all presented their interpretations of the life and times of Augustus, as we shall see.

Wolfgang Peterson's *Troy* (2004) suggests that Troy fell because of personal arrogance, misinterpretations of the gods, clever war technology, and cavernous depths of human hatred. Achilles is a demigod, obsessed with engraving his name in the annals of time. Being destined by the gods, he is somewhat difficult to empathize with. In his first scene, Achilles (Brad Pitt) lies nude with two beautiful women. He is only a few frames away from revealing how mosquito-free sleeping was in those days. No mention is made of his possible love affair with his companion, cousin Patroclus, because pagan bisexuality is not a theme in this movie. Besides, no actual data records a relationship, though no solid records exist of the sack of Troy, either.[52] Perhaps the legend and the answers lie several layers beneath the sands of time. This $170-million picture has male appeal, but skews toward women, as illustrated in the compromises made in the content and the substantial amount of promotion devoted to Pitt's dismount from his horse, revealing black briefs under his warrior uniform. Peterson's adventure was reported to do better at box offices overseas than in the United States. *Troy* is a stunning picture enhanced by beautiful computer effects, as well as a financial success.

For Oliver Stone's *Alexander* (2004), meager actual documentation exists, but interpretation is plentiful. Unlike Achilles, Alexander is not sure he is a god; therefore, he is conflicted in his struggle to carry out his destiny and his personal leanings. After several years, financing for the $160-million film became available through Warner Bros. and European backers, provided that homosexual references were minimal. Alexander (Colin Farrell), who is supposed to be the greatest general in history, tries to conquer the Middle East. He does a masterful job of conquering its geography, but he is not prepared to administer it in peacetime. He met an early death in Babylon (Iraq) in 323 B.C., and his remains, which may have been cremated, have never been found. At best, his legacy was the spread of Hellenistic culture at the expense of many lives and equally sophisticated civilizations. His family was killed and the land he had conquered was divided among his successors.

Alexander, like *Caligula*, deserves a second look as a movie. The story Oliver Stone is trying to tell is immense and unwieldy. Unless the viewer has read Mary Renault's fictional volumes on Alexander, his loves, and his campaigns, it will be difficult to appreciate the immense battles, the rugged, remote, panoramic locations, and the complex characters— his mother who says he is the son of Zeus, his father intent on conquest, several competitors, warriors, and enemies, and his lovers, including a possible homosexual relationship with Hephaestion (Jared Leto), his Persian wife, and a Persian boy. To this complicated story that travels from Macedonia to the Indus River in western India (Pakistan), viewers are asked to see the larger concept— Stone's attempt to show Alexander's desire to mold diverse cultures into one world.[53]

Alexander tries to include complexities; *Troy* omits them by sticking to the easily understood central battle over stealing Helen and conquering Troy and by leaving out religious motivations, some personal relationships, and character dimensions. Unfortunately, *Alexander*'s narrative is not easy to follow. It jumps back and forth in time and so the scenes seem disconnected. It could have had a compelling linear narrative— the more complex the drama, the more likely this simpler approach to telling the story will work. Granted, however, nonlinear narratives (*Crash*, *Babel*) are the currently popular approach. *Alexander* could have been a more magnificent picture — it is magnificent — opening with Alexander's mother seemingly giving birth to the son of Zeus, who was said to sometimes appear in the form of a snake. This is when the director and Hollywood should be commended for an expensive, valiant try that almost worked, especially for those who enjoy stories about ancient times.

Referring to homosexuality, supposedly an uncomfortable subject for many men and women, even if a story is set in pagan times when bisexuality was normal, *New York Times* culture critic Frank Rich told *The Advocate*: "Mainstream Hollywood may be the most conservative medium in this regard, [compared] to television, theater, and independent filmmaking." He attributed the general "dumbing down" of everything to Hollywood's dependence on pleasing an international market, an important consideration.[54] With *Alexander* failing to reach expectations at the box office, Stone quickly withdrew it, so that it could be reedited and returned to the marketplace on disk with the director's cut and to cable television, where it plays frequently. But viewers cannot trust cable channels to play the unexpurgated version. The theory is that the world market prefers less challenging movies with less intellectual value, that it prefers entertainment, but that conjecture needs study.

Producing ancient stories for television is different from producing them for the movies. Movies focus on successful men who attack problems and solve them, or go down trying. Television dramas, designed for women, require romance. For example, *Spartacus* (2004) starred young, good-looking, muscled Goran Visnjic in the title role. The remake of the 1960 film failed to get much attention as a four-hour mini-series on the USA Network. Set in 72 B.C., it tells about a man who was sold into slavery, but eventually rises up against Rome's legions, and fights valiantly before he is caught and crucified, and his followers meet their fate. Even so, the drama was respectable and encouraged ancient dramas to follow. ABC TV's *Empire* (2005) was a six-part entry costing $30 million. It is loosely based on the early life of Octavius, later called Augustus Caesar (Santiago Cabrera). While dying, Julius Caesar supposedly asks a gladiator, Tyrannus (Jonathan Cake), to train Augustus to be emperor, like Tiberius asks Nerva to educate Caligula. *Empire*'s story has more documentation to verify it, but that is not essential to create a stimulating drama. Augustus did become a great Roman ruler, whereas Caligula never realized his potential. These pictures are mainly promoted by means of their sexual innuendos or bloody violence in fight scenes, and of course, muscular leading men who look appealing in boots and tunics, preferably shorter than longer ones. Notice that Caligula's tunics are short and so are those in *Troy* and *Alexander*. In fact, these programs, designed mainly for women, are sustained by their love stories with romantic overtones and limited violence in fight scenes.

A great deal of effort and huge sums of money were spent on *Empire* and similar projects. Like *Caligula*, *Empire* was filmed in Rome (Cinecittà), and in south central Italy over five months. Three preliminary months were spent on Cake's physical regimen to tone him up and train him in sword fighting techniques. Fortunately, the leads were to a broad demographic, with Orlando Bloom as Paris of Troy, Helen's lover, appealing to "tween oglers."[55]

The gamble that was supposed to be the ultimate test for ancient-genre dramas on television was HBO's twelve-part, $100 million, heavily promoted series *Rome* (2006–2007). As the final season began after the murder of Julius Caesar, HBO and the BBC were trying to justify the largest-standing film set at Cinecittà studios. What happened to the grand dreams that resulted in public disappointment? What *Rome* needed most was a brilliant script like *I, Claudius*. Instead, it poked along, hinting weekly that something was going to happen. But, unlike a skillfully written soap opera, too little happens slowly and the overall direction of the episodes diminish in purpose, momentum, and interest. With *Cleopatra* and *Augustus* already released, why didn't HBO solve the problems they experienced? Numerous characters, who are mainly disagreeable men and women, are played by actors who are not well known to the general public (Ciarán Hinds, Kevin McKidd, Ray Stevenson, Lindsay Duncan, James Purefoy, Max Pirkis) and this hindered keeping track of the characters. These drawbacks contributed to lower viewer response and reduced the desire to invest time in a story that plodded along for several weeks. Although little is known about the lives of ordinary Romans, the writers did try to run a secondary plot about them. Unfortunately, they did not discover or reveal much that was compelling.

With a tedious storyline and characters having modest emotional rapport, who cares who won at Actium? Production values by themselves will not suffice. Perhaps *Rome* had four thousand multicolored costumes that more accurately reveals what the ancient Romans wore, with specially designed jewelry and dyed fabrics; none of this will substitute for the basic necessities. In 2007, silver-screen moguls were treated to a horde of muscle-bound men, mostly naked to the waist and in short skirts and boots, fighting the battle at Thermopylae, where three hundred dedicated soldiers delayed the inevitable by staving off an incredibly huge force of Persians in bloody hand-to-hand combat against a blue screen. The box office immediately told the story in a cash take of seventy million dollars for the opening weekend. The famous battle actually took place along a narrow pass in mountainous Sparta in 480 B.C. King Leonidas (Gerard Butler) makes love with his noble queen, Gorgo (Lena Headey), in what the *New Yorker* referred to as "the full splendor of their nakedness" before he led his dedicated army against King Xerxes (Rodrigo Santoro). The unreal and unbelievable Xerxes looked like an imaginary bisexual idol, combining masculine overall body strength and feminine traits, a giant god-king, not a realistic masculine warrior with big gonads. The financial backers won this battle. Warner Bros.' $60-million investment made more than $10 million over its production costs on the first weekend alone. The third highest grossing film since 2001 was *300*, with *The Passion of the Christ* coming in second and *Troy* in ninth. Three ancient genre films on the top ten list put real financial power and public approval behind them, as the twenty-first century began.

Just as the goddess Fortuna rolled the dice favorably to create Bob Guccione's fortune, she rolled them again to take it away. His close associate Franco Rossellini and Guccione's wife Kathy Keeton both died in the nineties. His children, who were employed by *Penthouse* from time to time, distanced themselves in deteriorating relationships. The twenty-first century brought losses in his far-sighted business ventures, including *Penthouse,* many possessions, and perhaps his home. His health was dealt a blow, but it has improved. By 2003, with a $40 million debt, Guccione's empire filed for Chapter 11 bankruptcy. Over a fifteen-year period *Penthouse* had steadily dropped from five million to a half million subscribers. The cause, some say, was a failure to diversify, or the public's loss of interest in softcore magazines and videos. An outside group of investors has purchased *Penthouse*, a subsidiary of General Media Communications, Inc.

Caligula is still alive, however. Caligula, in contemporary cinema, lives on as an existential character, in an undefined universe, a human being with no mandate, who had too much too soon, who was given more responsibility than he or those around him could grasp. Yet, he played his part as a solidifying figure who formalized the role of emperor for centuries to come. Just as he came to realize the potential of his power he was cut down for unknown reasons. Fortuna is capricious.

In the fall of 2007, a new DVD edition of *Caligula* was being offered to the marketplace in a three-disk version. There are some variations worth noting. The collection consists of the unrated edition, and two disks that include a documentary on the making of the film, and some interviews with Tinto Brass, Malcolm McDowell, and Helen Mirren, unseen but heard having a conversation against a screen playing the movie. There are interviews in the form of featurettes, omitted scenes, and behind-the-scenes documentaries. The producer of this edition also makes an appeal, in a printed folder to those who have the many missing miles of unseen footage, asking them to come forth and make it known, possibly for some future edition.

The most notable aspect of the 2007 edition is that the reproduction is now uniform in sound and color. The entire film is beautiful, lush, rich, and highly saturated in colors that more nearly resemble Caravaggio paintings than ever before. The color from the original negatives or from the printing process is about two f-stops too dark. The result is that faces, actions, and low-lit or spotlit scenes in earlier editions are lost to darkness. Blues and greens are especially vulnerable; consequently, some nudity is reduced or lost in the print. For instance, in Scene 19, lighting reduces the men ejaculating for Ennia's beauty preparation to one actor clearly identified. Caligula's face is often lost against a background of candles; his god declaration to the senate in Scene 42 is in cameo. The bedroom and courtyard shown during a storm, Scene 26, are dark to the level that Caligula's nudity is almost unnoticeable. Some characters' faces look older and tired. The editing, which has always been the biggest complaint about the film, appears to have been prudently adjusted in the transition between the storm scene and the Agrippina-Messalina tryst, Scenes 26 and 27, so that two additional back-and-forth inserts between the scenes make it smoother. The orgy in the galley, Scene 44, has been cleverly reedited so that all of the structural points where dialogue is involved are retained, but, in-between, shots have been added or rearranged. Earlier editions with poor composition and blank spaces have been eliminated.

Motion pictures and television document the world's cultural history. In this, *Caligula* is a benchmark. It is an omega-alpha film, marking the end of one era and the beginning of another era, in this instance, the end of a behavioral revolution and the beginning of a communications revolution. If *Caligula* is compared to other recent motion pictures about ancient life, its narrative is more complex but less well understood because of insufficient background; the cast was first-rate, and performed superbly under strenuous conditions. And, of course, Bob Guccione courageously made his appeal for greater artistic freedom without the benefit of expensive computer effects or a major studio's credit line. Furthermore, Caligula in cinema is a character who represents a contemporary icon: a popular leader, without moral direction, struck down for little or no reason by an unfathomable universe devoid of favorites, exemplifying an axiom: "Live now, for tomorrow never comes."

Perhaps the destruction of two of America's power centers, the twin towers of the World Trade Center in New York City on 11 September 2001, was also a benchmark, a cry from the depths of humanity. Many people think so, and therefore we must ask what caused it. Benchmarks are moments in history that give us pause to reflect and to adjust our moral compass. A moral compass points to both individual and collective good, to responsibility for the planet, to encouraging tolerance of diversity, and to respect for human life and all living things. Ancient stories are repeated frequently because we see compelling examples of human beings in conflict, mentally, physically, and spiritually. We see ourselves reflected in moments of glory and in funeral pyres. As Homer wrote in *The Iliad*:

> Like leaves on trees the race of man is found,
> Now green in youth, now withering on the ground:
> Another race the following spring supplies,
> They fall successive and successive rise.

CHAPTER NOTES

Chapter 1

1. Peter Bondanella, *Italian Cinema from Neorealism to the Present* (New York: Continuum Publishing Company, 2000), 3.
2. *Cabiria*. Directed by Piero Fosco (aka Giovanni Pastrone). Kino International Release, Eighteen Frames, Inc., 1990. Researchers have determined that ships could be destroyed by means of Archimedes' mirror device.
3. Richard Griffith and Arthur Mayer. *The Movies: The Sixty-Year Story of the World of Hollywood and Its Effect on America, from Pre-Nickelodeon Days to the Present* (New York: Simon and Schuster, 1957), 142. *Ben-Hur, A Tale of the Christ*. 1926. Directed by Fred Niblo. Written by Lew Wallace. 1926.
4. *Mutual Film Corporation v. Ohio Industrial Commission, 1915*. George N. Gordon, *Erotic Communications: Studies in Sex, Sin and Censorship* (New York: Hastings House, 1980), 166–169.
5. Eric Schaefer, *Bold! Daring! Shocking! True! A History of Exploitation Films, 1919–1959* (Durham, North Carolina: Duke University Press), 1999, 2.
6. Jeff Millar, "'Femme Fatale' Dietrich dies at Home in Paris at 90," *Houston Chronicle*, May 7, 1992.
7. Carol M. Ward, *Mae West: A Bio-Bibliography* (New York: Greenwood Press, 1989), 14–17; Molly Haskell, "Howard Hawks Masculine Feminine," *Film Comment*, March–April 1970, 39. Howard Hawks said West's personality was overwhelming; she thought her plays were literature.
8. *I, Claudius*. A BBC Television Production in association with London Film Productions Limited by arrangement with Gerry Blattner Productions, Ltd., 1976. Includes *The Epic That Never Was*, a documentary on the unfinished *I, Claudius*, 1937. Robin Wood, "Sternberg's Empress," *Film Comment*, March–April 1975, 6–12.
9. Michael Korda, *Charmed Lives: A Family Romance* (New York: Random House, 1979), 116, 118.
10. Albert Camus, *Caligula & Three Other Plays*, trans. Stuart Gilbert (New York: Vintage Books, 1962), vi. Spellings vary: Cherea/Chaerea.
11. Jon Solomon, *The Ancient World in the Cinema* (New Haven, Connecticut: Yale University Press, 2001), 162.
12. Fred Kaplan, Gore Vidal: *A Biography* (New York: Doubleday, 1999), 440–446.
13. Luke Ford, *A History of X: 100 Years of Sex in Film* (Amherst, New York: Prometheus Books, 1999), 66.
14. "Otto Preminger," *The Moviemakers*, PBS, 1996. Produced in association with Austrian Broadcasting Corporation. Distributed by Otto Preminger Films in association with TV Matters, Amsterdam/New York. Producer/director: Valerie A. Robins. Writer: Thomas J. Wiener.
15. Harold L. Nelson, ed. *Freedom of the Press from Hamilton to the Warren Court* (New York: Bobbs Merrill Company, 1967). *Roth v. United States*, pp. 299–305.
16. Lewis Segal, "Motion Pictures," *Show*, August 20, 1970, 41.
17. Gerald Mast and Bruce F. Kawin, *A Short History of the Movies*, 9th ed. (New York: Longman, 2006), 516–522.
18. Bondanella, *Italian Cinema from Neorealism to the Present*, 37.
19. Ibid., 229.
20. *The Magic of Fellini: A Biography*. Written and directed by Carmen Piccini. Turner Classic Movies Channel, 2004.
21. Bondanella, *Italian Cinema from Neorealism to the Present*, 235.
22. Patronius Arbiter, *Satyrica*, trans. Federic Raphael (London: Folio Society, 2003). *Satyrica*, the neuter plural, refers to satyrs. Many Greek sentimental tales of the Hellenistic period end in "-ica," as noted in the Introduction. Spellings in this book vary from some of the subtitles in *Fellini Satyricon*.

23. *Fellini Satyricon*. Directed by Federico Fellini. PEA Productioni Europee Associate, S.A.S., 1968.
24. John M. Culkin and Molly Haskell, "Both Sides Now: Pro and Con Reviews of Important Films, Fellini Satyricon," *Show*, April 1970, 21–22.
25. Bruce Williamson, "Porn Chic," *Playboy*, August 1973, 134–141, 153–154; Richard Hamner, "Playboy's History of Organized Crime," Part I, 89–94, 166–174.
26. Vivian Holland, "Playgirl's Top 10 Male Nude Scenes in Film," *Playgirl*, July 1997, 61. Seven of the ten mainstream films cited were post-1980.
27. *Television Digest* 20, no. 2 (January 14, 1980), 11.

Chapter 2

1. Jérôme Carcopino. *Daily Life in Ancient Rome: The People and the City at the Height of the Empire*, ed. Henry T. Rowell, trans. E. G. Lorimer (London: Folio Society, 2004), 23.
2. Ibid., 126–130, summarizes the quality of education from the time of Julius Caesar. As late as the fourth century, army recruits were typically illiterate.
3. The reign of the Julio-Claudian dynasty was preliminary to the peak years of the Roman Empire. Edward Gibbon, author of *The Decline and Fall of the Roman Empire*, wrote: "If a man were called to fix the period in the history of the world, during which the human race was most happy and prosperous, he would, without hesitation, name that which elapsed from the death of Domitian to the accession of Commodus." That was A.D. 96–180. Quoted in John Boardman, Jasper Griffin, and Oswyn Murray, *The Oxford Illustrated History of the Roman World* (Oxford: Oxford University Press, 1988), 440.
4. Carcopino, *Daily Life in Ancient* Rome, 266.
5. Patricia C. Johnson, "Of Myths and Monsters," *Houston Chronicle*, February 21, 2004; Suetonius, *The Twelve Caesars*, trans. Robert Graves (London: Penguin Books, 1979), 85.
6. Ibid., 147–148. A few days before his death, the lighthouse on Capri was damaged by an earthquake.
7. Cassius Dio, *The Roman History: The Reign of Augustus*, trans. Ian Scott-Kilvert (London: Penguin Books, 1987), 239.
8. "Caligula: Reign of Madness," *Biography*. History Channel, 1997. Scholars debate the attributes of Germanicus and his popularity. His persona and triumphs seem to shine in contrast to other leaders. I saw John F. Kennedy on the campaign trail in Fort Worth, Texas, in 1960. His qualities, previously seen only on black-and-white television, were undeniably greater in person.
9. Suetonius, *The Twelve Caesars*, 112.
10. Ibid., 121; Tacitus, *Annals*, Book IV, Chapter LVII, trans. John Jackson (Cambridge, MA: Harvard University Press/Loeb Library, 1998), 103.
11. Suetonius, *The Twelve Caesars*, 104.
12. Ibid., 131–132.
13. Cassius Dio, *The Roman History: The Reign of Augustus*, 249, 257.
14. Anthony A. Barrett, *Caligula: the Corruption of Power* (New Haven: Yale University Press, 1990), 85; Flavius Josephus, *The Works of Flavius Josephus*, Book XVIII, Chapter VI, trans. William Whiston (Philadelphia, PA: Winston Company, n.d.), 546. Translator Whiston cautions that Josephus reported some events with prejudice for he hated tyranny as exemplified by Caligula and had to depend on the records of Agrippa, whose father promoted the interests of Claudius.
15. Carcopino, *Daily Life in Ancient* Rome, xviii.
16. Suetonius, *The Twelve Caesars*, 155; Tacitus, *Annals*, Book VI, 233, 243–244. How Ennia's relationship with Caligula came about is uncertain.
17. Ibid., 142.
18. Ibid., 272.
19. Julius Agrippa is sometimes incorrectly referred to as Herod Agrippa. Barrett, *Caligula: the Corruption of Power* 34.
20. Herod became king under the Romans about 74 B.C. He built two palaces at Herodium, where his burial site was discovered in 2007. "Burial Site of King Herod Found Near Jerusalem," *Houston Chronicle*, May 8, 2007.
21. Josephus, *The Works of Flavius Josephus*, Book XVIII, 546–547.
22. Ibid., 549; Suetonius, *The Twelve Caesars*, 156–161.
23. Cassis Dio, *The Roman History: The Reign of Augustus*, 208.
24. The eighteen-year-old Pliny the Younger watched the eruption of Mt. Vesuvius from the relative safety of Misenum. His father Pliny the Elder sailed to help survivors; he died on the beach at Stabiae during the eruption. Thomas Noble Howe, "Power Houses," *Odyssey*, January/February 2005, 16–27.
25. Barrett, *Caligula: The Corruption of Power*, 74–75; *Ancient Discoveries — Ships*, History Channel, 2005. Pleasure ships were well known in ancient times. The Egyptians and the Hellenistic princes flaunted them as symbols of wealth.

26. Tacitus, *Annals*, 285.
27. Barrett, *Caligula: The Corruption of Power*, 93.
28. Suetonius, *The Twelve Caesars*, 159–160.
29. Ibid., 174–176.
30. Ibid., 164.
31. Barrett, *Caligula: The Corruption of Power*, 152–153.
32. Albert Camus, *Caligula & Three Other Plays*, trans. Stuart Gilbert (New York: Vantage Books, 1962).
33. Josephus, *The Works of Flavius Josephus*, Book XIX, 559–569.
34. Suetonius, *The Twelve Caesars*, 182; Josephus, *The Works of Flavius Josephus*, Book XIX, 571–572, 577–578. Herod the Great reigned as King of the Jews after being appointed by the senate in the days of Mark Anthony. He remained a friend of the Roman emperors and his sons became their friends. Herod Agrippa, the grandson of King Herod, had the kingdom restored to him by Claudius.
35. Linda Ann Nolan, "Emulating Augustus," *Odyssey*, May/June 2005, 39–47. The tomb of Augustus is adjacent to the restored Ara Pacis monument that stood on today's Via del Corso near the Tiber River.

Chapter 3

1. "The 12-minute Playboy Philosophy," *Playboy*, January 2004, 68.
2. Anthony Hayden-Guest, "Boom and Bust" (interview with Bob Guccione), *The Observer Magazine*, February 1, 2004. Online at http://observer.guardian.co.uk/magazine/story/0,11913,1136346,00.html.
3. *LFP Presents Larry Flynt, the Most Controversial Man That Nobody Knows* (Beverly Hills, CA: LFP, 1997), 17.
4. Bruce David, "Sexscene," *Screw*, May 6, 1974, 10.
5. Seth Mnookin, "The End of the Line for Penthouse?," Newsweek/MSNBC News, August 27, 2003, online.
6. "Macbeth," in *Variety Movie Guide 2000*, ed. Derek Eiley (New York: Perigee Books/Penguin Putnam, 2000), 18.
7. *Documentary on the Making of "Gore Vidal's Caligula."* Cinemedia West Corporation, 1981. Directed by Giancarlo Lui. Written by Alan Willis. This documentary is included with the twentieth anniversary edition of *Caligula*.
8. Ernest Volkman, "Bob Guccione: Penthouse Interview," *Penthouse*, May 1980, 116–118, 146–150.
9. Ibid., 114.
10. Fred Kaplan, *Gore Vidal: A Biography* (New York: Doubleday, 1999), 690.
11. W. I. Scorbie, "The Judgment of Vidal," *The Advocate*, March 9, 1977, 24–27.
12. Steven Austin, "Hail Caesar," *Adult Video News*, January 2000.
13. "Ben-Hur," *Variety Movie Guide*, 67.
14. Scorbie, "The Judgment of Vidal," 24.
15. Kaplan, *Gore Vidal: A Biography*, 690.
16. Ibid., 580.
17. Carol M. Ward, *Mae West: A Bio-Bibliography* (New York: Greenwood Press, 1989), 46.
18. William Scott Eyman, "Mae West: Hollywood Isn't Dead ... It's Taking a Siesta," *Take One*, September–October, 1974, 21.
19. Thomas W. Bohn and Richard L. Stromgren, *Light and Shadows* (Mountain View, CA: Mayfield Publishing Company, 1987), 337.
20. Ephraim Katz, *The Film Encyclopedia*, revised by Fred Klein and Ronald Dean Nolen (New York: HarperCollins Publishers, 1998), 1293; "*Jaws*," *E! True Hollywood Story*, E! Entertainment Network, 2002.
21. Tom Reck, "Huston Meets the Eye: A New Look at the Director," *Film Comment*, May–June 1973, 6–11.
22. Harlan Kennedy, "The Illusions of Nicholas Roeg," *American Film*, January–February 1980, 22.
23. Mario Gagliardotto, *Obiettivo Brass: Ii cinema secondo Tinto Brass* (Modena, Italy: Edizioni Ii Fiorino), 43–44; *The Documentary on the Making of "Gore Vidal's Caligula."*
24. John Walker, ed., *Halliwell's Who Is Who in the Movies* (New York: HarperCollins: 2003), 63.
25. Roger Ebert, "Russ Meyer King of the Nudies," *Film Comment*, January 1973, 35.
26. *Documentary on the Making of "Gore Vidal's Caligula."*
27. *Salon Kitty*, Coralta Cinematografica srl-Roma/Cinema Seven Film Gmb-Munich/Les Productions Fox Europe, 1975. Directed by Tinto Brass. Written by Ennio De Concini, Maria Pia Fusco, and Tinto Brass.
28. Joseph Conrad, *The Nigger of the Narcissus* (New York: Doubleday & Company, 1914).
29. Gagliardotto, *Obiettivo Brass*, 11.
30. Volkman, "Bob Guccione: Penthouse Interview," 150; Thomas Vinciguerra, "Porn Again: 'Caligula' Is Remastered in All Its Gross Glory," *New York Magazine*, September 6, 1999.
31. Bob Augustus interview, February 21, 2006.
32. Gagliardotto, *Obiettivo Brass*, 105, 110.
33. Ibid., 53–54.
34. Gideon Bachman, "The 120 Days of 'Salo': Pasolini's Last Film," *Film Comment*, March–April 1976, 40.

35. Gagliardotto, *Obiettivo Brass*, 53–54.
36. *Documentary on the Making of "Gore Vidal's Caligula."*
37. Suetonius, *The Twelve Caesars*, 275.
38. "Top twenty-five most controversial films of all time," *Entertainment Weekly*, June 16, 2006, 35–39.
39. "Peter O'Toole as T. E. Lawrence / Lawrence of Arabia [1962]," *Premiere*, April 2006, 72.
40. Stephen Whitty, "Not Unscathed but Unsurpassed," *Houston Chronicle*, May 16, 2004.
41. "Imperial Rome," Houston Museum of Natural Science, February 23–August 12, 2007. An assessment of Caesonia's appearance from a coin, even under magnification, is difficult. This exhibit included an attractive marble portrait/bust of Caligula.
42. Sheridan Morley, *John Gielgud: The Authorized Biography* (New York: Applause Theatre and Cinema Books, 2002), 419.
43. Ibid., 455.
44. *Ancient Discoveries — Ships*, History Channel, 2005. Directed by Stuart Clarke.

Chapter 4

1. Caligula visited Egypt in A.D. 18–19 with his father, Germanicus. Barrett, *Caligula: The Corruption of Power*, 14–15.
2. In the first two centuries, life expectancy was twenty-five to thirty years. Junia Caudilla, Caligula's first wife, died in childbirth. Carcopino, *Daily Life in Ancient Rome*, xix; Suetonius, *The Twelve Caesars*, 155.
3. *Love in the Ancient World* (A&E Television Networks, 1997).
4. John R. Clarke, *Roman Sex 100 BC to AD 250* (New York: Harry Abrams, 2003), 15.
5. Caligula had four wives and some male and female lovers. Suetonius, *The Twelve Caesars*, 179.
6. Men were sometimes nude; women were usually covered. Thomas Cahill, *Sailing the Wine Dark Sea: Why the Greeks Matter* (New York: Doubleday, 2003), 207.
7. Spartan women were the most likely to appear nude because they were trained as skilled athletes. Carl J. Richard, *Twelve Greeks and Romans Who Changed the World* (Lanham, Maryland: Roman and Littlefield, 2003), 32.
8. Kenneth Clark, *The Nude: A Study in Ideal Form* (Garden City, New York: Doubleday & Company, 1959), 23.
9. Ibid., 401–402.
10. Clever and colorful designs for the tunics and togas are used throughout the film. The ancient fabrics were probably wool, linen, or silk. The movie fabrics have the look and drape of various synthetics. The basic tunic consists of two cloth panels, gathered at the top of the shoulders and belted.
11. Excerpts from compositions by Khachaturian and Prokofiev add grandeur and significance to original work by Paul Clemente. The music reinforces the viewer's expectations of an epic film. An epic film usually tells about the heroic exploits of its extraordinary protagonist. For instance, Achilles was born to the Nereid, Thetis, and her mortal husband King Peleus. She tried to burn away the mortality of her children over the sacred fire, but only Achilles survived. He became the Greeks' greatest warrior. Caligula is not exactly an epic hero. Nevertheless, the majestic power of a film's musical score assists in elevating it.
12. Unlike Tiberius, Caligula lived well until his father died in A.D. 19. Then he lived with his mother to A.D. 27, while she tried to avenge his father's death. During his teen years he was with his great grandmother, Livia, and grandmother, Antonia, A.D. 27–31. Suetonius, *The Twelve Caesars*, 154–155.
13. Caligula was born 31 August A.D. 12. In A.D. 31, at age 18, he was summoned to Capri. Suetonius, *The Twelve Caesars*, 154.
14. John Boardman, Jasper Griffin, and Oswyn Murray, eds., *The Oxford Illustrated History of the Roman World* (New York: Oxford University Press, 2001), pp. 140–141, suggest the possibility that some exterior and panoramic shots could have been added. The palace is located too far from the stunning azure grottoes located on Capri's shore for the elderly Tiberius to have been able to make the trip conveniently. Villa Jovis had hot and cold water as explained on "Roman Vice," History Channel, 2005.
15. Tiberius, a different man in later life, commanded his legions on the northern front with discipline and moral standards. On Capri, Suetonius wrote that he liked to trick his soldiers into getting drunk so that he could charge them with some infraction and then tie the genitals with a knot, as shown in the film. Suetonius, *The Twelve Caesars*, 142.
16. Ibid., 147.
17. Tiberius was called a miser, but he managed to save enough money to carry on his lifestyle and to reign with little financial assistance from the senate. He did confiscate the wealth of some individuals and numerous foreigners. Ibid., 133.
18. While Tiberius lived, the Roman Empire was relatively stable and prosperous. Caligula inherited the wealth Tiberius had accrued during his reign.
19. After Caligula shaved in Scene 7, he be-

came an adult at age eighteen. By Scene 11, he is twenty-four; thus, Caligula lived about six years on Capri. Suetonius, *The Twelve Caesars*, 154.

20. Suetonius wrote that Tiberius was ill and traveling back to Capri when he died in a country house on 16 March A.D. 37 (ibid., 147). When Tiberius died, Macro was prefect of the Praetorian Guard, according to the movie. Various stories suggest that Tiberius may have been poisoned, strangled, or smothered by Macro. In early A.D. 37, Caligula is twenty-three. Ibid., 155.

21. Caligula asks equal allegiance for himself and his three sisters. Ibid., 157.

22. Caligula was very popular. The child of Germanicus was greeted with a personal response he had not seen since his father was alive. Ibid., 156–161; Caligula inherited Tiberius's entire fortune of 27 million gold pieces, which he squandered within the first year. Ibid., 171.

23. Tiberius found that his commander of the Praetorian Guards, Aelius Sejanus, was becoming dangerously popular. By pretending to accept his success, by extending high office to him, and by implying he would be able to marry into the imperial family, Tiberius led Sejanus unknowingly into a plot of alleged conspiracy. Sejanus was replaced by Macro, who switched his allegiance to Caligula and eventually was forced to commit suicide. Ibid., 164.

24. After his first wife died, Caligula seduced Ennia Naevia, Macro's wife, and put an oath in writing to marry her if he became emperor. Ibid., 155.

25. Supposedly unattractive (based largely on coinage that is difficult to assess), divorced with three daughters, and promiscuous, Melonia Caesonia attracted Caligula. Ibid., 163.

26. Caligula's first marriage was to Junia Claudilla, followed by brief marriages to Livia Orestilla and Lollia Paulina (ibid., 155, 163). Caesonia was his fourth wife.

27. Referring to these events might have helped to explain Caligula's warped mental state. In 1976, when the film was shot, post traumatic stress syndrome was little understood, but with the end of the Vietnam War and the eventual publicizing of PTSD due to its effect on soldiers returning from war, viewers could eventually empathize with him.

28. Caligula ordered that statues of gods, including Jupiter, have the heads replaced with his own. Usually, god status was not awarded by the senate until after a person died. In death, Augustus was recognized as a god. Caligula's move proved to be very unpopular. Ibid., 161. Gaius wanted to erect his statue in the temple of Jerusalem, but the Jews rejected it, saying that Roman soldiers would have to kill them first. Josephus, *The Works of Flavius Josephus*, Book XVIII, 549–553.

29. The death of Tiberius Gemellus was contrived by Caligula. Suetonius, *The Twelve Caesars*, 162.

30. Caligula and Caesonia lived promiscuous lives until she gave him a child, then he married her. Ibid., 164.

31. On what he thought was his deathbed, Caligula signed all he personally owned and the empire over to Drusilla (ibid., 163); Caligula was cruel his entire life (ibid., 155).

32. Caligula forced the senate to declare him a god. Ibid., 161.

33. Caligula used a room in the palace as a brothel. Ibid., 173.

34. Caligula had no real wars to fight; on trips to Germany and Gaul he engaged in faux skirmishes. Ibid., 173–176.

35. Caligula prepared to make up a battle story for presentation. He faced the Rhine river and told soldiers to gather seashells. He also picked out a few tall Gauls to represent captives. Ibid., 175.

36. On the shore of Gaul opposite the British Isles, he built a lighthouse and returned to Rome. Arriving on his birthday, he was joyfully received by the people. Ibid., 176.

37. Josephus cites at least three conspiracies brewing against Caligula. Cassius Chaerea's reasons for leading the conspiracy are speculation: He may have thought the deed was worthy of a free man, he may have been ashamed of the indignities Caligula imposed on him, and he lived in fear every day. He was in the best position to carry off the assassination and he may have believed authorities and the public might find it acceptable, even heroic. Josephus, *The Works of Josephis Flavius*, Book XVIX, 560–565.

38. The debate about the future of Rome was influenced greatly by the soldiers who wanted continuation of the monarchy, although some senators wanted a return to the republic. Ibid., 565–574.

39. Claudius, once regarded as incompetent, reigned from A.D. 41 to 51, and is believed to have been murdered by his wife Agrippina, Caligula's sister.

40. This is a translation from the Italian film credits.

41. Some artists and craftsmen did not get screen credits. They used pseudonyms such as Paul Clemente for Bruno Nicolai or spelled their names somewhat differently: Jole Cecchini for Iole Cecchini. Jack H. Silverman was executive producer, Masolino D'Amico was a translator, Paula Mitchell was a researcher, Giovanni Natalucci and Franco Velchi were ar-

chitects. Russell Lloyd and Bob Augustus were among many editors. Uncredited cast members include Patrick Allen for voice dubbing and about a dozen extras who served as priestesses and brothel workers. The various editions often required additional personnel.

Chapter 5

1. Arthur Knight, "Sex in Cinema—1977," *Playboy*, November 1977, 156–167.
2. These filmmakers, among others, visited Houston media and the University of Houston beginning in 1967, with director Norman Jewison screening *In the Heat of the Night*, a project initiated by MPAA president Jack Valenti.
3. *All the President's Men*, Warner Bros. and Wildwood Enterprises, 1976. The press kit includes biographies, photographs, audiotapes, and a film strip on building the *Washington Post* offices in Los Angeles.
4. "Done with 'Caligula,' Ready to Play Martha," *New York Times*, April 11, 2004. Mirren won an Emmy for HBO's *Elizabeth I* in 2006.
5. Nancy Debevoise, "No Violence, No Profanity, No Nudity," *American* Film, July–August 1976, 32.
6. Glenn Collins, "X-films Kiss of Death," *Houston Chronicle*, April 10, 1990.
7. Jeff Miller, "Breaking the Code of NC-17," *Houston Chronicle*, October 12, 1990.
8. In the early 1970s Georgina Spelvin said she had a difficult time as an actress in New York, so she turned to adult filmmaking. During the late 1970s I met Seka on tour when her prospects looked good.
9. The statement on preserving freedom for the adult video industry was played frequently at the beginning of many videos during much of the 1980s. It urged viewers to support the Free Speech Legal Defense Fund.
10. Bob Augustus, adult movie distributor, appeared as a guest in a class at the University of Houston School of Communication on 21 February 2006.
11. Adult Film Association of America, promotional packet, circa 1982.
12. Derek Elley, "Caligula," in *Variety Movie Guide 2000* (Berkley Publishing Group, 2000), 125. Penthouse Pet Lori Wagner said she went to Cannes for a screening.
13. Steve Austin, "Hail, Caesar," *AVN*, January 2000.
14. "Notes on a Few Movies" (*Caligula* review), *Les Cahiers du Cinéma* No. 315 (September 1980), 54.
15. Austin, "Hail, Caesar."
16. "Housecall," *Penthouse*, June 1980, 6.
17. "Anneka and Lori," *Penthouse*, June 1980, 141–153.
18. Dave Kehr, "The New Male in Melodrama," *American* Film, April 1983, 43.
19. Gordon Marino, "Real Men Shed Tears: Why It's All Right to Cry," *Newsweek*, August 27, 2007, 20; Samuel Osherman, *Finding Our Fathers* (New York: Free Press/Macmillan, 1985).
20. "The Myth of the 'Cool' Dad," *Details*, September 2007, 200. These articles say that the 2007 guy increasingly rejects invitations for sex and that fathers are more involved if they settle down, committed.
21. Rick Stewart, "Pushing Porn: The Selling of Sinema," *Starlet*, August 1981, 50.
22. "Cable TV 'Skin' Competition Gets Hot," *Broadcasting*, August 24, 1981, 22–23.
23. "You Can Turn the Tide," pamphlet, Texas Center for Media Awareness through Research and Education, Houston. From 1977 to 1997 I appeared in 15 trials as an expert witness. Texas, 1981. Dr. George Zenner, director, Family Services, University of Texas Medical School, Houston, and Chairman, Board of Directors. Unsigned circular asks Houstonians to contact the district attorney and the Houston Police Department vice division about the opening of *Caligula* on 16 October 1981.
24. Helen Gardner, *Art Through the Ages* (New York: Harcourt, Brace and Company, 1948), 515.
25. E. H. Gombrich, *The Story of Art* (New York: Phaidon Publishers/Oxford University Press, 1951), 328.
26. *Centurians of Rome*. Directed by John Christopher. Written by Timothy Michaels. Hand in Hand Uranus Films, Inc., 1981.
27. Robert Di Bernardo's demise is detailed in Legs McNeil and Jennifer Osborne, *The Other Hollywood: The Uncensored Oral History of the Porn Film Industry* (New York: HarperCollins/Regan Books, 2005), 431–434.
28. *Attorney General's Commission* on *Pornography: Final Report*. Washington, D.C.: United States Justice Department, 1095.
29. *Roommates* (1981) press kit.
30. Ibid.
31. *Attorney General's Report* on *Pornography. Final Report*, 74–75. For decades 35mm and 16mm reels of film were distributed through the U.S. mail to theater owners and individual customers.
32. *A History of X*, 190.
33. John Colapinto, "The Twilight of Bob Guccione," *Rolling Stone*, April 1, 2004, 64.
34. "Pubs to Publishing," in *LFP Presents Larry Flynt* (Beverly Hills, California: LFP), 17.
35. "Larry Flynt: Raw, Exposed, and Uncen-

sored," *E! True Hollywood Story,* E! Entertainment Network, April 2002.

36. Christopher Hitchens, "Hustler with Cause," reprinted from *Vanity* Fair, in *LFP Presents Larry Flynt,* 72.

37. "Networks Relax Rules on Censorship," *New York Daily News/Houston Chronicle,* December 28, 1988.

38. *The People vs. Larry Flynt* review. *DVD & Video Guide 2005,* 848.

39. Derek Elley, "Natural Born Killers," *Variety Movie Guide 2000,* 592.

40. Ephraim Katz, "Rob Lowe," in *The Film Encyclopedia,* ed. Fred Klein and Ronald Dean Nolen (New York: HarperCollinsPerennial, 1998), 850.

41. If Anderson and Lee were not famous, there would be little market for this poorly made, out-of-focus home video shot while on vacation in 1997. Minette Hillyer discusses it in "Sex in the Suburban: Porn Home Movies, and the Live Action Performance of Love in *Pam and Tommy Lee: Hardcore* and *Uncensored,"* in *Porn Studies,* ed. Linda Williams (Durham, North Carolina: Duke University Press, 2004), 50–76. Tommy Lee starred in *Tommy Lee Goes to College* (2005), an NBC-TV comedy; Pamela Anderson appeared on cable's *Comedy Central* in 2005.

42. *1 Night in Paris,* adult amateur video. Red Light District Video, 2004.

43. Bruce Westbrook, "1995 a Banner Year for Sales," *Houston Chronicle,* January 5, 1996.

44. Christine Spines, "Total Recall," *Entertainment Weekly,* April 6, 2007, 48–50.

45. Eric Schlosser, "Empire of the Obscene," *New Yorker,* March 10, 2003, 61–71.

46. Maria St. John, "How to Do Things with the Starr Report: Pornography, Performance, and the President's Penis," in Williams, *Porn Studies,* 27–29.

47. CBS *Evening News,* October 20, 2003.

48. According to the U.S. Census Bureau, 28.6 percent of adults age 45 to 59 were unattached in 2003, compared with only 18.8 percent in 1980. AARP claims that 20 percent of older singles have sex once a week or more. Sixty-one percent report that they are have unprotected sex. Barbara Kantrowitz, "Sex & Love: The New World," *Newsweek,* February 20, 2006, 51–60.

49. David Brooks, "Today's Tune Is One That Cole Porter Would Never Hum," *Houston Chronicle,* July 13, 2007.

50. "Young Women, Porn & Profits. Corporate America's Secret Affair," *Primetime Thursday,* ABC-TV, 2003–2004.

51. "Porn in the USA," *60 Minutes,* CBS-TV, 2003–2004.

52. *The True Story of Troy,* History Channel, May 16, 2004. This shows a scholars' reconstruction of the Troy site and what might have caused the Trojan War around 1250 B.C. They try to correlate their findings with Homer's *Iliad,* supposedly composed 500 years later.

53. Fred Schruers, "Oliver's Army," *Premiere,* September 2004, 55–57; Chris Heath, "Wild," *Gentleman's Quarterly,* November 2004, 232–239.

54. Michael Glitz, "The New Degaying of Hollywood," *The Advocate,* September 14, 2005, 41.

55. Gillian Flynn, "Empire Falls," *Entertainment Weekly,* Sumner 2005, 151.

BIBLIOGRAPHY

Books

Attorney General's Commission on Pornography. Final Report. Washington, D.C.: United States Justice Department, 1985.

Aurelius, Marcus. *Meditations.* Translated by Maxwell Staniforth. London: Folio Society, 2002.

Barrett, Anthony A. *Caligula: The Corruption of Power.* New Haven: Yale University Press, 1989.

Belton, John. *American Cinema, American Culture.* Boston: McGraw-Hill, 2005.

Blum, Daniel. *A Pictorial History of the Silent Screen.* New York: Grosset & Dunlap, 1953.

_____ and John Kobal. *A New Pictorial History of the Talkies.* New York: G. P. Putnam's Sons, 1958.

Boardman, John, Jasper Griffin, and Oswyn Murray. *The Oxford Illustrated History of the Roman World.* Oxford: Oxford University Press, 1988.

Bohn, Thomas W., and Richard L. Stromgren. *Light* and *Shadows: A History of Motion Pictures.* Mountain View, California: Mayfield, 1987.

Bondanella, Peter. *Italian Cinema: From Neorealism to the Present.* New York: Continuum, 2000.

Bordwell, David, and Kristin Thompson. *Film Art: An Introduction.* Boston: McGraw-Hill, 2004.

Bywater, Tim, and Thomas Sobchack. *Introduction to Film Criticism: Major Critical Approaches to Narrative Film.* White Plains, New York: Longman, 1989.

Cahill, Thomas. *Sailing the Wine-Dark Sea: Why the Greeks Matter.* New York: Doubleday, 2003.

Camus, Albert. *Caligula & Three Other Plays.* Translated by Stuart Gilbert. New York: Vintage Books, 1962.

Carcopino, Jérôme. *Daily Life in Ancient Rome: The People and the City at the Height of the Empire.* London: Folio Society, 2004.

Cawkwell, Tim, and John M. Smith. *The World Encyclopedia of the Film.* New York: World Publishing, 1972.

Cinema Year by Year: 1894–2004. The Complete Illustrated Guide to a Century of Cinema. London: Darling Kindersley Limited, 2004.

Clark, Kenneth. *The Nude: A Study in Ideal Form.* Garden City: New York: Doubleday Anchor Books, 1959.

Clarke, John R. *Roman Sex: 100 BC–AD 250.* New York: Harry N. Abrams, 2003.

Comfort, Alex, ed. *The Joy of Sex: A Gourmet Guide to Love Making.* New York: Simon and Schuster, 1972.

Community Standards Study, Houston, Texas. Prepared for Theatres West and Universal Amusement Company. Houston, Texas: Creative Research Group, 1979.

Cook, David A. *A History of Narrative Film.* New York: W. W. Norton, 2004.

Danville, Eric. *The Penthouse Erotic Video Guide: The Best of the XXX Adult Films Reviewed.* New York: Warner Books/ General Media Communications, 2003.

D'Aulaire, Ingri, and Edgar D'Aulaire. *Book of Greek Myths.* Garden City, New York; Doubleday, 1962.

De Franciscis, Alfonso. *Guide with Reconstructions: Pompeii-Herculaneum and the Villa Jovis, Capri, Past and Present.* Rome: Vision, S.R.L., 1964.

Dio, Cassius. *The Roman History: The Reign of Augustus.* Translated by Ian Scott-Kilvert. London: Penguin Books, 1987.

Dover, K. J. *Greek Homosexuality.* New York: Vintage Books/Random House, 1980.

Duckworth, George F., ed. *The Complete Roman Drama: All the Extant Comedies of Plautus and Terence, and the Tragedies of Seneca, in a Variety* of *Translations.* Two volumes. New York: Random House, 1942.

Elley, Derek, ed. *Variety Movie Guide 2000.* New York: Perigee, 2000.

Elsom, John. *Erotic Theatre.* New York: Delta/ Dell, 1973.

Fellini, Federico. *La Dolce Vita.* Translated by Oscar DeLiso and Bernard Shir-Cliff. New York: Ballantine Books, 1961.

Ford, Luke. *A History of X: 100 Years of Sex in Film.* Amherst, New York: Prometheus Books, 1999.

Franklin, Joe. *Classics of the Silent Screen.* New York: Citadel Press, 1959.

Freeman, Charles. *The Closing of the Western Mind: The Rise of Faith and the Fall of Reason.* New York: Alfred A. Knopf, 2003.

Gagliardotto, Mario. *Obiettivo Brass: Il clnema secondo Tinto Brass.* Modena, Italy: Edizioni Il Fiorino.

Gardner, Helen. *Art Through the Ages.* New York: Harcourt, Brace, 1948.

Gelmis, Joseph. *The Film Director as Superstar.* Garden City, New York: Doubleday, 1970.

Gibbon, Edward. *The Decline and Fall of the Roman Empire.* New York: Wise, 1943.

Gordon, George N. *Erotic Communications: Studies in Sex, Sin and Censorship.* New York: Hastings House, 1980.

Griffith, Richard, and Arthur Mayer. *The Movies: The Sixty-Year Story of the World of Hollywood and Its Effect on America, from Pre–Nickelodeon Days to the Present.* New York: Simon and Schuster, 1957.

Hartnoll, Phyllis, ed. *The Oxford Companion to the Theatre.* Oxford: Oxford University Press, 1990.

Hawes, William, ed. *Pornography Cinema Community Standards.* Houston: University of Houston, 1975.

_____. *Pornography Media Community Standards.* Houston: University of Houston, 1993.

Herodotus. *The Histories.* Translated by Aubrey de Selincourt. London: Folio Society, 2006.

Higham, Charles. *The Art of the American Film.* Garden City, New York: Anchor/Doubleday, 1974.

Hirshberg, Jack. *A Portrait of All the President's Men: The Story behind the Filming of the Most Devastating Detective Story of the Century.* New York: Warner Books, 1976.

Homer. *The Iliad.* Translated by Robert Eagles. London: Viking Penguin Books, 1996.

Hudson, Rock, and Sara Davidson. *Rock Hudson: His Story.* New York: Avon Books, 1987.

Jenkins, Ian. *Greek and Roman Life.* London: British Museum Press, 1986.

Josephus Flavius. *The Works of Josephus Flavius.* Translated by William Whiston. Philadelphia, Pennsylvania: John C. Winston, n.d.

Kaplan, Fred. *Gore Vidal: A Biography.* New York: Doubleday, 1999.

Katz, Ephraim. *The Film Encyclopedia.* Revised by Fred Klein and Dean Nolen. New York: HarperCollins, 1998.

Katz, Jonathan. *Gay American History: Lesbians and Gay Men in the U.S.A.* New York: Discus/Avon Books, 1978.

Kipnis, Laura. *Bound and Gagged: Pornography and the Politics of Fantasy in America.* Durham, North Carolina: Duke University Press, 1999.

Knight, Arthur. *The Liveliest Art: A Panoramic History of the Movies.* New York: New American Library, 1957.

Kolker, Robert. *Film, Form, and Culture.* Boston, Massachusetts: McGraw-Hill, 1999.

La Rue, Chi Chi, with John Erich. *Making It Big: Sex Stars, Porn Films, and Me.* Los Angeles: Alyson Books, 1997.

Lauro, Giuseppina. *Guide with Reconstructions of Ancient Ostia.* In collaboration with the Soprintendenza archeologica di Ostia. Roma: Vision, S.R.L., 1981.

Life Goes to the Movies. Alexandria, Virginia: Time-Life Books, 1975.

Linden, George W. *Reflections of the Screen.* Belmont, California: Wadsworth, 1970.

Lovelace, Linda, with Mike McGrady. *Ordeal.* Secaucus, New Jersey: Citadel Press, 1980.

Maltin, Leonard, ed. *Movie and Video Guide 1995.* New York: Plume/Penguin Books, 1994.

Man, Glenn. *Radical Visions: American Film Renaissance, 1967–1976.* Westport, Connecticut: Greenwood Press, 1994.

Martin, Mick, and Marsha Porter. *DVD & Video Guide 2005.* New York: Ballantine Books, 2004.

Mast, Gerald, and Bruce F. Kawin. *A Short History of the Movies.* New York: Pearson Longman, 2006.

Matyszak, Philip. *Chronicle of the Roman Empire: The Rulers of Ancient Rome from Romulus to Augustus.* London: Thames & Hudson, 2003.

McHam, David. *Law and the Press in Texas.* Houston: Texas Press Association, Texas Daily Newspaper Association, Texas Association of Broadcasters, 1996.

McNeil, Legs, and Jennifer Osborne, with Peter Pavia. *The Other Hollywood: The Uncensored Oral History of the Porn Film Industry.* New York: Regan Books/HarperCollins, 2005.

Michael, Paul, ed. *The American Movies Reference Book: The Sound Era.* Englewood Cliffs, New Jersey: Prentice-Hall, 1970.

Morley, Sheridan. *John Gielgud: The Authorized Biography.* New York: Applause Theatre and Cinema Books, 2002.

Nelson, Harold L., ed. *Freedom of the Press from Hamilton to the Warren Court.* Indianapolis, Indiana: Bobbs-Merrill, 1967.

Oates, Whitney J., and Eugene O'Neill, Jr., eds. *The Complete Greek Drama: All the Extant Tragedies of Aeschylus, Sophocles and Euripides, and the Comedies of Aristophanes and Menander, in a Variety of Translations. Two volumes. New York: Random House, 1968.

Osherman, Samuel. *Finding Our Fathers.* New York: Free Press/Macmillan, 1985.

Perkins, D. M.. *Deep Throat: A Novel.* New York: Dell/Quicksilver, 1973.

Petronius. *Petronius Arbiter: Satyrica.* Translated by Frederic Raphael. London: Folio Society, 2003.

Renault, Mary. *Fire from Heaven.* New York: Pantheon Books, 1969.

_____. *The Nature of Alexander.* New York: Pantheon Books, 1975.

_____. *The Persian Boy.* New York: Pantheon Books, 1972.

Richard, Carl J. *Twelve Greeks and Romans Who Changed the World.* Lanham, Maryland: Roman & Littlefield, 2003.

Rowse, A.L. *Homosexuals in History: A Study of Ambivalence in Society, Literature and the Arts.* New York: Dorset Press/Macmillan, 1983.

Russell, Paul. *The Gay 100: A Ranking of the Most Influential Gay Men and Lesbians, Past and Present.* New York: Citadel Press, 1995.

Sandford, John. *The New German Cinema.* London: Oswald Wolff Publishers, 1980.

Schaefer, Eric. *"Bold! Daring! Shocking! True!" A History of Exploitation Films, 1919–1959.* Durham, North Carolina: Duke University Press, 1999.

Sklar, Robert. *Film: An International History of the Medium.* Englewood Cliffs, New Jersey: Prentice Hall and Harry N. Abrams, 1993.

Solomon, Jon. *The Ancient World in the Cinema.* New Haven, Connecticut: Yale University Press, 2001.

Staccioli, R. A. *Rome Past and Present with Reconstructions of Ancient Monuments.* Roma: Vision, S.R.L., 1962.

Stanley, Robert Henry. *Making Sense of the Movies: Filmmaking in the Hollywood Style.* Boston: McGraw-Hill, 2003.

Suetonius. *The Twelve Caesars.* Translated by Robert Graves. London: Penguin Books, 1979.

Sundgren, Nils Petter. *The New Swedish Cinema.* Stockholm: Swedish Institute, 1970.

Tacitus. *Annals.* Books IV-VI, XI-XII. Translated by John Jackson. Cambridge, Massachusetts: Harvard University Press, 1998.

Thompson, Kristin, and David Bordwell. *Film History: An Introduction.* New York: McGraw-Hill, 2003.

Thucydides. *History of the Peloponnesian War, Selections.* Chicago, Illinois: Henry Regnery, n.d.

Tyler, Parker. *Classics of the Foreign Film: A Pictorial Treasury.* New York: Bonanza Books, 1962.

_____. *Screening the Sexes: Homosexuality in the Movies.* Garden City, New York: Anchor Books/Doubleday, 1973.

Tzachou-Alexandri, Olga. *Mind and Body: Athletic Contests in Ancient Greece.* Athens: Ministry of Culture, National Hellenic Committee, 1989.

Urdang, Laurence, ed. *The Timetables of American History.* New York: Touchstone Books, 1981.

Vermilye, Jerry. *The Great British Films.* Secaucus, New Jersey: Citadel Press, 1978.

Vidal, Gore. *A Thirsty Evil: Seven Short Stories.* San Francisco: Gay Sunshine Press, 1981.

Virgil. *Publius Vergilius Maro: The Aeneid.* Translated by David West. London: Penguin Books, 1991.

Walker, Alexander, Sybil Taylor and Ulrich Ruchti. *Stanley Kubrick, Director: A Visual Analysis.* New York: W. W. Norton, 1999.

Walker, John, ed. *Halliwell's Who's Who in the Movies.* New York: HarperCollins, 2003.

Ward, Carol M. *Mae West: A Bio-Bibliography.* New York: Greenwood Press, 1989.

Warhol, Andy. *The Philosophy of Andy Warhol: From A to B and Back Again.* New York: Harcourt Brace Jovanovich, 1975.

Wells, H. G. *The Outline of History: Being a Plain History of Life and Mankind.* New York: Garden City, 1920.

Williams, Linda. *Porn Studies.* Durham, North Carolina: Duke University Press, 2004.

Williams, Tennessee. *Memoirs.* New York: Anchor Press/Doubleday, 1983.

Wood, Edward D., Jr. *A Study in the Motivation of Censorship, Sex and the Movies.* Los Angeles, California: Gallery Press, 1973.

Wright, Basil. *The Long View: An International History of Cinema.* St. Albans, England: Paladin, 1976.

Ziegfeld, Richard, and Paulette Ziegfeld. *The Ziegfeld Touch: The Life and Times of Florenz Ziegfeld, Jr.* New York: Harry N. Abrams, 1993.

Periodicals

Abele, Robert, and others. "2005" [Movie Reviews], *Premiere*, February 2005: 72.

Acocella, Joan. "The Girls Next Door: Life in the Centerfold," *New Yorker*, March 20, 2006: 144–148. Review of *The Playmate Book: Six Decades of Centerfolds.*

Andriette, Bill. "Sodomy & the Supreme Court." *The Guide*, August 2003, 17–20.

"Animal Lovers/Pretty Doggie No. 2." *Houston Chronicle*, 28 May 1976: 18.

"Anneka and Lori." *Penthouse.* June 1980: 141–153.
"Are Music and Movies Killing America's Soul?" *Time,* June 12, 1995: 24–35, 37–39.
Austin, Steven. "Hail, Caesar." *AVN: The Adult Entertainment Monthly,* January 2000.
Baldwin, Barry. "Power Corrupts—and Absolute Power Is Even Nicer: New *Lives* of Caligula and Claudius." *Ancient History Bulletin* 4 (no. 6), 1990: 133–149.
Brady, Sara. "What Hollywood Makes." *Premiere,* March 2005: 91.
Brooks, David. "Today's Tune Is One That Cole Porter Would Never Hum." *New York Times,* July 13, 2007.
"Cable TV 'Skin' Competition Gets Hot." *Broadcasting,* August 24, 1981: 22–23.
"Caligula." *Penthouse,* May 1980: 69–89.
"Chicago May Bar Young at Superviolent Films." *Houston Chronicle,* May 10, 1976.
"Cinema Sex." *Film Comment,* January–February 1973.
Claessner, Verina, "Censorship in London." *Film Comment,* January 30, 1973: 31.
Colapinto, John. "The Twilight of Bob Guccione." *Rolling Stone,* April 1, 2004: 63.
Collins, Glenn. "X-films Kiss of Death." *New York Times,* April 10, 1990.
David, Bruce. "Sexscene." *Screw,* May 6, 1974: 10.
Debevoise, Nancy. "No Violence, No Profanity, No Nudity." *American Film,* July–August 1976: 32.
Diehl, Digby. "What We Have Here Is a Failure to Communicate." *Show,* July 9, 1970: 36.
"Done with 'Caligula,' Ready to Play Martha." *New York Times,* April 11, 2004: 8.
Ehrenstein, David. "Melodrama and the New Woman." *Film Comment,* September–October 1978: 59–61.
Eyman, William Scott. "Mae West. Hollywood Isn't Dead ... It's Taking a Siesta." *Take One,* January 22, 1974: 19–21.
Faber, Charles. "Young and Old in the World's Oldest." *The Advocate,* June 28, 1978: 38.
"Famous 'Nude Dudes!' The Men of Celebrity." *Sleuth,* June 9, 1997.
Farber, Stephen. "Censorship." *Film Comment,* January 1973: 32–33.
_____. "Russellmania," *Film Comment,* November–December 1975: 40–47.
Flynn, Gillian. "Empire Falls." *Entertainment Weekly,* Summer 2005: 151.
Flynt, Larry. *LFP Presents Larry Flynt: The Most Controversial Man That Nobody Knows.* Beverly Hills, California: LFP Inc., 1997.
Gage, Nicholas. "Probe Finds Mafia Is Involved in Pornographic Film Industry." *Houston Chronicle,* October 12, 1975: 4.
Glitz, Michael. "The New Degaying of Hollywood." *The Advocate,* September 14, 2005: 41.
Goldstein, Al. "X-Rated Video." *Penthouse,* February 1986: 133.
_____. "X-Rated Video." *Penthouse,* July 1987: 131.
Hamner, Richard. "Playboy's History of Organized Crime." *Playboy.* August 1973: 89–94, 166–174.
Haskell, Molly. "Howard Hawks Masculine Feminine." *Film Comment,* March–April 1970: 39.
Hayden-Guest, Anthony. "Boom and Bust" (interview with Bob Guccione). *The Observer Magazine,* February 1, 2004. Online at http://observer.guardian.co.uk/magazine/story/0,11913,1136346,00.html
Heath, Chris. "Wild." *Gentleman's Quarterly,* November 2004: 232–239.
Hitchens, Christopher. "Hustler with Cause." Reprinted from *Vanity Fair,* in Flynt, *LFP Presents Larry Flynt,* p. 72.
Holloway, Ron. "We Are Playing with Reality. A Conversation with Vigot Sjöman and Lena Nyman." *Film Journal,* Spring 1971: 2–22.
"Hooking Up, Finding Love." *The Advocate,* August 16, 2005: 24–33.
Howe, Thomas Noble. "Power Houses: The Seaside Villas of Stabiae." *Odyssey,* January–February 2005: 16–17, 50–51.
Kantrowitz, Barbara. "Sex and Love: The New World." *Newsweek,* February 20, 2006: 51–60.
Kehr, Dave. "The New Male in Melodrama." *American Film,* April 1983: 43.
Kennedy, Harlan. "The Illusions of Nicholas Roeg." *American Film,* January–February 1980: 22–27.
Knight, Arthur. "Sex in Cinema—1973. *Playboy,* December 1973: 150–160, 168–180.
_____. "Sex in Cinema—1977." *Playboy,* November 1977: 156–167.
_____. "Sex Stars of 1975." *Playboy,* December 1975: 178–190, 227–278.
_____. "The Story of O." *Playboy,* December 1975: 127–131.
Kolker, Phillip, "Ken Russell's Biopics: Grander and Gaudier." *Film Comment,* May–June 1973: 42–45.
Liu, Melinda, and Christopher Dickey. "Unearthing the Bible." *Newsweek,* August 30, 2004: 32–36.
Lubove, Seth. "The Player." *Forbes,* December 8, 2003: 114–126.
"Maryland Censors Prohibit 'Snuff.'" *Houston Chronicle,* March 5, 1976.
Mathews, Linda. "Obscenely on Stage." *Houston Chronicle,* March 23, 1975.
"Millennium Special: The Best of All Time: *Unzipped* Rates the Best Performers, Direc-

tors, and Films." *Unzipped*, January 4, 2000: 19.
Miller, Jeff. "Breaking the Code of NC-17." *Houston Chronicle*, October 12, 1990.
Mnookin, Seth. "The End of the Line for Penthouse?" *Newsweek* Web exclusive, August 27, 2003.
Morino, Gordon. "Why Men Shed Tears: Why It's All Right to Cry." *Newsweek*, August 20/27 2007: 20.
Nolan, Linda Ann. "Emulating Augustus: The Fascist-Era Excavation of the Emperor's Peace Alter in Rome." *Odyssey*, May–June 2005: 39–47.
"Notes and a Few Movies." *Les Cahiers du Cinéma*, no. 315 (September 1980): 54.
Pechter, William. "On the Wild Bunch." *Film Comment*, Fall 1970: 55–57.
"Penthouse Magazine Goes on the Block." *Sydney Morning Herald*, October 22, 2003.
Phillips, Gene D. "An Interview with Ken Russell." *Film Comment*, Fall 1970, pp. 10–17.
"Porn Kingpin Convicted of Racketeering." *Houston Chronicle*, October 22, 1979.
"The (Porn) Player." *Forbes*, July 4, 2005: 124–129.
Reisch, Walter. "Josef von Sternberg." *Action*, January–February: 6–7.
Romano, David Gilman. "When the Games Begin: Sport, Religion and Politics Converged in Ancient Olympia." *Odyssey*, July–August 2004: 12–20.
Sarris, Andrew. "Notes on the Auteur Theory in 1970." *Film Comment*, Fall 1970: 6–9.
Schiff, Frederick. "Nude Dancing: Scenes of Sexual Celebration in a Contested Culture." *Journal of American Culture* 22 no. 4 (1999): 9–16.
Schlosser, Eric. "Empire of the Obscene." *New Yorker*, March 10, 2003: 61–71.
Schrvers, Fred. "Oliver's Army." *Premiere*, September 2004: 55–57.
Scorbie, W. I. "The Judgment of Vidal." *The Advocate*, March 9, 1977: 24–27.
Scorsese, Martin. "Martin Scorsese's Guilty Pleasures." *Film Comment*, September–October 1978: 66.
Segal, Lewis. "Motion Pictures." *Show*, August 20, 1970: 41.
"Sex in Cinema 2003." *Playboy*, December 2003: 106–116.
Shales, Tom. "Sex on TV Gains as Public Concern Seems to Be Waning." *Houston Chronicle*, March 28, 1976: 9.
Sheff, David. "Playboy Interview: Oliver Stone." *Playboy*, November 2004: 63–64, 148–149.
Shocket, Dan. "Hard Times: The Root of Reel Raunch." *Starlet Magazine*, July–August 1981, 64–74.

Snyder, Gabriel. "Box Office Winners & Sinners." *Premiere*, February 2005: 62.
Spines, Christine. "Total Recall." *Entertainment Weekly*, April 6, 2007: 48–50.
Sullivan, Christopher. "Maryland Censors Snip Final Scenes from X-rated Films." *Houston Chronicle*, July 12, 1981.
Thomson, David. "The Art of the Art Director." *American Film*, February 1977: 12–30.
"The 12-minute Playboy Philosophy." *Playboy*, January 2004: 68.
Tynan, Kenneth. "In Praise of Hard Core." In *Dirty Movies: An Illustrated History of the Stag Film, 1915–1970*, by Al Di Lauro and Gerald Rabkin. New York: Chelsea House, 1976.
Tyre, Peg. "The Trouble with Boys." *Newsweek*, January 30, 2006: 44–52.
Vasc, Sparky, and Boz Crawford. "The Straight Skinny: Is Johnny Wadd Still with Us?" *Adult Cinema*, February 1982: 4.
Vinciguerra, Thomas. "Porn Again: 'Caligula' Is Remastered in All Its Gross Glory." *New York Magazine*, September 6, 1999.
Vinocur, John. "Pornography Business Is Dying in Denmark." *Houston Chronicle*, October 22, 1976.
Volkman, Ernest. "Bob Guccione: Penthouse Interview." *Penthouse*, May 1980: 112–118, 146–150.
Wellman, William, Jr. "Howard Hawks, the Distant Runner." *Action*, November–December 1970: 11.
Westbrook, Bruce. "1995 a Banner Year for Sales." *Houston Chronicle*, January 5, 1996.
White, Dave. "Video Companies That Produce Bareback Porn Are Thriving, but Do They Change the Way Gay Men Have Sex?" *Frontiers*, October 24, 2003: 37–42.
Wilder, Billy. "One Head Is Better Than Two." *WGAW/DGA Preston Sturges Award*, September 1991: 3.
Will, George. "Free Speech at the Skin Flick." *Houston Chronicle*, June 28, 1975.
Williamson, Bruce. "Porno Chic." *Playboy*, August 1973: 132–141.
Wood, Robin, "To Have and Have Not: Reflections on Authorship," *Film Comment*, May–June 1973: 30–35.
_____. "Rossellini" and "Ingrid Bergman on Rossellini," *Film Comment*, July–August 1974: 6–16.
_____. "Venus de Marlene," *Film Comment*, March–April 1978: 58–63.

Films and Television Programs

Alexander the Great: Murder Unsolved. Directed and written by Chris Lethbridge. Discovery Channel, 2003. Produced by Atlantic Productions for the Discovery Channel, Five and Granada International.

Ancient Discoveries — Ships. Directed by Stuart Clarke. History Channel, 2005. A Wild Dreams Films Production with S4C/S4C International SBS-TV Australia.

Anderson, Pamela, and Tommy Lee. Amateur video PTJVO1, 2006.

Augustus, Directed by Roger Young. Screenplay by Eric Lerner. RAI EOS Entertainment, and RAITRADE, 2002–2003.

Behind the Green Door. Directed by James Mitchell and Artie Mitchell. San Francisco: Mitchell Brothers Film Group, 1972. Released on VHS, 1992.

Ben-Hur: A Tale of the Christ. Directed by Fred Niblo. Written by Lew Wallace. 1926. Color sequences restored for Thames Television and Turner Entertainment Company.

Beyond the Valley of the Dolls. Directed by Russ Meyer. Written by Roger Ebert. 1970.

Broadway: The American Musical (1893–1927). Directed by Michael Kantor. PBS, 2004. The Educational Broadcasting Corporation and the Broadway Film Project, Inc. A coproduction of Green Light Films and Thirteen/WNET, New York, and the BBC.

Cabiria. Directed by Piero Fosco (aka Giovanni Pastrone). 1914. Kino International Release, Eighteen Frames, Inc., 1990.

Caligula. Principal Photography by Tinto Brass. Penthouse Films International, 1979.

Caligula. Tenth anniversary editions, rated and unrated. Principal Photography by Tinto Brass. Added scenes directed by Bob Guccione and Giancarlo Lui. 1989.

Caligula. Imperial edition. DVD. General Media Entertainment, Inc., 2007. This high-definition transfer of the unrated edition includes *The Making of Caligula* and others extras.

"Caligula: Reign of Madness." *Biography.* History Channel, 1997. A&E Television Networks. A Brian Roos Production by Film Roos, Inc.

Cecil B. DeMille: American Epic. Directed by Kevin Brownlow. Photoplay Productions, 2004. (Made for television.)

Celluloid Closet. Directed by Jeffrey Friedman. Home Box Office, 1996. Based on the book by Victor Russo. Narration written by Amistead Maupin.

Censored, Hollywood Real to Reel. American Movie Classics, 1999. Produced by Surreal Life Productions in association with American Movie Classics.

Centurians of Rome. Directed by John Christopher. Written by Timothy Michaels. Hand in Hand Uranus Films, Inc., 1981.

"Chippendales." Two parts. *E! True Hollywood Story.* Entertainment Channel, 2004.

Deep Throat. Directed by Gerald Damiano (credited as Jerry Gerard), 1972. Redistributed by Arrow Films on VHS, 1987.

Documentary on the Making of "Gore Vidal's Caligula." Directed by Giancarlo Lui. Written by Alan Willis. Cinemedia West Corporation, 1981.

"D. W. Griffith." *American Masters.* PBS. March 1993.

"The Education of Gore Vidal." Written and directed by Deborah Dickson. *American Masters.* PBS, 2002.

"Engineering an Empire." *Roman History Week.* History Channel, 2005.

Erotikus. A History of the Gay Movies. Directed by L. Brooks. Times Productions, 1972. Class X Video/Video Yesteryear, 1981.

Fellini Satyricon. Directed by Federico Fellini. PEA Produzioni Europee Associate, S.A.S., 1968.

Hearts of Darkness: A Filmmaker's Apocalypse. Written and directed by Fax Bahr and George Hickenlooper. American Zoetrope, 1991. A documentary based on Eleanor Coppola's diary written during the making of *Apocalypse Now.*

"Hitchcock-Selznik." *American Masters.* PBS, 1998.

Hitler's Children. Directed by Edward Dmytryk. Written by Emmet Lavery. RKO Radio Pictures, 1943.

"Homes of Roman Emperors, The." History Channel, 2004.

"Howard Hawks. American Artist." *Bravo Profiles.* Directed by Kevin MacDonald. Bravo Cable Television, 1997.

"Hugh Hefner: Girlfriends, Wives and Centerfolds." *E! True Hollywood Story.* Entertainment Television, 2006.

I Am Curious, Yellow. Directed by Vigot Sjögman..Film 8, S.A.G.A. Stockholms Allmanns Gymnastikakudelninger, 1968. An Evergreen Film, Grove Press, Electric Video, Inc., 1969.

Julius Caesar. Directed by Phil Grabsky and Peter Nicholson. History Channel, 1997. Produced by Seventh Art Productions for the BBC and the A&E Television Networks.

"Larry Flynt: Raw, Exposed, and Uncensored." *E! True Hollywood Story.* Entertainment Channel, 2002.

Last Tango in Paris. Directed by Bernardo Bertolucci. A co–production of PEA Produzioni Europee Associates S.A.S., Rome, and Les Productions Artistes Associes S.A., Paris, 1972. Distributed by MGA/UA Home Video, 1990.

Legacy of the Hollywood Blacklist. Produced and directed by Judy Chaikin. Written by Eve Goldberg. PBS, 1987. One Step Productions in association with KCET, Los Angeles.

"Life and Death in Rome—Gladiators & Slaves." *Roman History Week.* History Channel, 2005.

Love in the Ancient World. Written and directed by Christopher Miles. Arts & Entertainment Television Networks, 1997.

The Magic of Fellini. Written and directed by Carmen Piccini. Turner Classic Movies, 2004. A Puccini Production.

The Making of Rome. Home Box Office, Inc., in association with the BBC, 2005.

Midnight Cowboy. Directed by John Schlesinger. Jerome Hellman Productions, Inc., 1969.

"The Mitchell Bros." *E! True Hollywood Story.* Entertainment Television, 2003.

"The Monster That Ate Hollywood." Written by Alan Smithee. *Frontline.* PBS, 2001. Riot Pictures and WGBH Education Foundation.

1 Night in Paris. Red Light District Video, 2004.

"Otto Preminger." *The Moviemakers.* Directed by Valerie A. Robins. Written by Thomas J. Wiener. PBS, 1996. Produced in association with the Austrian Broadcasting Corporation.

"Porn in the USA." *60 Minutes.* CBS-TV, 2003–2004.

Quo Vadis? Directed by Mervin LeRoy. Loew's Incorporated, 1951. MGM, Incorporated, 1979.

Reel Radicals: The Sixties Revolution in Film. Directed by Don Fizzinoglia and Lewis Bogach. Written by Lewis Bogach. AMC Movie Classics, 2002. An AMC Original Production in association with Surreal Life Productions.

"The Roman Emperors." *History's Mysteries.* The History Channel, January 2006.

"Roman Vice."*Roman History Week.* History Channel, 2005.

Rome. Directed by Michael Apted. Written by Bruno Heller. 12 episodes, Home Box Office, Inc. in association with the BBC, 2005.

Salò: 120 Days of Sodom. Directed by Pier Paolo Pasolini. United Artists, 1975. Water Beaver Films, Inc., 1990. Based on the work of Marquis de Sade.

Salon Kitty. Directed by Tinto Brass. Coralta Cinematografica srl-Roma/Cinema-Seven Film Gmb-Munich/Les Productions Fox Europe, Paris, 1975.

Score. Directed by Radley Metzger. Audubon Films, Inc., 1972.

Scorpio Rising, Kustom Kar Kommandos, Puce Moment. Directed by Kenneth Anger. 1986. Magick Lantern Cycle, Volume 3. Mystic Fire Video.

Sebastiane. Directed by Paul Humfress and Derek Jarman. 1976.

The Secret History of the Other Hollywood. Courtroom Television Network, 2001. Produced by Frozen Television for Court TV. Producer Legs McNeil, based on his book.

Sensations. Written and directed by Alberto Ferro. A Lasse Braun Presentation. 1979.

The 75th Annual Academy Awards. Television broadcast. Motion Picture Academy of Arts and Sciences, May 30, 2003. Honorary Oscar: Peter O'Toole, includes *Caligula* in his film retrospective.

Sex in the Twentieth Century. Directed by Bonnie Peterson. History Channel, 2002.

Troy. Directed by Wolfgang Peterson. Warner Bros., 2004.

The True History of Alexander the Great. Written and directed by Jim Lindsay. History Channel, 2004.

The True Story of Hannibal. Directed by Mark Hufnail. History Channel, 2004.

The True Story of Troy. History Channel, 2004.

"Young Women, Porn & Profits. Corporate America's Secret Affair." *Primetime Thursday.* ABC Television, 2003–2004.

Press Kits

All the President's Men. Warner Brothers, 1976.

Roommates. Platinum Pictures Entertainment, 1981.

Internet Resources

"Bob Guccione." Internet Movie Database. us.imdb.com/name/nm0345579 (accessed February 13, 2008).

Fitzgerald, Tom. "The Weird World of Seventies Cinema." Pimpadelic Wonderland, http://www.pimpadelicwonderland.com/70s.html (accessed February 13, 2008).

INDEX

ABC Television 192, 210, 218–221, 223
Accius 70
Achilles 45, 221, 224
The Adult Film Association of America 41, 195
Adult Video News (AVN) 208
Adventures of Lucky Pierre 29
Advise and Consent (1962) 28
The Advocate 85, 223
Aeneas 46
The Aeneid 46
Agrippa, Herod (Julius) 5, 61, 73, 75
Agrippina (Caligula's mother) 39, 50, 55, 56, 58, 75
Agrippina Minor (Caligula's sister, Nero's mother) 56, 68, 76, 111, 150, 151, 226
Alexander (2004) 222, 223
Alexander the Great 5, 57, 58, 70, 125, 150, 222
All About Eve 213
All the President's Men (1976) 188, 190
Allen, Patrick 108
American Film 89, 200
American Gigolo 199
American Telephone and Telegraph Company 208
And God Created Woman (1956) 28
Anderson, John 106
Anderson, Lindsay 98
Anderson, Maxwell 85
Anderson, Pamela 212
Antioch 8, 58
Antonia (Caligula's grandmother) 49, 51, 53, 58, 61, 107, 129
Antonioni, Michelangelo 88
Antony, Mark/Marcus Antonius 50, 55, 207, 220
Apelles 69
Aphrodite 126
Apocalypse Now (1979) 81, 188, 190, 217
Appia, Adolph 108
Ara Pacis 64
art films 27
Asher, Bill 220
Asti, Adriana 109, 137, 140

Attorney General's Commission on Pornography 208–210, 212
Augustus (2003) 224
Augustus *see* Gaius Julius Caesar Octavianus
Augustus, Bob 195
auteur 30

Babel 222
Babylon, Iraq 6, 222
Bacchus 126
The Bachelor (2007) 218
Bad Influence (1990) 212
Badessi, Giancarlo 109, 138
Baiae 70
Baker, George 39
Ball, Lucille 2
Bara, Theda (Theodosia Goodman, 1890–1955) 6, 10
Bardot, Bridgitte 28
Barr, Candy 27
Barrett, Anthony A. 48, 59, 68, 72, 73
Basic Instinct (1992) 213
The Battle Over Citizen Kane (1996) 188
Baywatch 212
BBC Television 224
The Beast 29
Becket (1964) 101
Behind the Green Door (1973) 35, 193
Belasco, David 16
Belladonna 219
Ben-Hur (1907) 7
Ben-Hur (1959) 26, 81, 83, 84, 85
Ben-Hur: A Tale of the Christ (1926) 8
Berenice 61
Berger, Helmut 90, 190
Bergman, Andrew 213
Bergman, S.N. 85
Berkley, Elizabeth 213
Bernini, Lorenzo 201
Bertolucci, Bernardo 80
The Best Man (1970) 83
Beyond the Valley of the Dolls (1970) 29
The Bicycle Thief (1948) 31
Bijou Theatre/Video, Chicago 202

246 Index

Birdy (1985) 190
The Birth of a Nation (1915) 196
Black and White (1967) 89
Black bird 135, 139, 155, 163
Black Book (2006) 213
The Blair Witch Project (1999) 217
Blood Feast (1963) 29
Bloom, Orlando 224
Blowdry 190
The Blue Angel (1930) 11
Blue Lagoon 207
Bogart, Humphrey 2
Bogart, Paul 203
Bohn, Thomas W. 87
Bonacelli, Paolo 109
Bondanella, Peter 31, 32
Bonnie and Clyde (1967) 81
Boogie Nights (1997) 214
Boone, Richard 22
Borgnine, Ernest 24
Born, Max 32
Borowczyk, Walerian 29
Boyd, Steven 27
Brachman, Gideon 97
Brando, Marlon 80
Brass, Tinto 29, 31, 39, 84, 85, 87–89, 92, 94–98, 100, 103, 104, 106, 110, 122, 135, 146, 148, 190, 195, 201, 213, 225
Brazil (1985) 190
Breen, Joseph I. 13
Brenner, Joe 28
Brive, Bruno 109, 134
Brokeback Mountain 203
Brooks, David 218
Brown, Bryan 214
Buckley, Jim 35
Burgess, Anthony 98
Burstyn v. Wilson (1952) 20
Burton, Richard 22, 27, 101
Bush, George H.W. 210
Bush, George W. 215, 216
Bushman, Francis X. 8
Buster and Billie (1974) 36
Butler, Gerard 224
Butler, Jerry 207
Byrne, Patsy 39

Cabaret (1972) 90
Cabiria (1914) 7, 8
Cabrera, Santiago 223
Caesar, Julius *see* Gaius Julius Caesar
Caesar and Cleopatra (1945) 16, 17, 27
Caesonia 16, 18, 70, 72–74, 103, 105, 111, 144–146, 149, 150–153, 155, 156, 158, 160, 162, 164, 165, 205
Cage, Nicholas 190
La Cage aux folles (1978) 203
Cahiers du Cinéma 195
Cake, Jonathan 223, 224
Calendar Girls (2003) 103

Caligula *see* Gaius Caesar Augustus Germanicus
Caligula (1979) 1, 3, 4, 5, 10, 11, 17, 20, 24–26, 27, 30, 31, 32, 33, 37–39, 45, 53, 67, 68, 78, 81, 82, 85, 86, 87, 89, 90–92, 94–96, 98, 100, 104, 105, 110, 115, 117, 120–127, 149, 168, 188, 189, 190–192, 194–196, 198, 200–202, 205, 206, 210, 212–214, 217, 220, 222, 224, 125; censored scenes 172–180, 182, 183; poster/one sheet 197
Caligula (play, 1945) 17, 18, 153
Caligula: The Corruption of Power (1989) 48
Cameron, James 216
Campus Martius 75
Camus, Albert (1913–1960) 3, 17, 18, 19, 67, 73, 77, 153
Canby, Vincent 97, 106
Cannes Film Festival 95, 96, 212
The Canterbury Tales (1972) 204
Il capo al mondo — Chi lavora e perduto (1963) 89
Capri 22, 40, 51, 53–55, 57, 60, 61, 67, 91, 99, 111, 129, 138, 149, 202
Capucine 34
Caravaggio, Michelangelo 108, 201, 226
Caserini, Mario 18
Catholic Legion of Decency 13
Cavalcanti, Alberto 89
CBS Television 210, 215
Centurians of Rome (1981) 202
Chaerea (Cherea), Cassius 17, 18, 25, 40, 73, 74, 109, 141, 152, 159, 162, 163, 165
Chambers, Marilyn 35
Chapman, Edythe 7
Charicles 62, 110, 138, 153
Chattanooga Free Press 214
Chicago World's Fair, 1933 27
Chinatown (1974) 81, 88, 188
Christ 22, 127
Churchill, Frank 2
Cicero 48, 57
Cinderella 190
Cinecittà Studios 26, 32, 115, 224
CinemaScope 22, 23
Cinémathèque Française 89
Cinerama 22
Circus Maximus 8, 45, 50
Citizen Kane (1941) 96, 129, 188
Citizens for Decency through Law (CDL) 195
The City and the Pillar (1948) 82
Clark, Kenneth 127
Clarke, John R. 126
Claudius (10 B.C.–A.D. 54) 5, 14–16, 24–26, 39, 40, 59, 61, 73, 75, 76, 99, 109, 111, 117, 131, 138, 141, 159
Clemente, Paul 129
Cleopatra 72, 103
Cleopatra (1918) 6
Cleopatra (1963) 27, 81, 115

Cleopatra (1999) 220, 224
Clinton, William (Bill) 214, 215
A Clockwork Orange (1971) 81, 98, 100, 140
Closing of the Western Mind: The Rise of Faith and the Fall of Reason 125
Coblenz, Walter 191
Cocktail (1988) 214
Colbert, Claudette 11, 21
Collins, Glen 192
Columbia/Sony 221
Commission on Obscenity and Pornography, 1970 3
Commodus, Lucius Aelius Aurelius 221
Cooke, Alistair 39
Cooper, Gary 2
Coppola, Francis Ford 81
Crash 222
Crist, Judith 35
Cross, Marcia 218
Crowe, Russell 221
Cruise, Tom 214
Culkin, John M. 34
Custer, Gen. George A. 81

Dalton, Timothy 220
Damiano, Gerard 34
The Damned (1969) 91
Dangelo, Mirella 110, 148
D'Annunzio, Gabriele 7
Dante 97, 191
Dastor, Sam 40
Day, Doris 203
Dear Studios 32, 81, 115
Death in Venice (1971) 65
The Decameron (1971) 82, 204
The Deep 190
Deep Throat (1972) 30, 34, 35, 120, 121, 193, 206
Demetrius and the Gladiators (1954) 23, 24, 25, 26
De Mille, Cecil B. (1881–1959) 6, 7, 10, 11, 13, 15, 20, 26, 70, 81, 110, 112, 127
De Santis, Giuseppe 88
De Sica, Vittorio (1902–1974) 31, 88
Desperate Housewives (2004–) 218
Details 200
The Devil in Miss Jones (1972) 35, 193
Diamond Lil (play, 1928) 86
Diana 67
Diana, Princess of Wales 103
Di Bernardo, Robert 206, 207
Dido, Queen 46
Dietrich, Marlene (1901–1992) 11, 12
Di Lorenzo, Anneka 95, 111, 151, 198
Dio, Cassius (c. A.D. 163–235) 48, 51
Diocletian 36
Dionysus 126
Disney, Walt/Walt Disney Company 2, 3, 217, 220
La dolce vita (1960) 31, 82

Donaldson, Roger 214
Donati, Danilo (1926–2001) 34, 56, 67, 112, 114, 117, 129, 142, 196
Dorian Gray 140
Douglas, Lloyd C. (1877–1951) 22
Downey, Robert, Jr. 211
Dracula 100
Dreamworks 217
Drusilla 17, 40, 56, 59, 65, 69, 70, 91, 92, 100, 104–108, 111, 127, 129, 130, 135, 136, 141, 142, 144–146, 149–151, 153–156
Drusus (brother of Caligula) 56, 58
Drusus (son of Tiberius) 53, 56, 62
Duke, Doris 83
Dunaway, Faye 81
Duncan, Lindsay 224
Dunne, Philip 22, 24

The Earth Trembles (1948) 31
Eastwood, Clint 190
Ebert, Roger 90
Ecstasy (1933) 120, 213
Edward the 8th (1894–1972) 15
Egan, Richard 25
8½ (1962) 31, 88
Eisenstein, Sergei 95
Elizabeth I (2003) 103
Empire (2005) 221, 223
Empire of Caesar 207
Ennia 68, 91, 100, 108, 109, 136, 137, 142, 226
Entertainment Weekly 100
Episcopal Committee on Motion Pictures 13
Equus 190
Esquire 77
Euripides 68
Evander, King 46

The Fall of Troy (1910) 7
"Falling in Love Again" 11
Falwell, Jerry (1933–2007) 210
Le farò da padre (1974) 106
Farrell, Colin 222
Federal Bureau of Investigation (FBI) 207, 210
Federal Communications Commission (FCC) 19, 192, 210, 215
Felix Cinematografica 82, 97, 205
Fellini, Federico (1922–1994) 88, 31, 32, 82, 84, 86, 95, 112
Fellini Satyricon (1969) 30, 31, 32, 34, 112, 132, 159
Fellini's Roma (1972) 84
femme fatale 11, 12
Film Comment 97
Finding Our Fathers 200
First Amendment 2, 10, 19, 20, 194, 195, 210
Fleming, Victor 95
Flent, Michael 202
Flesh (1968) 30
Flynt, Althea Leisure 203, 210

Flynt, Larry 28, 79, 80, 203, 209–211
Fonda, Henry 2
A Fool There Was (1914) 6
Ford, Luke 28
Fortuna 72, 155, 200, 225
42nd Street (1933) 2
Fox, Samantha 207
Franklin, Joseph Paul 210
Free Speech Legal Defense Fund 194
Freedman, Charles 125
Freedman, David 41
Freedman v. Maryland (1965) 20
Friedman, Davis 28, 29
Fry, Christopher 26, 85

Gaetulicus, Cornelius Lentius 70–72
Gagliardotto, Mario 96
Gaius Caesar Augustus Germanicus (Caligula A.D. 12–41) 3–5, 9, 11, 15–18, 22–26, 39, 40, 42, 44–47, 49–52, 55, 57–65, 67, 69, 70, 72–75, 87, 88, 91, 93, 94, 96, 99, 100, 102, 103, 105, 106–108, 110, 114, 117, 119, 124–131, 133–147, 188–190, 195, 200, 201, 217, 219, 223, 225; British invasion 159–162; brothel 157–158; death 163–168; illness 151–156
Gaius Julius Caesar (100 B.C.–44 B.C.) 14, 47–50, 163, 207, 220, 223, 224
Gaius Julius Caesar Octavianus (Augustus 63 B.C.–A.D. 14) 14, 15, 47–51, 53, 54, 57–59, 61, 63, 64, 65, 70, 72, 75, 131, 142, 150, 215, 221, 223
Galba, Savicus Sulpicius 70, 71
Gallagher, Peter 212
The Game of Love 28
Gardner, Helen 201
Garland, Judy 2
Gemellus 59, 61, 64, 68, 74, 102, 109, 110, 117, 133–135, 138, 139, 141, 149, 150, 153
General Della Rovere (1959) 89
General Media Communications, Inc. 205, 225
Gere, Richard 199
Germanicus 39, 50, 52, 55, 56, 57, 58, 59, 64, 75, 188
Germany Year Zero (1947) 31
Germi, Pietro (1914–1974) 88
Giacomo, Laura San 212
Giant 110, 156, 157, 160, 161
Giant (1956) 203
Gibson, Mel 26
Gielgud, John 93, 98, 104–106, 114, 136, 137
Gilliam, Terry 190
Gladiator (2000) 147, 221
The Godfather (series 1972, 1974, 1990) 81
Godfrey, Arthur 85
golden age: adult cinema 31, 193; American cinema 187, 188; Italian cinema 30, 31
Goldstein, Al 207
Goldstein, Allen A. 100
Gombrich, E.H. 201

Gone with the Wind 95, 119, 120
Goodbye Emmanuelle 190
Gore Vidal (1999) 85
Gore Vidal's Caligula 83, 84
Gosling, Ryan 217
Gospel According to St. Matthew (1964) 204
Grable, Betty 2
Grant, Michael 48
Graves, Robert 3, 5, 14, 16, 39, 48
The Great War (1952) 112
Greed 92
Greenaway, Peter 106
Griffith, David Wark (1875–1948) 6, 7, 15, 17, 196
Grimaldi, Alberto 97
Guazzoni, Enrico 8
Guccione, Anthony (Bob Guccione's son) 77
Guccione, Nicholas 77
Guccione, Nina (Bob Guccione's daughter) 77
Guccione, Robert Charles Joseph Edward Sabatini (Bob) 1, 4, 28, 30, 31, 34, 37–39, 41, 77–79, 80–90, 95, 96, 98, 99, 100, 102–104, 106, 111, 112, 118–124, 146, 150, 188, 189, 191, 193, 195, 196, 198, 200, 201, 205, 209, 211, 214, 220, 225, 226
Guccione, Robert, Jr. 77
Guccione, Tonina 77

Hammanet Studios, Tunisia 221
Hannibal 8
Hanson, Curtis 212
hardcore 4, 28, 34, 190
Harlow, Jean 11
Harrelson, Woody 210
Harris County v. Landmark River Oaks Theatre (1983) 204
Hart, Veronica 207
Haskell, Molly 34
Hatcher, Teri 218
Hays, Will (1879–1954) 13
Hayward, Susan 23, 24
HBO (Home Box Office) 218, 221, 224
Headey, Lena 224
Hearst, William Randolph 188
Heat (1970) 30
Hector 45
Hefner, Hugh 28, 78, 193, 209, 210
Henie, Sonja 2
Henry & June (1990) 123, 193
Hephaestion 222
Hera 57
Hercules 57, 202, 217
Hercules, the Legendary Journey 217
Herod the Great 61
Herostratus 103
Heston, Charlton 26, 190
Hiller, Arthur 203
Hilton, Paris 212
Hinds, Ciarán 224

Index

A History of X 28
Hitchcock, Alfred 94
Hitler, Adolf 92
Hoffman, Dustin 191
Holmes, John (Johnny Wadd) 3, 203, 214
Homer 45, 227
Honeypie 190
Hooking Up (2005) 218
Hope, Bob 2
Houston Chronicle 193
Houston Police Department 201, 203
"How to Do Things with the Starr Report: Pornography, Performance, and the President's Penis" 215
Hudd, Ron 207
Hudson, Muriel 77
Hudson, Rock 203
Huffman, Felicity 218
Humfress, Paul 36
Human Immunodeficiency Virus/Acquired Immunodeficiency Syndrome (HIV/AIDS) 203, 210, 212
Hurt, John 39
Hustler 79, 80, 202, 209–211
Huston, John 81, 88
Hutchens, Christopher 210

I, Claudius (BBC, 1976) 39, 40, 41, 53, 58, 69, 102, 108, 224
I, Claudius (1937) 16, 25
I, Claudius (novel, 1934) 5, 14, 15
If (1968) 98
The Illiad 45, 227
The Immoral Mr. Teas 29
In the Realm of the Senses (1976) 38
Incitatus 40, 100, 117, 128, 151
India (1958) 89
Inside the Sexes 210
Intolerance (1916) 6, 17
Io, Caligola (1984) 83, 98, 120, 122, 124, 125, 128, 129, 144, 165, 168, 205, 206
Ippoliti, Silvano 91, 96
Isherwood, Christopher 90
Isis 111, 138, 142, 143, 163
Italian Cinema from Neorealism to the Present 31

Jackson, Janet 215
Jacobi, Derek 39
Jannings, Emil 11
Jarman, Derek (1942–1994) 36
Jaws (1975) 87
Jenkins, George 191
Jensen, Elizabeth 210
Jesus 5, 8, 9, 21, 24, 61, 217
Johnson, Pres. Lyndon B. 3, 79
Jones, Barry 24
Josephus 64, 74
Joy, Leatrice 7
Juba 72

Judith of Bethulia (1914) 6, 21
Julia (Augustus's daughter) 50, 53, 221
Julia (Claudius's niece) 68
Julia Drusilla (Caligula's daughter) 16, 74, 105, 155, 165
Juliet of the *Spirits* (1965) 31
Julius *see* Gaius Julius Caesar
Junia Claudilla (Caligula's wife) 58, 59
Juno 46
Jupiter 46, 73, 82
Jurassic Park (1993) 216

Kael, Pauline 80
Kaplan, Fred 26, 85
Kaufman, Philip 193
Kawin, Bruce F. 30
Keeton, Kathy 77, 78, 225
Kehr, Dave 200
Keller, Hiram 32
Kennedy, Pres. John F. 52
Kerr, Deborah 21
Khachaturian, Aram 129
The King of Kings (1927) 7, 127
Kipling, Rudyard 88
Klaw & Erlanger 3
Knight, Arthur 190
Knoll, Kip 3
Korda, Alexander (1893–1956) 14, 15, 16
Korean War 2, 28
Koster, Henry 22
Krim, Dr. Matilda 203
Kubrick, Stanley 81, 98, 100

La Bare 213
Lamarr, Hedy (1913–2000) 20, 21, 213
Landi, Elissa 11
Landmark River Oaks Theatre 201, 204
Lasky, Jesse 81
Last Days of Pompeii (1913) 8
Last Tango in Paris (1972) 80, 92, 106
The Last Temptation of Christ (1988) 196
Laughton, Charles (1899–1962) 11, 14, 15, 16, 99
Lavinia (Evander's daughter) 46
Lawrence of Arabia (1969) 89, 101
Lean, David 89, 94, 101
Lee, Ang 204
Lee, Tommy 212
Leigh, Vivien (1913–1967) 2, 16
Leonard, Gloria 3
Leonidas, King 224
Lepidus, Marcus 59, 72
LeRoy, Mervin 21
Leto, Jared 222
Lewinsky, Monica 215
Lewis, Juliet 211
The Lickerish Quartet (1970) 35
Light and Shadows 87
The Lion in Winter (1968) 101
The Lion King 3

250 Index

Little Big Man (1970) 81
Livia (Caligula's grandmother) 15, 19, 40, 42, 44, 47, 48, 51, 53, 58, 61, 102, 107
Livia (Proculus's fiancée) 91, 110, 144, 146–149, 154, 205
Livilla (Caligula's sister) 56
Livilla (Tiberius's daughter) 54
Logic of Utopia, Power, and Folly 96, 140, 148, 156, 167, 168
London American 77
London Times 85
Longinus, Lucius Cassius 59, 110, 146, 151, 152, 154, 156, 157, 163
Longoria, Eva 218
Lord Jim (1965) 101
Lorna (1964) 29
Lovelace, Linda (1949–2002) 35
Lowe, Rob 212
Lubitsch, Ernst (1892–1947) 7
Lucas, George 86
Lui, Giancarlo 95, 150, 198
Lux Radio Theatre (1936–1945) 127

MacArthur, Gen. Douglas 85
Macbeth 30
Macbeth (1971) 80, 81
MacDowell, Andie 212
Macedonia 222
macho male 29, 79, 98, 199, 200, 215, 216220
Macro, Quintus Naevius 25, 40, 59–63, 68, 74, 108, 109, 117, 129, 130, 132, 134, 136–139, 141, 142, 146
Mad Hercules 68
Magnani, Anna 20
The Magnificent Seven Deadly Sins 80
Making Love (1980) 203
The Making of Caligula 216
Male and Female (1919) 7
The Maltese Falcon (1940) 88
Mankiewicz, Joseph L. (1909–1993) 27
The Man Who Would Be King (1975) 88
The Man with the Golden Arm (1955) 28
Mannari, Guido 108, 137, 139
March, Frederic 11
Mark, gospel of 127, 221
Mars 42
Marshall, William 24
Marvin Miller v. California (1973) 37
"M*A*S*H" 188
Mast, Gerald 2, 30
Masterpiece Theatre 39
Mature, Victor (1915–1994) 20, 21, 22, 24
McDowell, Malcolm 48, 81, 85, 91, 93, 98–100, 110, 117, 132–134, 137, 146, 160, 161, 191, 196, 199, 202, 225
McKidd, Kevin 224
McNeil, Legs 207
Medea (1970) 82
Meese, Edwin 208–210, 212
Meighan, Thomas 7

Messalina 11, 14, 15, 23, 24, 25, 26, 40, 111, 150, 151, 226
Messalina (1923) 8
Messalina, Messalina (1977) 83
Messiah 5
Metzger, Radley 29, 35, 36
Meyer, Russ (1922–2004) 29, 90, 91
Mickey Gilley's, Pasadena, Texas 199
Midnight Caller 210
Midnight Cowboy 192
Miller, Jeff 193
MIPORN 207
The Miracle (1948) 20
Mirren, Helen 92, 98, 103, 104, 152, 160, 191, 225
Mishkin, Bill 28
Mitchell, Artie 35
Mitchell, Jim 35
Mitchell, Paula 110
Mnester 69, 110, 156
Modine, Mathew 190
Molinaro, Edouard 203
Monicelli, Mario 112
Monroe, Marilyn 28
The Moon Is Blue (1953) 28
Moore, Demi 213
Morley, Sheridan 105
Morrissey, Paul 2, 30, 121
Moses 26
Mother Lode (1982) 190
Motion Picture Association of America (MPAA) 192, 193
Motion Picture Producers and Distributors Association (MPPDA) 13
Motion Picture Production Code 8, 13, 14, 28, 30
Mozzato, Umberto 8
Murray, Don 28
Mussolini, Benito 67, 97, 204
Mutual Film Corporation v. Ohio Industrial Commission (1915) 10
Myra Breckinridge (1970) 86
Myrick, Daniel 217

"Naked Moon" 11
Naldi, Nita 17
Nata di marzo (1957) 82
National Board of Censorship of Motion Pictures, 1909 9
National Football League Superbowl, 2004 215
Natural Born Killers (1994) 211
NBC Television 210, 220
Neame, Ronald 190
Nemi, Lake 67, 117
neorealism 31
Nero (Caligula's brother) 56, 58
Nero, Emperor 11, 14, 21, 32, 76
Nerva 102, 105, 109, 130, 136–138, 144, 154, 223

New American Cinema 2
New Amsterdam Theatre 3
New York Daily News 210
New York Newsday 106
The New York Times 97, 106, 191, 218, 223
New Yorker 224, 225
Newman, Alfred 22
Niblo, Fred 8
Nichols, Kelly 207
Nicholson, Jack 81
Night After Night (1931) 13
Night Must Fall (1935) 16
Nijinsky 83
Nin, Anaïs 193
Nixon, Pres. Richard M. 3, 37, 85
Not Tonight, Henry 39
Novarro, Ramon 8
The Nude: A Study in Ideal Form 127
nudie-cutie 29

O Lucky Man (1973) 98
Oberon, Merle (1911–1979) 14–16
obscenity 28, 37, 41
Octavia (Augustus's sister) 50, 56
Odysseus 45
The Odyssey 45
The Odyssey (TV, 1997) 220
Olcott, Sidney 7
Olivier, Laurence 14
Omni 83
One Flew Over the Cuckoo's Nest 188
1 Night in Paris 212
The Opening of Misty Beethoven (1975) 35, 193
Orestilla, Livia 70
Osborne, Jennifer 207
Osherman, Samuel 200
Oshima, Nagisa 38
Osiris 126, 163
Ostia 65, 204
The Other Hollywood 207
O'Toole, Peter 98, 100, 101, 102, 130, 132–134, 137, 139, 221
The Outlaw (1943) 123

Pact with the Devil 100
Padgett, J. Michael 46
Pagano, Bartolomeo 8, 24
Paget, Debra 24
Paisan (1946) 31
Pakula, Alan 190, 191
Palatine Hill 8, 42, 43, 45, 48, 50, 51, 58, 76
Pallus 46
Paramount 7, 81
Paramour, Ted 29
Parets, Richard 110
Parker, Al 3
Parker, Alan 190, 191
Pascal, George (1894–1954) 17, 27
Pasolini, Pier Paolo (1922–1975) 82, 88, 91, 97, 112, 204

The Passion of the Christ 26, 225
Pastrone, Giovanni 7
Patrocius 221
Paul 21, 36
Payne, George 202
Peckinpah, Sam 94
Penn, Arthur 81
Penthouse 11, 30, 37, 77–80, 83, 86, 97, 111, 112, 118, 120, 124, 144, 145, 150, 190, 198, 199, 209, 213, 225
Penthouse East Theatre 3, 196, 198
Penthouse Entertainment Network/Pet Network 200
Penthouse Film International 98, 205
Penthouse Forum 209
Penthouse Pets 39, 82, 91, 94, 95, 97, 104, 111, 112, 118, 24, 143, 144, 149, 151, 154, 159, 191, 205, 211
The People vs. Larry Flynt (1996) 211
Peraino, Anthony 206, 207
Peraino, Louis 206, 207
Peter 21–26, 36
Peterson, Wolfgang 221
Petronius (Gaius Petronius Arbiter) 21, 32, 34, 73
Pevarello, Osiride 110
Phaedre 68
Philip of Macedon 58
Philipe, Gerard 17
Phillips, Sian 39, 102
Philo Judaeus (30 B.C.–A.D. 45) 47
Phoenix, Joaquin 221
Pietrangeli, Antonio 82
Pilate, Pontius 22, 26
Pillow Talk (1959) 203
Pirkis, Max 224
Piso, Gnaeus (governor of Syria) 39, 58
Pitt, Brad 221, 222
Placido, Donato 110, 148
Play Misty for Me (1971) 190
Playboy 28–30, 77–80, 84, 190, 200, 208–210, 213
Pliny, the elder (A.D. 23–79) 47
Pliny, the younger (A.D. 62–110) 48, 66
Polanski, Roman 80, 81
The Police Gazette 77
Polina, Lollia 70
Pompeii 66, 67
Poppaea 11, 13, 21
"porno chic" 35
pornography 4, 27, 28, 112
Pornography (1970) 37
Portrait of Constanza Buonarelli 201
The Poseidon Adventure (1972) 190
Potter, Martin 32
Preminger, Otto (1905–1986) 28
Presley, Elvis 2
Priapus 80, 126
Prime Suspect (2003) 103
The Prince of Egypt (1998) 217

Proculus 110, 144, 146, 147, 153, 154, 167, 205
Prokofiev, Sergei 129
Prospero's Books (1991) 106
Pullman, Jack 39
Purefoy, James 224
Pussycat Theatres 206
Puteoli 67, 70

The Queen 103
Queer as Folk (TV series 2000–2005) 204, 217
Quo Vadis? (1913) 8
Quo Vadis? (1951) 21

Rabbit Test (1978) 190
Rains, Claude (1889–1967) 16, 17
Rampling, Charlotte 221
Rand, Sally 27
ratings 36, 37, 98, 112, 121, 124, 192, 193, 205, 206, 213
Reagan, Ronald 195, 203
The Real World (2003) 219
Reams, Harry 35
Redford, Robert 191
Reed, Rex 86
Reeves, Steve 202
Rehnquist, William 210
Remus 42–44, 48, 57
Renault, Mary 222
Rennie, Michael 22, 24
Report to the Presidential Commission on Obscenity and Pornography (1970) 37
Reynolds, Bert 214
Rhy-Davies, John 40
Rich, Frank 223
The Rise and Fall of the Roman Empress 203
Rivers, Joan 190
The Robe (1953) 22, 23, 24
The Robe (novel, 1941) 22
Robinson, Jay 22–24, 26, 99, 202
Robson, Flora 15
Roeg, Nicholas 89
Roman Sex 126
Rome (2006–2007) 221, 224
Rome, Open City (1945) 31
Romeo and Juliet (music) 129
Romulus 42, 43, 44, 48, 57
Roommates (1981) 207
Ross, Frank (1904–1990) 22
Rossellini, Franco (1935–1992) 82, 83, 97, 110, 120, 125, 205, 206
Rossellini, Remo (1908–1982) 82, 129
Rossellini, Roberto (1906–1977) 20, 31, 82, 88, 89, 92, 94
Royal Shakespeare Company 98, 103
Russell, Ken 103
Ryan, Eric 202

Sade, Marquis de 97, 204
St. John, Maria 215

Salò— The One Hundred Days of Sodom (1975) 91, 97, 204
Salomé 61
Salon Kitty (1976) 89, 91, 92, 96, 106, 109, 110, 190
Samson and Delilah (1949) 20, 21
Samuel Roth v. United States (1957) 20, 28
Sánchez, Eduardo 217
Santoro, Rodrigo 225
Sarne, Michael 86
Satyrica (Satyricon) 32, 86, 115, 117, 132
Savage Messiah (1972) 103
Savoy, Teresa Ann 90, 92, 106, 107, 140, 146, 190
Sawyer, Diane 219
Schneider, Maria 80, 92, 106
Score (1973) 35, 36
Scorpio 202
Scott, Ridley 221
Screen Writers' Guild 27, 85
Screw 35
Scribonia 50
Sebastiane (1976) 36, 159
Second Punic War 8
Segal Lewis 29
Sejanus, Lucius 40, 54, 58, 59, 60, 108
Selene 72
Selznick, David O. 119
Seneca, the elder 68
Seneca, Lucius, the younger (4 B.C.–A.D. 65) 47, 68
Seven Beauties (1976) 88
7-Eleven 209
Sex in the City 207, 218
sex, lies and videotape (1989) 212
Shakespeare, William 50, 103, 105, 106, 220
Shampoo 190
Shaw, George Bernard 16, 17
Shields, Brooke 207
Shoeshine (1946) 31
A Short History of the Movies 30
Show 29, 34
Showgirls (1995) 213
Showtime 204
The Sign of the Cross (1932) 11, 21, 110
Simmons, Jean 23
Sinatra, Frank 28
Smart Aleck 27
Smith, Phil 207
Snow White and the Seven Dwarfs (1937) 2
"snuff" film 38
Soderbergh, Steven 212
softcore 35, 190, 200
Sonny, Dan 28
The Sopranos 212
Sorbo, Kevin 217
Spader, James 212
Spartacus (music) 129
Spartacus (1960) 147
Spartacus (2004) 223

Spelvin, Georgina 3, 35
Spiegel, Joe 3
Spielberg, Steven 87, 216
spintriae 61, 64, 149
The Spy Who Loved Me 190
Stabiae 66
Staller, Ilona 203
Star Wars (1977) 86, 188, 202
Starr, Kenneth 215
Steiner, John 91, 110, 146, 154
Sternberg, Josef von 11, 12, 14–16, 92
Stevenson, Ray 224
Stewart, Patrick 40
Stone, Oliver 210, 222
The Story of Art 201
The Story of O 29
Striptease (1996) 213
Stroheim, Eric von 92
Strom, Richard L. 87
Sturman, Ruben 28, 214
Sudura Singer 110
Suetonius (Gaius Suetonius Tranquillus) (A.D. 69–130) 5, 14, 17, 39, 48, 52
Sundance Film Festival 217
Swank 207
Swanson, Gloria (1899–1983) 7

Tacitus, Publius (A.D. 62–110) 14, 47, 53, 58, 68
Take One 86
Tarantino, Quentin 211
Tate, Sharon 81
Taylor, Elizabeth 27, 83, 203
Taylor, Robert 21
The Tempest 106
The Ten Commandments (1923) 7, 127
The Ten Commandments (1956) 26
Teorema (1968) 82
Texas Center for Media Awareness 201, 204
Theatre of the Absurd 19
Thermopylae, Sparta 224
Thesiger, Ernest 22
"A Thirsty Evil" (1956) 83
thirtysomething 210
Thrasylla, Ennia 59
300 (2007) 225
The Three Little Pigs (1933) 2
Thulin, Ingrid 90
Tiber River 42, 46, 62, 141
Tiberias 61
Tiberius (Tiberius Claudius Nero) (42 B.C.–A.D. 37) 14, 15, 22, 33, 39, 40, 42, 44, 47–49, 51–53, 55, 56, 59, 60, 61, 63, 65, 67, 69, 70, 91, 99, 100, 101, 102, 105, 108–111, 115, 124, 128, 130–134, 136–142, 188–190, 195, 221, 223
Timberlake, Justin 215
Times Square 3, 8
Titanic (1997) 216
toga virilis 60, 136

Torch Song Trilogy (1988) 203
Trash (1970) 2, 30
Travolta, John 199
Trieste, Leopoldo 110, 139
Trojan War 46
The Trojan Women 68
Tropic of Cancer 193
Tropic of Capricorn 193
Troy 45, 65, 222
Troy (2004) 102, 221, 223, 225
Tunberg, Karl 26, 85
Turnus 46
The Twelve Caesars (1957) 5, 39, 48
20th Century–Fox (TCF) 22

Umberto D (1951) 31
United States Supreme Court 2, 3, 10, 20, 28, 30, 37, 120, 192, 194, 210
Universal Pictures 220
Urban Cowboy 199, 215, 216
USA Network 223
Ustinov, Peter 21

The Vacation 89
Vadim, Roger 28
Valenti, Jack 192
Vanity Fair 210
Varela, Leonor 220
Variety 31, 81, 195, 211
Varus, Publius Quintilius 51
Venus 18, 46, 126
Venus (2006) 102
Verhoeven, Paul 213
Vestal Virgins 127, 144
Vesuvius, Mt. 66
Vidal, Gore 26, 48, 82–87, 89, 92, 99, 105, 122, 126, 163, 195, 201, 214
Vietnam War 3, 79
Villa Jovis, Capri 52, 54, 55, 67, 113, 129, 130
Village Voice 122
Vincent, Chuck 207
Vincent, Jan-Michael 36
A Violent Life 204
Virgil (70–19 B.C.) 46
Visconti, Luchino (1906–1976) 31, 65, 88
The Vision of St. Theresa 201
Visnjic, Goran 223
Vispania 53
"Visit to a Small Planet" (1955) 83
Vitellius, Aulus 60, 61, 99, 149
Vivid Video 220
Vixen (1968) 29
Vulcan 46

Wagner, Lori 95, 111, 151, 198
Walberg, Mark 214
Waldrop, Rika 201
Walker, Fiona 39
Warhol, Andy (1927–1987) 2, 29, 83, 121
Warner Bros. 220, 222, 225

254   Index

Washington Post 190
Welch, Rachael 86
Welles, Orson 96
Wertmuller, Lina 88, 95
West, Mae (1892–1980) 2, 11, 86
White, Shiela 40
Whitehead, T.A. 99
"Who's Afraid of the Big Bad Wolf" 2
Williams, Emlyn 15, 16
Willis, Gordon 191
Wise, Herbert 39
Wise, Robert 96
The Wizard of Oz (1939) 95
World Trade Center, New York 226
World War I 10

World War II 2, 26, 19
Wuthering Heights (1939) 14
Wyler, William 26, 27

Xerxes, King 225

Young Hercules (1998) 217

Zaffarano, Michael 206, 207
Zane, Billy 220
Zefferelli, Franco 88, 112
Zeus 57, 126, 223
Ziegfeld, Florenz, Jr. 3, 27
Zimbalist, Sam 26
Zukor, Adolph 81

www.ingramcontent.com/pod-product-compliance
Ingram Content Group UK Ltd.
Pitfield, Milton Keynes, MK11 3LW, UK
UKHW041934140426
5217IPUK00014B/478